浙江省普通本科高校"十四五"重点教材

现代会展翻译实用教程
Practical Coursebook on Modern Exhibition Translation

朱越峰　高　乾　编著

苏州大学出版社

图书在版编目(CIP)数据

现代会展翻译实用教程 = Practical Coursebook on Modern Exhibition Translation / 朱越峰，高乾编著. -- 苏州：苏州大学出版社，2024.8. --（浙江省普通本科高校"十四五"重点教材）. -- ISBN 978-7-5672-4849-6

Ⅰ. G245

中国国家版本馆 CIP 数据核字第 2024PD9970 号

书　　名	现代会展翻译实用教程 Practical Coursebook on Modern Exhibition Translation
编　　著	朱越峰　高　乾
责任编辑	汤定军
策划编辑	汤定军
封面设计	吴　钰
出版发行	苏州大学出版社（Soochow University Press）
社　　址	苏州市十梓街1号　邮编：215006
印　　装	镇江文苑制版印刷有限责任公司
网　　址	www.sudapress.com
邮　　箱	sdcbs@suda.edu.cn
邮购热线	0512-67480030
销售热线	0512-67481020
开　　本	787 mm×1 092 mm　1/16　印张：15.75　字数：345千
版　　次	2024年8月第1版
印　　次	2024年8月第1次印刷
书　　号	ISBN 978-7-5672-4849-6
定　　价	58.00元

凡购本社图书发现印装错误，请与本社联系调换。服务热线：0512-67481020

　　会展是现代服务业的重要组成部分,能够反映一个国家社会、经济与文化的综合发展水平。"十一五"时期,国家政策支持规范发展商务服务业,包括合理规划展馆布局,发展会展业。"十二五"时期,商务部从多方面提出对会展业的发展要求,包括加快市场化和专业化进程、扶持品牌展会发展、加强对外交流合作等。"十三五"时期,中国规划打造多个市场化、专业化、国际化的重点文化产业展会。"十四五"时期,国家明确提出要办好中国国际服务贸易交易会等国际经贸类展会。

　　近年来,随着我国现代会展业的兴起和迅猛发展,由我国主办的各类国际会展数量呈大幅上升趋势。根据《中国展览经济发展报告2023》,2023年中国共举办经贸类展会3923场,较2022年增长117.1%,较2019年增长10.6%;办展总面积1.41亿平方米,较2022年增长153.3%,较2019年增长8.25%。在北京奥运会和上海世博会之后,我国会展业进入繁荣发展时期,会展人才供不应求的矛盾也日益突出,而融会展管理、会展英语应用两种技能于一体的会展翻译人才更是北京、上海、广州等国内主要会展城市的紧缺人才。但是,国内以"会展翻译"为主题的专业教材严重缺乏,只有诸如《会展英语》《商务英语翻译》等类似教材,专业相关度不高,实用性较弱,无法有效指导会展实务翻译,这在很大程度上影响我国现代国际会展的服务质量和高校会展相关专业的建设水平。本教材有效弥补了当前专业教材缺乏的不利状况,对国内会展行业的复苏和发展、与国际接轨起到较好的推进作用,并对会展翻译复合型人才培养起到积极作用。

　　《现代会展翻译实用教程》为高等学校外国语言文学类专业教材,供英语专业、翻译专业、商务英语专业、会展经济与管理专业本科高年级学生使用。本教材以"新文科"理念为纲,在系统讲述会展实务内容的基础上,聚焦翻译策略与实践,并将机器翻译技术融入其中。本教材共八章,分理论篇(会展概述和会展文本类型与翻译)与实践篇(会展实务翻译、会展申请报告翻译、会展评估报告翻译、会展功能性文案翻译、会展合同与规章翻译、译后编辑)。理论篇中的"会展概述"主要介绍会展定义与分类、国际国内会展专业组织、重要国际会展、知名会展企业、会展业发展概况及会展翻译研究;"会展文本类型与翻译"阐述文本类型、目的功能、文案格式等相关概念,以及翻译的基本方法和技巧。实践篇第三章至第八章为主题单元,分别围绕会展实务与机器翻译技术展开,帮助学生灵活应用多种翻译策略及翻译技术,提高语言表达与传播能力。其中,朱越峰负责第一章至第七章的编撰工作,高乾负责第八章的编撰工作。

本教材的编撰主要遵循以下五项原则:

(1) 以教师为主导,以学生为主体:以教师讲解原文内容与翻译策略为基础,引导学生强化翻译策略训练;将教师阐释与学生学习体验相结合,帮助学生掌握会展实务核心要义,认识会展翻译的特点与规律。

(2) 突出基础,强化对比:重视汉语与英语的基础知识学习,关注中外会展的文本语言特色及文化差异。

(3) 以标准为纲,以创新为领:坚持以国际会展行业术语标准化为根本,兼顾受众理解与接受,灵活应用多样化翻译策略与方法,积极发挥学生翻译创新性。

(4) 以实践为本,以反思为要:基于大数据语料平台,将翻译实践感悟与理论阐释相结合,引导学生系统总结与理性分析会展翻译实践,认识会展翻译的专业性与复杂性。

(5) 技术革新,翻译转型:顺应当前人工智能技术趋势,以传统翻译转型为目的,实现机器翻译与人工翻译有效融合——译后编辑。

本教材的编撰以大数据平台为依托,以语料驱动为导向,以最新机器翻译技术为支撑,以质量标准化为纲要,多学科专业融合交叉,通过情景设定强调业务实操,符合国家"新文科"建设理念与浙江省普通本科高校"十四五"首批新工科、新文科、新医科、新农科重点教材建设项目要求。该教材的主要特色与创新点有以下四个:

(1) 基于大数据平台的语料驱动素材:编撰素材选自"UTH 国际、上海外语音像出版社、杭州师范大学合作共建多功能复合语料库平台(2019)",语料的真实性、时效性、实用性强,能为行业提供较好的语言服务素材。

(2) 行业术语翻译国际标准化:会展行业术语翻译采用"国际标准化组织标准规范 25639-1:2008:展览、展会、交易会和大会——第 1 部分:词汇",通过已建成英汉平行语料库(术语库),有效控制翻译质量,实现术语翻译国际标准化。

(3) 多学科专业融合交叉:翻译学、语言学、经济学、传媒学、社会学、计算机科学等多学科专业融合交叉,突破现有文科人才培养的学科专业限制,在更大范围内实现文理交叉、文科各学科专业之间的交叉。

(4) 基于情景设定的业务实操:通过会展实务各个环节的情景设定,定向阐述、实操相关翻译技能,真正培养学生解决问题的能力。

(5) 机器翻译技术导向下的传统翻译转型:以译后编辑技术为依托,以机器翻译与人工翻译的有效融合为目的,实现传统翻译转型,为专业人才快速转入行业提供高速通道。

本教材在编撰过程中参考了大量的行业资料和文献,尤其需要指出的是,滕超所著《会展翻译研究与实践》(浙江大学出版社,2012)一书使编撰者受益匪浅,谨在此向这些作者表示衷心的感谢! 同时,也向本书编撰过程中给予支持与帮助的杭州师范大学外国语学院师生致以诚挚的谢意! 由于学识有限,书中难免会有疏漏和不当之处,恳请不吝赐教和指正。我们的联系邮箱:20021870@hznu.edu.cn 和 20100070@hznu.edu.cn。恳盼交流。

目录 CONTENTS

理论篇

☞ **第一章 会展概述** ⋯⋯⋯⋯⋯⋯⋯⋯⋯⋯⋯⋯⋯⋯⋯⋯⋯⋯⋯⋯⋯⋯⋯⋯⋯⋯⋯⋯⋯⋯ 3
 第一节 会展定义与分类 ⋯⋯⋯⋯⋯⋯⋯⋯⋯⋯⋯⋯⋯⋯⋯⋯⋯⋯⋯⋯⋯⋯⋯⋯⋯ 4
 第二节 国际、国内会展专业组织 ⋯⋯⋯⋯⋯⋯⋯⋯⋯⋯⋯⋯⋯⋯⋯⋯⋯⋯⋯⋯⋯ 6
 第三节 重要国际会展 ⋯⋯⋯⋯⋯⋯⋯⋯⋯⋯⋯⋯⋯⋯⋯⋯⋯⋯⋯⋯⋯⋯⋯⋯⋯⋯ 11
 第四节 知名会展企业 ⋯⋯⋯⋯⋯⋯⋯⋯⋯⋯⋯⋯⋯⋯⋯⋯⋯⋯⋯⋯⋯⋯⋯⋯⋯⋯ 14
 第五节 会展业发展概况 ⋯⋯⋯⋯⋯⋯⋯⋯⋯⋯⋯⋯⋯⋯⋯⋯⋯⋯⋯⋯⋯⋯⋯⋯⋯ 17
 第六节 会展翻译研究概况 ⋯⋯⋯⋯⋯⋯⋯⋯⋯⋯⋯⋯⋯⋯⋯⋯⋯⋯⋯⋯⋯⋯⋯⋯ 19

☞ **第二章 会展文本类型与翻译** ⋯⋯⋯⋯⋯⋯⋯⋯⋯⋯⋯⋯⋯⋯⋯⋯⋯⋯⋯⋯⋯⋯⋯ 27
 第一节 文本与功能类型 ⋯⋯⋯⋯⋯⋯⋯⋯⋯⋯⋯⋯⋯⋯⋯⋯⋯⋯⋯⋯⋯⋯⋯⋯⋯ 28
 第二节 语义翻译和交际翻译 ⋯⋯⋯⋯⋯⋯⋯⋯⋯⋯⋯⋯⋯⋯⋯⋯⋯⋯⋯⋯⋯⋯⋯ 30
 第三节 会展文本翻译 ⋯⋯⋯⋯⋯⋯⋯⋯⋯⋯⋯⋯⋯⋯⋯⋯⋯⋯⋯⋯⋯⋯⋯⋯⋯⋯ 31
 第四节 国际标准化组织标准规范 25639-1:2008:展览、展会、交易会和大会——
    第1部分:词汇 ⋯⋯⋯⋯⋯⋯⋯⋯⋯⋯⋯⋯⋯⋯⋯⋯⋯⋯⋯⋯⋯⋯⋯⋯ 37

实践篇

☞ **第三章 会展实务翻译** ⋯⋯⋯⋯⋯⋯⋯⋯⋯⋯⋯⋯⋯⋯⋯⋯⋯⋯⋯⋯⋯⋯⋯⋯⋯⋯⋯ 47
 第一节 招展书翻译 ⋯⋯⋯⋯⋯⋯⋯⋯⋯⋯⋯⋯⋯⋯⋯⋯⋯⋯⋯⋯⋯⋯⋯⋯⋯⋯⋯ 48

第二节　参展商手册翻译 ………………………………………… 63

☞ **第四章　会展申请报告翻译** ……………………………………… 94
　　第一节　会展申请报告篇章布局 ………………………………… 95
　　第二节　英文会展申请报告语言特征 …………………………… 98
　　第三节　会展申请报告翻译实践 ………………………………… 104

☞ **第五章　会展评估报告翻译** ……………………………………… 121
　　第一节　会展评估概述 …………………………………………… 121
　　第二节　会展评估报告文本分析 ………………………………… 123
　　第三节　会展评估报告翻译实践 ………………………………… 127

☞ **第六章　会展功能性文案翻译** …………………………………… 141
　　第一节　致辞翻译 ………………………………………………… 142
　　第二节　信函翻译 ………………………………………………… 149
　　第三节　会议背景板标识语翻译 ………………………………… 158
　　第四节　会议台签翻译 …………………………………………… 161

☞ **第七章　会展合同与规章翻译** …………………………………… 165
　　第一节　会展合同与规章概述 …………………………………… 165
　　第二节　会展合同与规章翻译实践 ……………………………… 168

☞ **第八章　译后编辑** ………………………………………………… 183
　　第一节　机器翻译的发展历史与技术更迭 ……………………… 184
　　第二节　机器翻译评价方法 ……………………………………… 187
　　第三节　译后编辑的类型与原则 ………………………………… 193

☞ **参考文献及重要会展网站** ………………………………………… 203
☞ **参考答案** …………………………………………………………… 206
☞ **附录一** ……………………………………………………………… 216
☞ **附录二** ……………………………………………………………… 226
☞ **附录三** ……………………………………………………………… 237

理论篇

第一章 会展概述

学习目标

- 掌握会展的定义和分类
- 知晓国际、国内的重要会展专业组织
- 熟悉重要国际会展与知名会展企业
- 了解会展业发展概况
- 了解会展翻译研究概况

核心词汇

* 会展(Meeting, Incentive Tour, Conventions, Exhibitions and Events, MICE)
* 国际展览局(Bureau International des Expositions, BIE)
* 国际大会及会议协会(International Congress and Convention Association, ICCA)
* 国际会议中心协会(International Association of Convention Centers, AIPC)
* 全球展览业协会(The Global Association of the Exhibition Industry, UFI)
* 国际展览与项目协会(International Association of Exhibitions and Events, IAEE)
* 国际专业会议组织者协会(International Association of Professional Congress Organizers, IAPCO)
* 中国国际贸易促进委员会(China Council for the Promotion of International Trade, CCPIT)
* 香港展览会议业协会(Hong Kong Exhibition & Convention Industry Association, HKECIA)
* 中国进出口商品交易会(Canton Fair / China Import and Export Fair)
* 中国国际进口博览会(China International Import Expo, CIIE)
* 世界互联网大会(World Internet Conference, WIC)
* 会展管理国际认证课程(Exhibition Management Degree, EMD)
* 注册会展经理证书(Certified in Exhibition Management, CEM)

第一节　　会展定义与分类

一、会展定义

会议、展览会、博览会、交易会、展销会、展示会等是会展活动的基本形式,世界博览会为最典型的会展活动。欧洲是会展的发源地,在欧洲会展被称为 C&E（convention and exposition）或 M&E（meeting and exposition）。

会展概念的内涵是在一定地域空间,许多人聚集在一起形成的、定期或不定期的、制度或非制度的传递和交流信息的群众性社会活动;其概念的外延包括各种类型的博览会、展览展销活动、大型会议、体育竞技运动、文化活动、节庆活动等。

会展汇聚了产业链上下游及衍生产业的商流和人流。这一集聚效应不仅推动了会展的衍生产业发展,还促进了需求的迭代升级和信息的实时交互。大型的国际性展览和会议直接带动了高品质会展上下游产业的集聚,同时也吸引了高端人流,进而推动了本地消费的升级。

会展的本质是展示宣传活动,其目的是交易合作,而国家级会展还肩负政策导向和国际合作的重任。因此,会展宣传的深度、广度、高度、持久性和各方参与的便捷性与互动性等都会对展会的效果有很大影响。会展经济生态体系和会展行业产业链全景分别如图1.1和图1.2所示。

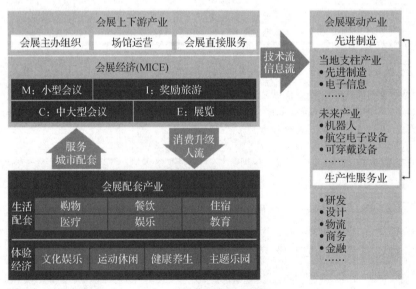

图1.1　会展经济生态体系

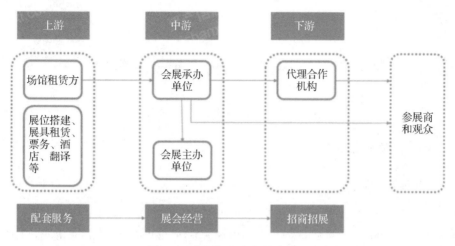

图1.2 会展行业产业链全景图

二、会展分类

狭义的会展仅指展览会和会议;广义的会展是会议、展览会、节事活动和奖励旅游的统称,即通常所说的MICE(M:Meeting;I:Incentive Tour;C:Conventions;E:Exhibitions and Events)。

M(Meeting):会议,主要指公司会议等,如董事会、研讨会、经销商会、发布会等。

I(Incentive Tour):奖励旅游,专指以激励、奖励特定对象为目的而进行的旅游活动,如招待会、答谢会、表彰仪式、拓展培训、考察等。

C(Conventions):中大型会议,主要指协会、社团组织的会议等,如国际性会议、行业峰会、论坛、学术会议等。

E(Exhibitions and Events):展会/商品交易会、文化体育活动等,如演唱会、电影节、比赛联赛、展览会、交易会等。

第二节　国际、国内会展专业组织

一、国际会展专业组织

（一）国际展览局

● 网址：https://www.bie-paris.org/site/en/

国际展览局（Bureau International des Expositions，简称 BIE）是政府间组织，负责监督和规范所有持续超过3周且具有非商业性质的国际展览，总部位于巴黎。国际展览局主要赞助组织四种类型的世界博览会：世界博览会、专业博览会、园艺博览会和米兰三年展。国际展览局的使命是保证上述世界性活动在确保质量的前提下成功举办，保护组织者和参与者的权利，并维护其教育、创新和合作的核心价值观。国际展览局成员已从1928年创建时的31个国家发展到2024年的184个国家。中国于1993年正式加入国际展览局，中国国际贸易促进委员会一直代表中国政府参与国际展览局的各项工作。

International Exhibitions Bureau

（二）国际大会及会议协会

● 网址：http://www.iccaworld.org

国际大会及会议协会（International Congress and Convention Association，简称 ICCA）是目前国际会议行业最知名的协会，创建于1963年，总部位于荷兰阿姆斯特丹，现拥有来自近100个国家的1000多名会员。国际大会及会议协会作为国际会议领域的先导，其目的是通过有关教育培训或实践活动，开发各种类型的国际性会议，并进一步提高协会成员的专业技能，不断改善及提高服务和接待水准，提升会议、展览及奖励旅游业的水平。

国际大会及会议协会尽力促使其会员成为合格的国际会议组织者及倡导者，为成员提供如下服务：按照资格标准向国际会议主办者和组织者推荐国际大会及会议协会成员；提供国际会议方面的数据，包括所需设施、目的地和联系地址；为会员提供业务机会；通过积极的教育计划，进一步开发会员的专业技能。

（三）国际会议中心协会

- 网址：https://aipc.org/

国际会议中心协会（International Association of Convention Centres，简称 AIPC）于 1958 年成立于罗马，总部位于比利时布鲁塞尔，是一个专业的非营利性协会，会员来自 60 多个国家的 172 个主要会议中心，是全球专业会议和展览中心管理人员的行业协会。国际会议中心协会致力于为国际会议和会展场馆提供优质的服务，通过其高质量的行业分析、教育培训和所拥有的关系网络，为会员单位提高管理水平和服务质量提供支撑，在行业术语的释义、统计数据以及国际会议等方面起着非常重要的作用。

（四）全球展览业协会

- 网址：https://www.ufi.org

国际展览联盟（Union of International Fairs，简称 UFI）是国际展览行业最重要的国际组织之一，1925 年成立于意大利米兰，总部设在法国巴黎。为了适应发展的需要，2003 年更名为"全球展览业协会"（The Global Association of the Exhibition Industry，仍简称 UFI），目前获得认证的展会总数近 1000 个，会员数量为 800 多家。截至 2020 年，中国境内和中国境外自主办展共有 159 个展会项目通过全球展览业协会认证。

作为非政府、非营利的组织，全球展览业协会的宗旨是促进国际贸易，提升其成员主办的博览会和展览会水平，使之在世界贸易服务中起到更有效的作用。全球展览业协会成员在本国的博览和展览行业中均占据领先地位，一旦博览会和展览会的名称与全球展览业协会联系在一起，即被认为是高品质的象征，经全球展览业协会认可的博览会和展览会，80%以上是专业性的博览会和展览会。

（五）国际展览与项目协会

- 网址：https://www.iaee.com

国际展览与项目协会（International Association of Exhibitions and Events，简称IAEE）成立于1928年，前身是国际展览管理协会（International Association for Exhibition Management，简称IAEM），代表着商贸展览从业经理人的权益，总部设于美国达拉斯，是国际展览业重要的行业协作组织，涵盖来自全球50多个国家的将近12000多名个人和1400多个组织。国际展览与项目协会的使命是在全球范围内推广展览和活动的独特价值，致力于提供渠道、促成合作。据统计，至2020年年底，国际展览与项目协会在中国大陆地区的企业会员达68个，个人会员累计299人。国际展览与项目协会推出的"注册会展经理证书"（Certified in Exhibition Management，简称CEM）已成为会展业专业人士全球性顶尖证书。

（六）国际专业会议组织者协会

- 网址：https://www.iapco.org

国际专业会议组织者协会（International Association of Professional Congress Organizers，简称IAPCO）是会议组织者和国际性会议管理人员的专业协会，创立于1968年，总部在比利时布鲁塞尔，目前拥有40多个国家的130多名成员。协会的目的在于制定高等级的专业化标准，在组会方面保持高专业化的水准。国际专业会议组织者协会作为一个卓越的标志已被客户及会议行业广泛认可，成为国际性活动，特别是会议组织方面的全球性品牌。

除了上述协会外,全球领先的会展协会或国际组织还有国际会议专家联合会(Meeting Professionals International,简称 MPI)、国际会议观光局协会(International Association of Convention and Visitor Bureaus,简称 IACVB)、独立组展商学会(Society of Independent Show Organizers,简称 SISO)、奖励旅游管理者协会(Society for Incentive Travel Excellence,简称 SITE)、亚洲会议和旅游局协会(Asian Association of Convention and Visitors Bureaus,简称 AACVB)、亚洲太平洋地区展览会及会议联合会(Asia Pacific Exhibition and Convention Council,简称 APECC)、欧洲会展旅游城市联盟(European Federation of Conference Towns,简称 EFCT)、欧洲展览馆管理协会(European Major Exhibition Centres Association,简称 EMECA)、贸易展览参展商协会(Trade Show Exhibitors Association,简称 TSEA)、国际展览物流协会(International Exhibition Logistics Associates,简称 IELA)等。

二、国内会展专业组织

(一)中国国际贸易促进委员会

- 网址:https://www.ccpit.org

中国国际贸易促进委员会(China Council for the Promotion of International Trade,简称 CCPIT)成立于1952年,是全国性对外贸易投资促进机构,其宗旨是开展促进对外贸易、利用外资、引进外国先进技术及各种形式的中外经济技术合作等活动,促进中国同世界各国、各地区之间的贸易和经济关系的发展,增进中国与世界各国人民以及中外经贸界之间的了解与友谊。截至2022年5月,中国国际贸易促进委员会已与世界200多个国家和地区的工商企业界建立了广泛的经贸联系,与160多个对口组织签订了合作协议,并与一些国家的商会建立了联合商会。

(二)香港展览会议业协会

- 网址:https://exhibitions.org.hk

香港展览会议业协会(Hong Kong Exhibition & Convention Industry Association,简称 HKECIA)前身为香港展览业协会,于1990年5月由当时10家主要展览会主办机构创立。作为行业的代表,该协会与政府及法定机构协商,维护会员的商业利益。香港展览会议业协会的宗旨是通过精心策划的培训及教育课程,提升从业人员的专业知识及操作水平;与其他有关团体或组织紧密合作,从而提高本行业的声誉和地位,并推动香港成为东亚地区及全球的主要国际展览及会议之都。

(三) 中国展览馆协会

- 网址：http://www.caec.org.cn/

中国展览馆协会(China Association for Exhibition Centers,简称CAEC)成立于1984年，是我国目前唯一的全国性展览行业组织，为国家AAA级协会，也是国际展览业协会的国家级会员。中国展览馆协会主要由展览主办机构、展览场馆、展览中心、展览工程公司、展览运输公司、展览媒体、高等院校、展览科研机构以及与展览行业相关的且具有法人资格的企事业单位自愿参加组成。截至2024年6月，会员单位为5000多家。

(四) 中国城市会议展览业协会联盟

- 网址：http://www.ccace.luckhr.com/

中国城市会议展览业协会联盟(China Union of City Convention and Exhibition Industry Associations,简称CCACE)成立于2013年，是全国地(厅)级以上城市会展业社团法人机构的联盟体。联盟宗旨是立会为公，服务各城市会展企业，服务政府，服务中国各城市会展经济的发展，促进各地会展业的大联合、大合作、大发展。联盟现有成员近百家，所属会展企业(团体会员)超过10000家，是中国会展业发展的重要力量。

另外，国内重要的会展协会或专业组织还有中国商务会展联盟（China Business Event Federation，简称 CBEF）、中国会展产业联盟（China Exhibitions Industrial Cooperation Alliance，简称 CEIA）、中国会展直播产业联盟（China Exhibition Live Industry Alliance，简称 CELIA）等。

第三节　重要国际会展

一、综合类

• 世界博览会

世界博览会（World Exposition），又称"国际博览会""世博会"，是一项由主办国政府组织或政府委托有关部门举办的国际性博览活动。按照国际展览局的规定，世博会按性质、规模、展期分为两种：一种是注册类（也称"综合性"）世博会，展期通常为 6 个月，从 2000 年开始每 5 年举办一次；另一种是认可类（也称"专业性"）世博会，展期通常为 3 个月，在两届注册类世博会之间举办一次。注册类世博会不同于一般的贸易促销和经济招商的展览会，是全球最高级别的博览会。中国申请的 1999 年昆明世博会与 2019 年北京世博会属于认可类世博会，2010 年上海世博会则属于注册类世博会。

世博会的起源是中世纪欧洲商人定期的市集。到 19 世纪，商界在欧洲地位提升，市集的规模渐渐扩大，商品交易的种类和参与的人员愈来愈多，影响范围愈来愈大，到 19 世纪 20 年代，这种规模的大型市集便成为博览会。最早的现代博览会是"万国工业博览会"，在英国伦敦的海德公园举行，展期是 1851 年 5 月 1 日至 10 月 11 日，主要内容是世界文化与工业科技。世博会已经先后举办 40 多届。

2020 年迪拜世博会中国馆华夏之光

二、文化体育类

• 奥林匹克运动会

奥林匹克运动会(Olympic Games),简称"奥运会",是国际奥林匹克委员会主办的最大的世界规模综合性运动会,每四年一届,会期不超过16日,是世界上影响力最大的体育盛会,"更快、更高、更强——更团结"(Faster, Higher, Stronger—Together)为奥林匹克格言。

奥林匹克运动会分为夏季奥林匹克运动会、夏季残疾人奥林匹克运动会、冬季奥林匹克运动会、冬季残疾人奥林匹克运动会、夏季青年奥林匹克运动会、冬季青年奥林匹克运动会、世界夏季特殊奥林匹克运动会、世界冬季特殊奥林匹克运动会、夏季聋人奥林匹克运动会、冬季聋人奥林匹克运动会十个运动会。奥林匹克运动会中,各个国家和地区用运动交流各国文化,以及切磋体育技能,其目的是鼓励人们不断进行体育运动。

奥林匹克运动会发源于两千多年前的古希腊,因举办地在奥林匹亚而得名。古代奥林匹克运动会停办了1500年之后,法国人顾拜旦于19世纪末提出举办现代奥林匹克运动会的倡议。1894年成立奥委会,1896年希腊雅典举办了首届奥林匹克运动会,2021年在日本东京举办了第三十二届夏季奥林匹克运动会,2022年在北京举办了第二十四届冬季奥林匹克运动会。

国家速滑馆,又称"冰丝带"(2022年北京冬奥会唯一新建冰上竞赛场馆)

三、商品交易类

• 中国进出口商品交易会

中国进出口商品交易会(Canton Fair / China Import and Export Fair),简称"广交会",创办于1957年,每年春秋两季在广州举办,由商务部和广东省人民政府联合主办,中国对外贸易中心承办,是中国历史最长、层次最高、规模最大、商品种类最全、到会采购商最多且分布国别地区最广、成交效果最好的综合性国际贸易盛会,被誉为"中国第一展"。

广交会贸易方式灵活多样,除传统的看样成交外,还举办网上交易会。广交会以出口贸易为主,也做进口生意,还可以开展多种形式的经济技术合作与交流,以及商检、保险、运输、广告、咨询等业务活动。广交会展馆总面积达62万平方米,是全球最大的会展综合体之一。

广交会展馆四期项目东北角鸟瞰

- 中国国际进口博览会

中国国际进口博览会(China International Import Expo,简称CIIE),简称"进博会",由商务部和上海市人民政府主办,中国国际进口博览局、国家会展中心(上海)承办,为世界上第一个以进口为主题的国家级展会。举办中国国际进口博览会由国家主席习近平亲自谋划、亲自提出、亲自部署、亲自推动,是中国着眼于推动新时代高水平对外开放作出的一项重大决策,是中国主动向世界开放市场的重大举措。

2018年11月5日至10日,首届中国国际进口博览会在上海国家会展中心成功举办,国家主席习近平出席开幕式并发表主旨演讲。经过近六年发展,进博会让展品变商品、让展商变投资商,交流创意和理念,联通中国和世界,发挥国际采购、投资促进、人文交流、开放合作的平台功能,成为全球共享的国际公共产品。

四、专业/行业类

- 世界互联网大会

世界互联网大会(World Internet Conference,简称WIC)是由中华人民共和国倡导、每年在浙江省嘉兴市桐乡乌镇举办的世界性互联网盛会,大会由中华人民共和国国家互联网信息办公室和浙江省人民政府共同主办,旨在搭建中国与世界互联互通的国际平台和国际互联网共享共治的中国平台,让各国在争议中求共识、在共识中谋合作、在合作中创共赢。大会主要邀请国家和地区政要、国际组织的负责人、互联网企业领军人物、互联网名人、专家学者,涉及网络空间各个领域,体现多方参与。首届世界互联网大会于2014年11月在乌镇举办,现已举办十届。

第四节　知名会展企业

一、德国汉诺威展览公司

成立于1947年的德国汉诺威展览公司(Deutsche Messe AG, Hannover/Germany)总部位于德国汉诺威市,拥有世界最大的展览场馆——汉诺威展览中心。公司的展览主题主要是资本货物,每年举办的汉诺威国际信息及通信技术博览会是世界规模第一的展览会,而汉诺威工业博览会则是全球最有影响力的展览会。汉诺威展览公司的核心业务是在德国汉诺威及由其选定的国家举办领先的国际贸易展览会。凭借丰富的办展经验和不断创新的办展理念,德国汉诺威展览公司每年举办逾150场专业贸易展览。

二、法兰克福展览有限公司

法兰克福展览有限公司(Messe Frankfurt Exhibition GmbH)总部设于德国法兰克福市,2008年12月是公司成立一百周年。事实上,法兰克福的展览业拥有超过800年的悠久历史,是全球最大规模从事贸易展览业务的主办单位之一。公司在法兰克福市拥有10个展厅和会议中心,展地面积约为32.1万平方米,仅次于汉诺威展览公司和米兰展览公司,位居世界前列。其主要业务是在国内外举办各种展览,每年在世界28个城市举办的贸易展览有100多个。

三、克劳斯国际展览公司

克劳斯国际展览公司(E. J. Krause & Associates, Inc.)成立于1984年,现已发展成为美国最大的展览公司之一。公司总部位于美国首都华盛顿,在美洲、欧洲和亚洲十余个国家和地区设有代表处或分公司,形成了全球性的展览业务网络。克劳斯公司是中国改革开放后最早来华开拓展览业务的先行者之一,直接与国家各部委合作。克劳斯公司每年在全球举办约10个国际展览及会议。鉴于在展览界的出色表现,克劳斯公司曾荣获美国总统布什授予的杰出荣誉奖。这一奖项是颁发给那些在本行业表现出色、对美国出口贸易有卓越贡献的企业。在过去的四十多年中,克劳斯公司是全美第二家获得此殊荣的展览公司。其主要展会包括巴黎航空展、荷兰国际石油技术展览会、国际调味品食品添加剂博览会、食品行销协会亚洲展、中国国际通信设备技术展览会等。

四、励展博览集团

励展博览集团(Reed Exhibitions)总部位于英国,是励德爱思唯尔集团的成员之一,是全球最大的展览及会议活动主办机构,已积淀逾百年的全球品质展览会的开发、策划、推广及销售经验,并赢得"品质、知名、权威展览会主办者"的美誉。励展博览集团早于20世纪80年代就进入中国办展,现已发展为中国最活跃的国际展览及会议主办者。励展博览集团每年主办的一流国际展览会超过460个,涵盖52个行业,足迹遍及美洲、欧洲、中东及亚太区的34个国家,主要展会包括:亚洲国际航展、电子生产设备暨微电子工业展、英国酒店展、伦敦国际图书展、影视设备展、法国国际船展、国际专业高尔夫球展、英国国际旅游展等。

五、中国国际展览中心集团公司

中国国际展览中心集团（China International Exhibition Center Group Limited，简称 CIEC），简称"中展集团"，是中国国际贸易促进委员会直属企业，成立于1985年。现已发展成为拥有展馆经营、国内组展、境外出展、展览设计与工程、展览运输、展览信息广告、住宿餐饮等展览全产业链的集团性展览企业，是中国展览馆协会理事长单位、中国国际商会会展委员会主席单位、国际展览业协会（UFI）成员和国际展览会管理协会（IAEM）成员。其主要展会包括北京国际印刷技术展、北京国际汽车展、中国国际石材展、北京国际门窗幕墙博览会、中国（北京）国际建筑装饰及材料博览会等。

六、中国对外贸易中心

中国对外贸易中心（China Foreign Trade Centre，简称CFTC）是商务部直属事业单位，主要负责承办广交会。中国对外贸易中心以其60多年的专业办展经验、卓越的业绩、专业的服务在中国会展业中占有举足轻重的地位。近年来，中国对外贸易中心下设的中国对外贸易中心集团有限公司经营收入位列世界各大展览机构前列，所经营的广交会展馆办展面积达752.4万平方米（含广交会），列世界展馆之首，自主举办的家博会、建博会、汽车展均为世界知名品牌大展。

七、香港贸易发展局

香港贸易发展局（Hong Kong Trade Development Council，简称HKTDC），简称"香港贸发局"，成立于1966年。根据《香港贸易发展局条例》，香港贸发局是专责拓展香港特别行政区全球贸易的法定机构，为香港制造商、贸易商及服务出口商服务。其主要展会包括香港电子展、香港国际珠宝展、香港国际影视展、香港玩具展、香港国际时尚荟萃、香港国际体育用品博览会、香港国际文具展、香港家庭用品展、香港专利授权展等。

第五节　会展业发展概况

会展业作为一个国家综合经济实力和经济总体规模的重要反映,已经成为全球经济发展的重要驱动力。发达国家凭借其综合优势在会展业中占据了主导地位,并向全球各地扩张。根据全球新闻专线(GlobeNewswire)的数据,2022年全球会展市场规模估计为197亿美元,预计到2030年将达到607亿美元,复合年增长率为15.1%。其中,欧洲,尤其是德国,作为全球会展业的领头羊,已经形成了强大的品牌效应,并在全球范围内展现了其专业化的优势。

目前在我国会展业与旅游业等被称为新经济产业。会展业在调整经济结构、开拓市场、促进消费、加强合作交流、扩大产品出口、推动经济快速持续健康发展等方面发挥重要作用,在城市建设、精神文明建设、和谐社会构建中显示出其特殊的地位和作用。

第一,能产生强大的互动共赢效应。会展业不仅能带来场租费、搭建费等直接收入,而且能拉动或间接带动数十个行业的发展,直接创造商业购物、餐饮、住宿、娱乐、交通、通信、广告、旅游、印刷、房地产等相关收入;不仅能集聚人气,而且能促进各大产业的发展,对一个城市或地区的经济发展和社会进步产生重大影响和起到催化作用。

第二,能获得优质资源。会展业汇聚巨大的信息流、技术流、商品流和人才流。因此,各行业在开放潮中,在产品、技术、生产、营销等诸方面获取比较优势,优化配置资源,增强综合竞争力。会展业发展可以不断创造出"神话",博鳌效应就是其中一个典型范例,穷乡僻壤的博鳌镇建成国际会议中心后,以其良好的生态、人文、治安环境,吸引了众多海内外会议组织者、参会者、旅游者等。

第三,能提升支持力度。各产业要发展,特别是制造业要生存和提升竞争力,需要相关服务行业的协作,加快新型工业化、新农村建设,更离不开会展业的支持和助力。会展是一个特殊的服务行业,会展经济能够增强城市对周边地区的辐射力和影响力。

第四,能增加就业机会。随着近年来办展活动的增多,会展业不仅能提供就业机会,而且能拉动和促进就业。

第五,能成为经济发展的"风向标"。会展紧扣经济,展示经济发展成果,会展经济的发展将直接刺激贸易、旅游、交通、运输、金融、房地产、零售等行业的市场景气,大型和专业性会展往往是产品或技术市场占有率及盈利前景的晴雨表,推动商品贸易、投资合作、服务贸易、高层论坛、文化交流等各方面的发展与进步。

一、国际会展业

随着经济全球化程度的日益加深,会展业已发展成为新兴的现代服务贸易型产业,成为衡量一个城市国际化程度和经济发展水平的重要标准之一。作为会展业的发源地,欧美地区实力仍然领先,但行业的发展重心正在逐渐向亚洲等新兴市场转移。这一转变得益于行业的品牌化、集团化趋势,以及其在国际化和信息化方面的迅速发展。国际组织在增强行业规范性和自律性方面也发挥了积极作用。

目前,国际会展行业形成了以欧美国家为中心,辐射亚太、中南美、中东非的格局。亚太地区、中东非地区会展市场占比不断提升,其原因在于:一方面,随着国际会展行业的不断发展,众多国际知名的会展品牌纷纷进入亚太、中东非市场,通过行业细分和跨地域的协调、延伸来巩固自身地位;另一方面,亚太、中东非地区经济的高速发展以及人民生活水平的日益提升促使当地贸易需求增加,当地会展市场规模亦随之增长。近年来,国际会展项目更加注重展与会的结合,会展内容趋于专业化、品牌化。越来越多的展览公司和会议公司涌现,且呈现集团化趋势。信息技术开始应用在会展方面,与实物展览相结合也是现在国际会展发展的新趋势。

二、国内会展业

与此同时,中国的会展业也在迅速崛起。自20世纪80年代以来,我国会展业经历了从无到有、从小到大,以年均近20%的速度递增,行业经济效益逐年攀升,场馆建设日臻完善,已成为国民经济的助推器和新亮点。全国以北京、上海、广州为一级会展中心城市,初步形成三大会展经济产业带:以广州为中心的华南—珠三角会展经济产业带、以上海为中心的长三角会展经济产业带、以北京为中心的环渤海会展经济产业带。随着会展业市场化程度的提高,会展城市内部场馆之间、会展城市之间的竞争日益明显。法治建设、品牌意识、现代化场馆建设、人才培养成为普遍共识。与此同时,数字经济和"互联网+"的推动也为会展业开创了新的局面,为行业的未来发展带来了更多的机遇。

作为世界第二大经济体,预计到2030年,中国的会展业市场规模将达到83亿美元,2022年至2030年分析期内的年均复合增长率为18.1%。这种高速增长的背后是政策环境的持续优化、行业向市场化的改革,以及行业品牌化、专业化和企业规模集团化运作的趋势。

三、会展业未来发展趋势

1. 世界会展产业"东移"趋势更加明显

伴随着亚太、中东非、中南美等新兴市场国家经济发展的提速,国际会展产业出现了重心由发达国家向发展中国家转移的趋势。欧美国家在保持行业主导地位的同时,市场增速放缓,而亚太、中东非地区因居民人均可支配收入和生活水准的提升,其会展行业市场正以较高的年复合增长率快速增长。

步入"新常态"的中国更加渴望有更多、更大的平台进行自我展示,一系列国际会展的成功举办也为会展行业带来了难得的机遇,作为世界第二大经济体的中国的展览市场将越来越令世界展览业瞩目。近年来,国际展览业巨头纷纷在中国移植或者举办新的展览会,成绩斐然。可以预见,中国经济的进一步转型将为国际市场带来更加巨大的机会,国际市场和中国市场的双向需求将带动世界展览业加速"东移"。与此同时,为了展现中国制造,中国也将充分利用出国展览平台,将中国企业的形象输出到国外,国内的出国展览行业也将迎来历史性机遇。

2. 专业性展览会已成未来趋势

综合与细分是设定展会内容的两种思路。从展览业的发展看,展会的内容从综合到细分,是展览业发育成熟并迈向专业化的重要标志。欧美展览大国已经开始细分行业之后的"再细分",展览内容极具专业性,使采购商能够以最快的速度找到所需的产品。在我国,由于追求展览经济的规模效应和"大而全"的展示效果,偏综合性的展会仍大量存在。近几年,许多综合性展会开始将内容细分成专业性主体展览会或主题馆。虽然与欧美相比这种划分仍显粗放,却已体现出中国展览业专业化进程的加速。随着政府介入的逐步减少,中国展会将在市场的要求下对内容进行更合理、更专业的细分,许多大型展览会有可能分为规模更小、专业性更强的展览会,与国际展览业的发展更为紧密地联系在一起。

第六节 会展翻译研究概况

相较于会展业近年来的迅猛发展,会展翻译的研究就显得有些相形见绌,主要原因有:其一,会展翻译是会展业和语言服务业相互交叉的领域,但在实际应用中会展业作为主角更受学术界的青睐,而语言服务业作为配角相对来说不像会展业那样受重视,相关研究也就少之又少。其二,会展翻译类属应用翻译系列中的商务英语翻译,这种类属身份不可避免地制约其研究地位,继而影响其研究角色取舍。一般来说,研究人员更倾向于其商务英语翻译的研究。其三,会展翻译的对象是会展操作中的具体实务,内容更多涉及具体的实践细节,从应用性角度来看,理论研究意义不如实践操作重要,这也导致了近年来学者们对会展翻译研究的忽视。

以中国知网2010—2023年近十四年的期刊学术论文为例,主题词为"会展翻译研究"的相关论文共72篇,年均不到5篇(图1.3),主要主题分布在"会展英语"(17篇)、"会展外宣材料"(7篇)、"翻译策略"(5篇)、"汉英翻译"(4篇)、"目的论视角"(4篇)、"翻译目的论"(3篇)、"国际会展"(3篇)、"会展翻译"(3篇)、"会展英语翻译"(3篇)等20个方向(图1.4);次要主题分布在"翻译策略"(4篇)、"翻译方法"(4篇)、"翻译问题"(3篇)、"翻译人员"(3篇)、"翻译要求"(2篇)等20个方向(图1.5);文献来源类别分布(图1.6)显示期刊整体水平不高,其中北大核心期刊10篇,中文社会科学引文索引(Chinese Social Sciences Citation Index,简称CSSCI)期刊5篇。

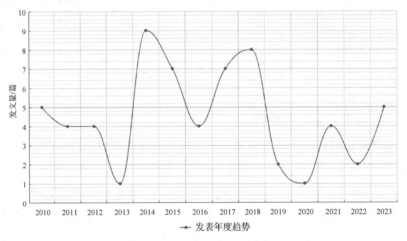

图1.3 论文发表数总体趋势

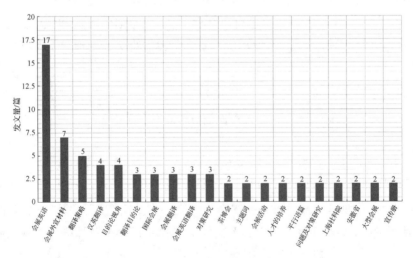

图1.4 主要主题分布

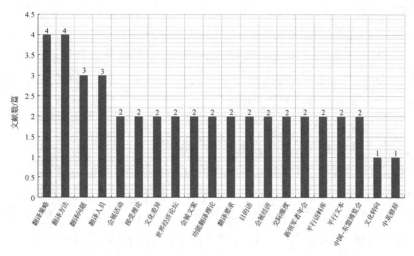

图1.5 次要主题分布

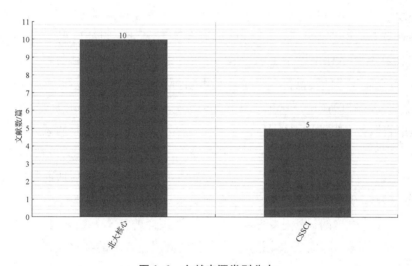

图1.6 文献来源类别分布

再以专著为例,比较有代表性的会展翻译著作也是凤毛麟角,有2012年浙江大学出版社出版的"新世纪翻译学R&D系列著作"分册《会展翻译研究与实践》(滕超)和2018年世界图书出版公司出版的"学术文库"系列之一《会展英语翻译技巧与教学实践研究》(李燕华)。《会展翻译研究与实践》内容包括"理论"与"实践"两大模块:第1章至第4章侧重"理论探索",首先总揽我国会展翻译研究的社会背景与发展现状,从而引出关注焦点:汉语会展文案的英译理论与实践。作者通过相当篇幅探讨以文本类型学为基础、以目的论为核心的功能翻译流派,构建了会展翻译框架下的文本分析模型,从文本内、外两个层面勾勒了会展语篇要素的独特性,揭示了会展文案语言功能的多重效果。第5章至第9章关注的则是理论研究成果在会展文案翻译实践中的具体运用,深入细致地对申请报告、规章与合同以及指南类、评估类和事务类等各种类型文案进行导向性文本分析,融入了大量生动的、具有普遍意义的实例。在选材上,力求撷取北京奥运会、上海世博会、广交会、博鳌亚洲论坛等最具影响力的项目结构完整的国际会展文案。《会展英语翻译技巧与教学实践研究》在对会展和会展翻译进行概述的基础上,就会展英语的教学实践进行了分析;之后对会展翻译的文本功能、特点以及翻译的理论和方法进行了介绍,并就会展词汇、名称、文案、企业简介等方面进行翻译实践;最后对会展推广和服务类信息方面的资料进行整体翻译,凸显其中的翻译技巧。上述两本专著的共同之处在于,在论述过程中,强调会展翻译的理论指导及具体的实践操作,并与现实场景相结合,凸显会展翻译的应用型特征。

相较于会展翻译学术论文和专著的乏善可陈,有较多的会展翻译相关教程可供参考,如 2008 年大连理工大学出版社出版的《会展英语翻译》(杨自力)、2010 年武汉大学出版社出版的《会展英语现场口译》(黄建凤)、2013 年北京对外经济贸易大学出版社出版的《商务会展英汉互译实训》(赵惠)等;或以"商务英语翻译"为主题的相关教程,其中部分内容涉及会展英语翻译,如 2023 年高等教育出版社出版的《商务英语翻译(英译汉)》(李明)、2013 年武汉大学出版社出版的《商务英语翻译》(王森林、肖水来)、2018 年清华大学出版社和北京交通大学出版社出版的《商务英语翻译案例教程》(董晓波)、2020 年浙江大学出版社出版的《商务英语翻译实务》(陈娟)、2020 年安徽大学出版社出版的《商务英语翻译》(丁立福)、2021 年商务印书馆出版的《新编商务英语翻译教程》(彭萍)等。上述教程都从应用的视角对会展翻译的实操部分做了非常生动、真实的阐述,但也存在一些不足,如读者层次普遍不高,大多为高职高专类学生;又如,切入点角度多为特殊用途英语(ESP)或会展业,而不是语言服务业。为弥补上述不足,本教程是基于语言服务业的翻译实践研究与应用进行编写,读者对象为本科高年级学生。通过该教程的学习,学生可以接触、了解会展翻译各种相关知识,对会展翻译的原则、分类、方法等有较全面的认识,从而把握会展翻译中的各种现象,理解会展翻译的基本要素和不同要求;同时,在教授翻译文本类型、目的功能和文案格式等相关概念的过程中,使学生切实掌握翻译的基本方法和技巧,进一步适应文化多样化、经济一体化、信息全球化语境,能够胜任会展场景下的英汉互译与跨文化交流工作,具备专业会展翻译人才所需的从业实力和职业素养。

思考题

1. 辨析"会展"概念的内涵和外延。
2. 讨论杭州会展业实现《杭州市会展业发展"十四五"规划》中"国际化水平"目标的优势与劣势。

国际化水平进一步提升。到 2025 年,新增国际展览业协会(UFI)认证会展项目 5 个,每年举办国际性展览 20 个左右,占全部展览的比重达到 10% 左右;列入国际大会及会议协会(ICCA)公布在杭举办的国际会议数量达到 50 个左右,举办国际性会议 1000 个左右,占全部会议的比重达到 5% 左右,全球会议目的地城市排名争取进入前 60 位,打响"开会观展到杭州"品牌。

（一）
《中华人民共和国国民经济和社会发展第十四个五年规划和2035年远景目标纲要》（摘编）

第十章 促进服务业繁荣发展

聚焦产业转型升级和居民消费升级需要，扩大服务业有效供给，提高服务效率和服务品质，构建优质高效、结构优化、竞争力强的服务产业新体系。

第一节 推动生产性服务业融合化发展

以服务制造业高质量发展为导向，推动生产性服务业向专业化和价值链高端延伸。聚焦提高产业创新力，加快发展研发设计、工业设计、商务咨询、检验检测认证等服务。聚焦提高要素配置效率，推动供应链金融、信息数据、人力资源等服务创新发展。聚焦增强全产业链优势，提高现代物流、采购分销、生产控制、运营管理、售后服务等发展水平。推动现代服务业与先进制造业、现代农业深度融合，深化业务关联、链条延伸、技术渗透，支持智能制造系统解决方案、流程再造等新型专业化服务机构发展。培育具有国际竞争力的服务企业。

第三节 深化服务领域改革开放

扩大服务业对内对外开放，进一步放宽市场准入，全面清理不合理的限制条件，鼓励社会力量扩大多元化多层次服务供给。完善支持服务业发展的政策体系，创新适应服务新业态、新模式和产业融合发展需要的土地、财税、金融、价格等政策。健全服务质量标准体系，强化标准贯彻执行和推广。加快制定重点服务领域监管目录、流程和标准，构建高效协同的服务业监管体系。完善服务领域人才职称评定制度，鼓励从业人员参加职业技能培训和鉴定。深入推进服务业综合改革试点和扩大开放。

第十三章 促进国内国际双循环

立足国内大循环，协同推进强大国内市场和贸易强国建设，形成全球资源要素强大引力场，促进内需和外需、进口和出口、引进外资和对外投资协调发展，加快培育参与国际合作和竞争新优势。

第一节 推动进出口协同发展

完善内外贸一体化调控体系，促进内外贸法律法规、监管体制、经营资质、质量标准、检验检疫、认证认可等相衔接，推进同线同标同质。降低进口关税和制度性成本，扩大优质消费品、先进技术、重要设备、能源资源等进口，促进进口来源多元化。完善出口政策，优化出口商品质量和结构，稳步提高出口附加值。优化国际市场布局，引导企业深耕传统出口市场、拓展新兴市场，扩大与周边国家贸易规模，稳定国际市场份额。推动加工贸易转型升级，深化外贸转型升级基地、海关特殊监管区域、贸易促进平台、国际营销服务网络建设，加快发展跨境电商、市场采购贸易等新模式，鼓励建设海外仓，保障外贸产业链供应链畅通运转。创新发展服务贸易,推进服务贸易创新发展试点开放平台建设,提升贸易数字化水平。实施贸易投资融合工程。办好中国国际进口博览会、中国进出口商品交易会、中国国际服务贸易交易会等展会。

(资料来源:新华社)

(二)

陈泽炎:对会展业在"十四五"高质量发展的10点思考

"十四五"时期,我国会展业将在"十三五"发展的基础上更上一层楼。指导我国会展业在"十三五"时期发展的规划性文件就是2015年3月发布的《国务院关于进一步促进展览业改革发展的若干意见》(国发〔2015〕15号,以下简称"15号文件"),强调促进展览业发展,关键要坚持专业化、国际化、品牌化、信息化。在此基础上,高质量发展将成为会展业"十四五"的主基调和主旋律。笔者对此有以下相关思考:

第一,会展业的大格局背景:党中央对我国发展大格局和大背景的判断是,我国发展环境面临深刻复杂变化;我国发展仍然处于重要战略机遇期。当今世界正经历百年未有之大变局,要善于在危机中育先机、于变局中开新局。为此,我们的会展业一定要服务好国家"十四五"的发展任务。按照"十四五"规划建议,这些任务包括:6个"新"的发展目标;作为1个核心地位的"创新";11项重要的"举措";等等。围绕这些国家发展任务和发展目标,会展业应当进一步发挥好"搭建平台,提供服务"的功效与作用。

第二,会展业的发展总要求:可以理解为这一总要求就是要在"十四五"时期实现会展业的高质量发展。那么,什么是会展业的高质量发展呢?本文认为这就是,随着我国进入高质量的发展阶段,会展业必须不断提升水平,通过更加深入的供给侧结构性改革,输出更高质量的服务供给。为此,在"十四五"时期新发展格局、新发展阶段、新发展形势之下,将15号文件的内容予以进一步补充、完善、提升、改进,则是实现会展业高质量发展的基本路径。

第三,会展业的更完备体系:15号文件提出的"建设展览业体系"发展目标需要逐步完成、逐步深化。"十四五"时期,应在"基本建成"的基础上做到"更加完善""更有提升",也就是要在构成展览业体系的各方面获得新进展、做出新描述、达到新高度。

第四,会展业的三模式创新:2020年中央常委会提出"创新展会服务模式"。2020年4月13日商务部发出《关于创新展会服务模式培育展览业发展新动能有关工作的通知》,要求推进展会服务模式创新、管理模式创新、业态模式创新,加快培育行业发展新动能。"十四五"时期,会展业的"三模式创新"应当进一步予以落实和推进。譬如,在"服务模式创新"方面的利用新技术,实现O2O;"管理模式创新"方面的"放管服"改革,市场化取向;"业态模式创新"方面的会展新经济、多业态融合等。

第五,会展业的双循环对应:"十四五"规划建议提出,坚持创新驱动发展,全面塑造发展新优势;加快发展现代产业体系,推动经济体系优化升级;形成强大国内市场,构建新发展格局;畅通国内大循环,促进国内、国际双循环;全面促进消费,拓展投资空间。我国会展业与"双循环"战略的对应就体现在所搭建的一系列会展活动平台上,如进博会(上海)、广交会(广州)、服贸会(北京)以及中国—东盟、中国—东北亚、中国—南亚、中国—阿拉伯、中国—中东欧、中国—非洲、中国—俄罗斯、中国—蒙古国、中国—亚欧等博览会项目。

第六,会展业的文化大功效:15号文件已经提到"明确展览业经济、社会、文化、生态功能定位"。"十四五"规划建议又提出,坚定文化自信,围绕举旗帜、聚民心、育新人、兴文化、展形象的使命任务,促进满足人民文化需求和增强人民精神力量相统一,推进社会主义文化强国建设。"十三五"时期我国先后举办了"砥砺奋进的五年"大型成就展(2017)、"伟大的变革——庆祝改革开放40周年大型展览"(2018)、"伟大历程 辉煌成就——庆祝中华人民共和国成立70周年大型成就展"(2019)等,还有北京国际设计周展览会、艺术上海国际博览会、各大博物馆的常年展览和临时展览(譬如,在国家博物馆举办的"众志成城——抗疫主题美术作品展")。这些展览都属于文化宣传展览的范畴,都需要策展、布展等会展专业的技术支持和技术服务。同时,在发展会展业的过程中,关于中国特色会展文化的构建也不能被忽视。这些都是会展业文化大功效的体现。

第七,会展业的基础性建设:会展业的基础性建设当然包括场馆设施等硬实力方面的建设,但更为重要的还有关于管理方面的软实力建设。15号文件提出的完善展览业标准体系、完善行业诚信体系、加强知识产权保护、打击侵权和假冒伪劣、优化展览业布局、落实财税政策、改善金融保险服务、提高便利化水平、健全行业统计制度、加强人才体系建设、发挥中介组织作用等多方面工作,都属于基础性建设的内容。在"十四五"时期,这些基础性建设工作需要进一步予以加强与夯实。

第八,会展业的国际话语权:15号文件提出,我国在国际展览业中的话语权和影响力要显著提升。"十四五"时期必须进一步有所进展、有所作为,具体将涉及对会展业中国特色的阐释、对中国会展项目品牌标准的构建、对中国会展业"走出去"的支持、对发展"一带一路"共建国家和地区会展业合作的推进、对既有会展国际合作项目的经验总结与效果评估等多方面。

第九,会展业的安全化管理:"十四五"规划提出要全面推进健康中国建设,把保障人民健康放在优先发展的战略位置。完善突发公共卫生事件监测预警处置机制,提高应对突发公共卫生事件能力。保障人民生命安全。全面提高公共安全保障能力。"十四五"时期,会展业要加强安全化管理的主要工作是,做好新冠疫情防控常态化下的会展活动组织管理,做好会展场馆人流的管控和应急事件的预防应对,做好对展览搭建工程的标准审核与展会期间的日常巡检等。

第十,会展业的多层次规划:可以肯定的是,在全国"十四五"规划中要提到发挥进博会等重要展会的作用。我们进一步希望,国务院再发一个像15号文件那样的关于会展业的指导性文件;或者我们要求,商务部编制《关于"十四五"时期会展业发展的指导意见》。我们认为,商务部在参与全国"十四五"规划的编制过程中可以明确写入关于会展业的内容。当然,商务部会在《"十四五"现代服务业发展规划》中部署会展业的工作。相应的,全国会展城市会结合各自实际制定本地区的"会展业'十四五'规划"。在此基础上,还需要做好全国的统筹与协调。与"十四五"规划相衔接,我们设想的中国会展业2035年远景目标是"建设成为世界领先的会展强国"。

  "十四五"时期,会展业要牢记党中央的指示:实现"十四五"规划和2035五年远景目标,意义重大,任务艰巨,前景光明。为此,我国会展业一定要勇于担当,不辱使命,为完成国家"十四五"规划,实现会展业"十四五"规划而努力奋斗。

(资料来源:经济日报—中国经济网,有改动)

第二章 会展文本类型与翻译

学习目标

- 了解莱斯和纽马克的文本分类
- 熟悉不同文本翻译的基本原则和方法
- 了解语义翻译和交际翻译的差异与关注点
- 合理运用文本类型理论进行会展文本分析与翻译

核心词汇

* 文本类型理论(Text Typology Theory)
* 表达型(expressive)
* 信息型(informative)
* 呼唤型(vocative)
* 语义翻译(semantic translation)
* 交际翻译(communicative translation)
* 凯瑟琳娜·莱斯(Katharina Reiss)
* 彼得·纽马克(Peter Newmark)
* 国际标准化组织(International Standard Organization, ISO)

20世纪至今,由于现代科技的发展和影响,世界经济趋向一体化,各国间的经济活动交流更加密切。作为新兴服务业的重要内容,会展业有着无限的商机与发展潜力。同时,会展文本的翻译需求也在不断增长。一方面,会展翻译为会展活动提供必要的服务;另一方面,精准的会展翻译能够有效地搭建经济文化交流的桥梁,提升会展活动的影响力。因此,会展业对翻译人才的需求是刚性的、多样的、巨大的。

相较于我国经济现状、经济地位,我国会展翻译人才仅能够满足10%的国际会展活动需求,缺口高达90%,无法满足我国会展业的迅速发展所带来的翻译人才需求,这其中包含翻译人才的数量缺少和翻译人才的质量欠缺两方面。会展服务是综合性的,需要的是既懂专业技术、组织管理技能又通晓外语的职业翻译人才,这对译员提出了非常严苛的专业知识挑战,而专业技术及组织管理技能的习得又需要较长的周期。另外,会展翻译的职业化程度不高,绝大多数译员为兼职翻译,职业认可度不高,直接影响专业水平和职业发展。

第一节　文本与功能类型

文本类型翻译理论的创始人凯瑟琳娜·莱斯(Katharina Reiss)将文本分为信息型(informative)、表情型(expressive)和操作型(operative)三大类型,并在此基础上提出了以文本为导向的翻译策略(表2.1)。

表2.1　文本类型的功能特点及其与翻译方法之间的联系(Munday, 2001: 74)

文本类型	信息型	表情型	操作型
语言功能	信息的(表达事物与事实)	表情的(表达情感)	感染的(感染接受者)
语言特点	逻辑的	审美的	对话的
文本焦点	侧重内容	侧重形式	侧重感染作用
译文目的	表达其内容	表现其形式	诱出所期望的反应
翻译方法	简朴的白话文,按要求做到简洁明了	仿效,忠实于原作者	编译,等效

从图2.1可看出,莱斯不仅将文本分为三大类型,还阐述了各种文本类型与翻译方法的总体关系。换言之,翻译策略的选择有了自己的理据。

根据莱斯的观点,信息型文本主要表现事实、信息、知识、观点等,其语言特点是逻辑性较强,文本的焦点是内容而不是形式,翻译时应以简朴明了的白话文传递与原文相同的概念与信息;表情型文本用于表达信息发送者对人、对物的情感和态度,其语言具有美学的特征,侧重点是信息发送者及其发送的形式。表情型文本的翻译应采用仿效法,使译文忠实于原作者和原文;操作型文本旨在感染或说服读者并使其采取某种行动,以读者和效果为导向,其语言形式通常具有对话的性质,关注点是信息的接受者及对他们的感染作用。翻译操作型文本时,可用编译或适应性的方法以达到感染读者的目的。

莱斯还举例说明了哪些文本属于她所说的三种类型,切斯特曼(Chesterman)用图表描绘了她的文本分类(图2.1)。根据该图,参考用书是最典型的信息型文本,诗歌最具表情功能,广告则是最具感染力的类型。在参考用书、诗歌和广告三者之间,还有一些具有多重功能的文本类型。例如,传记可能是信息型与表情型兼备的类型,布道则是既有信息性又具感染力的多功能文本类型。虽然不少文本具备多种功能,但是它们总是有主次之分。莱斯(1977/1989:109)认为,翻译方法应该根据文本类型的不同而不同。芒迪指出,"莱斯理论的重要之处是,它超越了纯语言的层面,超越了纸上的文字及其意义,把视野拓宽到翻译的交际目的"(Munday,2001:76)。

图 2.1　莱斯的文本类型与文本种类(Reiss,1989:105)

功能语言观认为语言是一个社会文化系统,在这个系统中人们根据社会生活的目的来使用语言,语言是表达功能意义的载体。就语言功能而言,除了极少数简短公告类文案表现为单一功能的纯信息文本外,其他会展文案都表现出多重语言交际功能的特征。

在功能语言学的基础上,英国翻译理论家彼得·纽马克(Peter Newmark)在《翻译问题探讨》(*Approaches to Translation*,1988)一书中,将各类文本体裁划分为表达型文本(expressive)、信息型文本(informative)和呼唤型文本(vocative)三大类,并明确指出语言的主要功能表现为表达功能、信息功能及呼唤或诱导功能三大类型,而语言的酬应功能、元功能和美学功能为次要功能。

表达功能的核心在于说话者或作者运用一些话语来表达其思想感情,作者独特的语言形式和内容同等重要。典型的表达型文本包括严肃的、富有想象力的文学作品,权威性言论,作者个人情感的宣泄或无直接读者群的文本。表达型文本强调原作者的权威,在翻译时要遵循"原作者第一"的原则,既要忠实于原作者表达的思想内容,又要忠实于原作者的语言风格,无须考虑目标语读者的反应,所采用的翻译方法是"字面"翻译。

信息功能的核心是外部情况,即一个话题的全部信息,或者说言语之外的现实情况。信息型文本可以涉及任何知识领域,如工、农、商、教育、科技、经济等方面,其形式往往是标准化的。信息型文本的核心是内容的"真实性"(authenticity),作者的语言是次要的。在翻译时应遵循"真实性第一"的原则。译者在语言应用上可以不以原文本为标准,而以目标语读者的语言层次为标准,力求通顺易懂,所采用的翻译方法是等效翻译。

呼唤型文本强调以读者为中心,目的是"号召读者去行动、去思考、去感受"。告示、产品说明书、宣传手册、广告以及以取悦读者为目的的通俗小说等都属于这一范畴。呼唤型文本的语言特别强调可读性,讲究通俗易懂。译者可以充分发挥译入语的优势,不拘泥于原文的表达方式,使译文的语言尽量达到与原文语言同样的表达效果,所采用的翻译方法是等效再创作。

第二节　语义翻译和交际翻译

基于上述功能语言观,针对不同的文本类型,纽马克提出相应的翻译策略——语义翻译和交际翻译。

语义翻译的目的是"在目的语语言结构和语义许可的范围内,把原作者在原文中表达的意思准确地再现出来"(Newmark,1981/1988:22)。语义翻译重视的是原文的形式和原作者的原意,而不是目的语语境及其表达方式,更不是要把译文变为目的语文化情境中的事物。由于语义翻译把原文的一词一句视为神圣,因此有时会产生前后矛盾、语义含糊甚至是错误的译文。语义翻译通常适用于文学、科技文献和其他视原文语言与内容同等重要的语篇体裁。然而,需要指出的是,纽马克本人也认为,语义翻译并非一种完美的翻译模式,而是与交际翻译模式一样,在翻译实践中处于编译与逐行翻译之间的"中庸之道"(Hatim & Mason,1990:7)(图2.2)。

图 2.2　语义翻译 vs 交际翻译

从上图可以看出,"字对字翻译"(word-for-word translation)和"归化"(adaptation)译文之间的差距最大,其次是"直译"(literal translation)和"意译"(free translation),再其次是"忠实翻译"(faithful translation)和"地道翻译"(idiomatic translation),差距最小的是"语义翻译"(semantic translation)和"交际翻译"(communicative translation)。这八种方法是一个连续体,各种方法相辅相成,并不能被完全割裂开来。不过,语义翻译拥有逐字翻译、直译和忠实翻译的优势,交际翻译拥有归化、意译和地道翻译的优势。

交际翻译的目的是"努力使译文对目的语读者所产生的效果与原文对源语读者所产生的效果相同"(Newmark,1988:22)。也就是说,交际翻译的重点是根据目的语的语言、文化和语用方式传递信息,而不是尽量忠实地复制原文的文字。译者在交际翻译中有较大的自由度去解释原文、调整文体、排除歧义,甚至是修正原作者的错误。由于译者要达到某一交际目的,有其特定的目的读者群,因此他的译文必然会打破原文的局限。通常采用交际翻译的文体类型包括新闻报道、教科书、公共告示和其他很多非文学作品。

交际翻译与语义翻译有许多不同。交际翻译的关注点是目的语读者,尽量为这些读者排除阅读或交际上的困难与障碍,使交际顺利进行。在语义翻译中,译者仍然以原文为基础,只是解释原文的含义,帮助目的语读者理解文本的意思。交际翻译强调的是译文的"效果",而语义翻译强调的是保持原文的"内容"。语义翻译与交际翻译的区别与联系见图2.3。

视角	语义翻译	交际翻译
语言侧重	客观(屈从于源语文化,讲究准确性)	主观(屈从于目标语文化,译文地道、流畅)
表达形式	超额翻译(Overtranslation) 复杂、笨拙、具体、浓缩	欠额翻译(Undertranslation) 通顺、简朴、清晰、直接
信息内容与效果发生矛盾时	重内容,不重效果	重效果(译文一般优于原文)
翻译工作	一门艺术(Art),只能由一人单独承担	一门技巧(Craft),常由多人合作承担
适用文本类型	表达型文本	信息、呼唤型文本
联系	相辅相成,互为补充	

图2.3 语义翻译与交际翻译的区别与联系

第三节 会展文本翻译

会展文本,指的是因会展活动的需要,在会展管理和举办过程中使用语言文字记载会展信息的各种文书材料及其整理归档后的所有文本文案。国际会展业务基本流程主要分为策划(展前)、运作(展中)和测评(展后)三个阶段。不同阶段涉及不同功能的文本写作:策划阶段的会展申请类报告文案;运作阶段的会展规章、合同类文案和会展指南类文案;测评阶段的会展评估类文案;贯穿会展全过程的事务类文案。

会展文本既包括服务类信息,又含有宣传推介广告的成分。它具备信息传递以及宣传劝导两大基本功能,以实现预期的收益与效果为目的,因此需要把参加会展的益处传递出来,以便尽可能地吸引国内外企业前来参展或给予赞助。按照上述文本类型理论的观点,会展服务类信息文本传递基本的服务性信息,目的在于告知读者,属于信息型文本,翻译时要力求忠实再现;会展推介广告文本,关注的是劝说的宣传效果,目的在于争取读者,属于呼唤型文本,翻译策略要灵活变通。这两种文本的翻译方法不管是忠实再现,还是灵活变通,根据纽马克的观点,都需要采用交际翻译。而诸如致辞等表达型文本所要表达的核心是作者的思想,它在文本中的地位是神圣的。处理此类文本,要尽可能使用贴近原文的语义及句法结构,将原文的语境意义准确表达出来,因此语义翻译更为有效。

综上所述,翻译会展文本时,先要界定文本类型,然后确定翻译策略——语义翻译或交际翻译,再采取相应的翻译方法,如直译、意译、编译、仿译等,其中还应施以具体的翻译技巧,如增词法、省略法、转态法、分句法等,最终达到有效翻译的目的。

一、表达型文本

表达型文本的主旨是表明作者的态度、思想感情和价值取向,带有鲜明的个人印记。典型的表达型文本主要包括严肃文学作品、官方文告、法律法规文献,权威学者撰写的科学、哲学、学术著作以及自传和个人信函。

例1 商机无限 合作共赢

译文:BOUNDLESS OPPORTUNITIES, WIN-WIN COOPERATION

该文本通过"无限"与"共赢"表达文案撰写者的强烈行动指令,号召和激发消费行为,同时在语言形式上体现该标语言简意赅、富含修辞的特点。译文在语义及句法结构上(名词性短语的排比结构)与原文相似,并辅以英文字母的大写(引起读者注意),符合原文文本功能。

例2 南宁国际民歌艺术节成为南宁市一张亮丽的名片,成为向世界展示南宁魅力之城、活力之城、开放之城的窗口。

译文:Nanning International Folk Song Festival has become a brilliant business card of Nanning and a window displaying the charm, vitality and openness of the city.

表达型文本文案撰写者通过使用评价色彩浓重的修辞语(如"亮丽的""魅力之城""活力之城""开放之城"等)表达主观评价。译文在语义表达、词序安排及句法结构上力求接近原文形式,突出文本的"表达性"要素特征。例如,将"亮丽的"译为 brilliant 比译为 beautiful 更准确、到位;the charm, vitality and openness of the city 与"魅力之城、活力之城、开放之城"皆为名词性短语,表达具体有力。

二、信息型文本

信息型文本关注的焦点是信息传达的真实性,而信息交流是会展的核心。就会展文本翻译而言,"语言信息功能主要有告知和指令两种形式"。告知功能旨在告知读者不了解的事实或状态。在进行此类文本翻译的时候,译者应注意译文语言的规范性、客观性、严谨性和可读性。指令功能用于规定正确的行为方式,如规章类、合同类会展文案等。为了确保内容传递过程中不发生任何信息损益,译文在内容上应忠实于传递源语信息,在形式上应遵循目的语习惯,便于读者更透彻、更直观地接收源语信息。

例3 各展位布展须按规定申领施工证。不得涂改、复制、转借、转让或倒卖施工证,不得超出本展位范围施工。

译文:The CAEXPO Pass for Contractor for booth setup is requested. The Pass shall not be altered, duplicated, lent to other people, transferred or speculatively sold out. Booth setup and decoration can only be done in your own booth.

原文为具有指令功能的信息类文本,译文在内容上完全忠实于原文信息,同时为确保内容传递过程中不发生任何误解,采用了"增词法"的方式,明确说明"施工证"为the CAEXPO专用。此外,形式上译文采用了"转态译法",把主动语态变为被动语态,更符合目的语习惯。

例4 由于海关要求运输总代理对每件展品负责,因此如果没有通过我公司向海关作事先安排,参展商不得在展会开幕前、展会期间及结束后将任何展品带出展览中心。我公司对由此造成的任何展品没收和罚款不予负责。

译文:As the Customs requires the official forwarder to be responsible for every exhibit, exhibitors should not be allowed to take any of their exhibits out of the exhibition site before, during and after the exhibition without prior arrangement with the Customs through us. We shall not be responsible for any confiscation and fines arising therefrom.

原文为具有指令功能的会展规章条款,行文高度严谨,为确保内容在翻译过程中准确传递,译文采用了具有规章类文本文体特征的表达方式,如古语词 therefrom、高频词 shall、书面语 prior、专有名词 the Customs 等,有效兼顾原文与译文在内容和形式两方面的对等。

例5

新闻中心

负责广交会期间记者邀请、接待、重要采访活动的安排以及组织召开新闻发布会;负责编辑出版《广交会通讯》中文版;负责收集、整理《舆情快报》;负责宣传品发放管理。

电话:020-89130465

新闻中心日常办事机构设在外贸中心办公室(电话:020-89138489)。

译文:

Press Centre

Press Centre is responsible for receiving journalists and arranging interviews, management of publications, and arrangement of meeting rooms for all kinds of news release and seminars, editing and publishing *The Canton Fair Dispatches* (Chinese Version), collecting *Media Report Briefing* and managing promotion publications.

Tel: 86-20-89130465

The standing office is set up in Executive Dept., China Foreign Trade Centre (Tel: 86-20-89138489).

原文为具有告知功能的信息类文本,译文为了在内容上忠实传递原文信息、在形式上遵循目的语习惯,采取了一系列翻译技巧。首先,通过增加 management of publications 和 meeting rooms,清晰界定了原文所指内容;其次,为使译文形式符合目的语习惯,便于读者理解,译文采取了诸如省略法(省略 responsible for)、增词法(增加中国大陆国际区号 86)、转态译法(使用被动语态 is set up)等翻译技巧。

三、呼唤型文本

呼唤型文本关注的焦点是信息的传递效果和读者的情感呼应,其目的在于"唤起"读者去"思考"、去"感受"、去"行动"。因此,为实现此类文本的"呼唤"功能,译者应顺从译文读者的欣赏习惯与心理感受,尽量使用其所熟悉的语言表达形式以获得预期的效果。

例 6

i-分享——更多优质采购商,更好参展效果

如果您是广交会的参展企业,可在广交会官方网站"参展易捷通"平台向您的客户发出与会采购的邀请,也可在您发给客户的信件中添加"广交会参展企业编码"定制邀请,让您的朋友共享广交会商机。同时,您还有机会获得广交会电子商务专享服务与好礼。

译文:

JOIN i-share

Enjoy more opportunities and high-quality services of Canton Fair i-share—more convenient, more considerate.

If you are a Canton Fair buyer, you can send invitations to your friends via the BEST (Buyer E-Service Tool) platform on the fair's official website. Regular buyers can also send their "i-share" exclusive entry tickets to their friends, who may also enjoy business opportunities of Canton Fair. Meanwhile, you also have the chance to receive the Fair's VIP services and premium gifts.

广交会的参展企业最关心的是展会能提供的那些优质、便利的服务。译文紧紧抓住此核心要素,通过增词法(增加 more convenient 和 more considerate)、引申法(使用 exclusive,

VIP services, premium gifts)及大写字母(引起读者注意)等翻译技巧,极大地激发起参展企业参展并邀请其客户采购的"行动"。

例7 《中国-东盟博览会会刊》是中国-东盟博览会秘书处的唯一正式会刊,汇集了中国及东盟十国的名企、名品及各省市最新、最翔实丰富的资讯。《第三届中国-东盟博览会会刊》在中国-东盟博览会期间公开发行,并惠赠给来自20多个国家和地区的客商、各国驻华使馆商务处、海内外企业驻华机构、各国政府贸易机构等。

译文:The China – ASEAN Expo Journal is a unique official publication of China – ASEAN Expo Secretariat, collecting abundant and the latest information on well-known enterprises, brand products and excellent cities in China and 10 ASEAN countries. The 3rd China – ASEAN Expo Journal will be publicly issued during the Expo and be distributed to the business clients, commercial offices of embassies in China, resident offices of domestic and foreign enterprises in China and trading departments of governments, involving more than 20 countries and regions, for free.

该文作为中国-东盟博览会官网上的会刊简介,其目的是"唤起"更多的读者(参展商)去"行动",即订购会刊广告。其诉求功能需要通过提供详细的会刊信息(客观事实的描述)并配以明确的主观评价才能得以实现。因此,译文通过使用专业术语(China – ASEAN Expo Secretariat)和被动语态(will be issued, will be distributed),体现原文的规范性和客观性。同时,通过使用评价色彩浓重的修辞语(unique, abundant, latest)表达主观评价,"唤起"参展商的订购会刊广告的愿望。

例8 作为2011年西博会重要项目和杭州综合性人才交流会的重头戏之一,本届人才交流会着眼于深入实施《杭州市中长期人才发展规划纲要(2010—2020年)》,加快建设"一基地、四中心"的目标,本着服务社会与服务求职者、用人单位和毕业生就业的原则,以"一体化、市场化、层次化、专业化、精品化"为交流模式,突出"广纳英才、服务发展"的主题,为吸引更多创新创业人才、调整当地产业结构、推动经济发展方式转变和统筹城乡区域发展提供有益的助力。

译文:As a major program of the 2011 West Lake Expo and a leading part of the job fairs of Hangzhou, and taking " being integrated, market-oriented, tiered, specialized, selected" as its guidelines and "extensive recruitment of professionals for the city's development" as its theme, the fair has contributed to the pooling of more creative and business-minded professionals, restructuring of the local industries, furthering the transformation of the mode of economic growth, and consolidating rural and urban regional development of Hangzhou.

作为呼唤型文本,原文通过对人才交流会的政府背景及政策介绍达到推介的目的。由于原文中"程式化"口号文字过多,考虑到西方读者"重事实、忌空洞"的接受习惯,译文采用了省略法,删减"本届人才交流会着眼于深入实施《杭州市中长期人才发展规划纲要(2010—2020年)》,加快建设'一基地、四中心'的目标,本着服务社会与服务求职者、用人单位和毕业生就业的原则"这部分内容,只保留了"一体化、市场化、层次化、专业化、精品化"和"广纳英才、服务发展"等重要信息,这有利于实现译文与原文文本宣传功能的对等。

例9 近年来,每届投洽会都吸引了100多个国家和地区的10000多名境外客商参会,在已经举办的十二届投洽会中,共签订各类投资合作项目13568个,合同利用外资908.9亿美元。

译文:At the end of the 12th CIFIT, we are very pleased to see that many overseas investors have signed contracts with their Chinese partners, involving 13,568 projects and an investment amount of 90.89 billion US dollars in China.

中国国际投资贸易洽谈会(简称"投洽会")经中华人民共和国国务院批准,于每年9月8日至11日在中国厦门举办。投洽会以"引进来"和"走出去"为主题,以"突出全国性和国际性、突出投资洽谈和投资政策宣传、突出国家区域经济协调发展、突出对台经贸交流"为主要特色,是中国唯一以促进双向投资为目的的国际投资促进活动,也是通过国际展览业协会(UFI)认证的全球规模最大的投资性展览会。原文中文版会展推介广告偏重于介绍政府的功绩,是一种政府主导型的宣传模式;而国外的会展则多是展示企业的诉求点,直观明了,辞藻朴实,是一种市场主导型的推广模式。中国的会展宣传文字外译时需要把政府主导型的宣传模式转换成市场主导型的推广模式,这才符合外商投资者的心理期待。如果忽视这一点,就会出现如下译文:* At the 12th CIFIT (China International Fair for Investment and Trade) which is just concluded, many contracts have been signed, involving 13,568 investment cooperation projects, and 90.89 billion US dollar foreign capitals have been utilized。这个译文虽然内容与语言形式都与原文相符,但句子焦点是政府主导的行为,而这不是市场主导型的推广方式。换言之,外商对投资对象国引入多少海外资金和项目并无多少兴趣,他们的兴趣点在于市场现有可利用的外资和项目。因此,译文从心理和语言习惯上更容易被外商接受。

第四节　国际标准化组织标准规范 25639-1：2008：展览、展会、交易会和大会——第1部分：词汇

2008年11月15日由国际标准化组织发布的"国际标准化组织标准规范25639-1：2008：展览、展会、交易会和大会——第1部分：词汇"（International Standard ISO 25639-1：2008：Exhibitions, Shows, Fairs and Conventions—Part 1：Vocabulary）对国际会展领域中的专业术语进行了标准化界定，为英法双语版，中文版暂时空缺。附录一为试译双语（英中）平行语料，仅供参考。

思考题

1. 如何理解纽马克的观点"语义翻译与交际翻译一样，是翻译实践的'中庸之道'"？
2. 运用文本类型理论分析以下实例。
（1）原文：请于截止日期前将有关表格填妥，连同全部款项直接交回有关机构。
译文：Please COMPLETE and RETURN all related forms, WITH FULL PAYMENT, to the related parties directly.
（2）原文：让我们以杭州为新起点，引领世界经济的航船，从钱塘江畔再次扬帆起航，驶向更加广阔的大海！
译文：Let's make Hangzhou a new departure point and steer the giant ship of the global economy on a new voyage from the shore of the Qiantang River to the vast ocean.
（3）原文：凭借地处沿海、交通便利、工商业发达、城市繁荣等天时地利之优，本着多年来遵循的平等互利、广交朋友、优质服务、信誉至上的宗旨，竭诚同世界各国发展贸易关系。
译文：With the convenient transport along the coast and the prosperous commerce in the city, we spare painstaking efforts to do business with countries and regions all over the world on the basis of equality and mutual benefits.
（4）原文：The Contractor shall co-operate with the Site Security Services with respect to reporting of security incidents, closing and locking of gates, visitors, vehicles and any other matters to be reasonably requested.
译文：承包商应与现场安全服务部门合作处理以下事项：报告安全事故，关门锁门，管理访客和车辆进出现场，以及处理其他可能提出的合理要求。
（5）原文：At the concluding press conference of the 125th session of the Canton Fair, Xu Bing, Deputy Secretary General and Spokesperson of the Canton Fair and Deputy Director General of China Foreign Trade Centre, introduced the achievements made in stabilizing the size, improving the quality and shifting growth impetus of foreign trade.

译文：在第 125 届广交会闭幕新闻发布会上，广交会副秘书长、新闻发言人、中国对外贸易中心副主任徐兵介绍了广交会在服务稳规模、提质量、转动力方面取得的成效。

3. 分析并翻译以下段落。

诞生于 20 世纪 80 年代末的虎豹集团信守孜孜矻矻、永不言退的发展理念，在市场经济的大潮中，任凭浊浪排空、惊涛拍岸，独有胜似闲庭信步的自信，处变不惊，运筹帷幄。尽握无限商机于掌间，渐显王者之气于天地。

虎豹人以其特有的灵气，极目一流，精益求精，集世界顶尖服装生产技术装备之大成。裁天上彩虹，绣人间缤纷，开设计之先河，臻质量之高峰，领导服装潮流，尽显领袖风采。

（浙江虎豹集团宣传资料）

Semantic and Communicative Translation: Guided Reading

Peter Newmark (1916) is an accomplished translation scholar as well as an experienced translator. He has translated a number of books and articles and published extensively on translation. His publications on translation include *Approaches to Translation* (1981), *About Translation* (1983), *Paragraphs on Translation* (1985), *A Textbook of Translation* (1988), and *More Paragraphs on Translation* (1993).

In his work *Approaches to Translation*, Newmark proposes two types of translation: semantic translation and communicative translation. Semantic translation focuses primarily upon the semantic content of the source text whereas communicative translation focuses essentially upon the comprehension and response of receptors. This distinction results from his disapproval of Nida's assumption that all translating is communicating, and the overriding principle of any translation is to achieve "equivalent effect". For Newmark, the success of equivalent effect is "illusory", and that "the conflict of loyalties, the gap between emphasis on source and target languages will always remain as the overriding problem in translation theory and practice" (1981: 38). To narrow the gap, Newmark formulates his concepts of "communicative translation" and "semantic translation", which in a sense are similar to Nida's "dynamic equivalent translation" and "formal equivalent translation". Newmark admits "communicative translation" is a common method and could be used in many types of translation. Nevertheless, he justifies the legitimacy of "semantic translation" in the following three aspects. Firstly, all translations depend on the three dichotomies, namely, the foreign and native cultures, the two languages, the writer and the translator. Hence, it is unlikely to have a universal theory that could include all these factors. Secondly, previous discussions on methods of translation, either Nida's "dynamic equivalence" or Nabokow's "literal translation", does not reflect the actual reality of translation method, for each of them either recommends one or disparages the other. Thirdly, the social factors, especially the readers of the second language, only play a partial role in translation. Some texts, such as an expressive one, require a "semantic translation" (1981: 62). It can be seen that by proposing the coexistence of "communicative translation" and "semantic translation", Newmark suggests a correlation between translation method and text type.

It should be pointed out that Newmark's semantic translation differs from literal translation because the former "respects context", interprets and even explains while the latter sticks very closely to source text at word and syntax level (1981: 62). Literal translation, however, is held to be the best approach in both semantic and communicative translation, "provided that equivalent effect is secured, the literal word-for-word translation is not only the best, it is the only valid method of translation" (1981: 39). Here Newmark seems to only take account of literary translation rather than non-literary translation, which is often rendered more freely in order to communicate the meaning. But he also states that when there is a conflict between semantic translation and communicative translation, the latter would win out. For instance, it is better to render communicatively the public sign "bissiger Hund and chien mechant" into "Beware the dog!" in order to communicate efficiently the message, but not semantically as "Dog that bites! And bad dog!" (1981: 39). Nevertheless, it is difficult for a translator to follow Newmark's translation methods in practice, which should be adopted flexibly according to the specific context and text type.

A Textbook of Translation is an expansion and a revision of *Approaches to Translation* in many aspects. In this book, Newmark, following the German linguist Karl Buhler's functional theory of language, proposes three main types of texts (i.e. expressive, informative and vocative) as well as methods of translating them (Chapters 4 and 5). Although he lists many translation methods from word-for-word translation to adaptation, he insists that "only semantic and communicative translation fulfill the two main aims of translation, which are first, accuracy, and second, economy". While semantic translation is used for expressive texts, communicative translation is for informative and vocative texts although he admits that few texts are purely expressive, informative or vocative. By stressing the wide applicability of these two translation methods, Newmark seems to overlook the function of other translation methods frequently adopted in translation practice.

Newmark's semantic and communicative translation have been quoted frequently among translation scholars. His concern about the coexistence of semantic and communicative translation shows that in his view effect-oriented translation such as Nida's dynamic equivalence should not be overstressed in translation practice, but is just one type of translation. Newmark's types of translation, however, are less influential than Nida's dynamic equivalence in the field of translation studies because they "raise some of the same points concerning the translation process and the importance of the TT reader" (Munday, 2000: 46). Further, his views and comments are still very traditional and prescriptive, bearing some traces of traditional translation theories. The strength of his writing lies in that his discussion on translation covers a wide range of topics, and he always provides useful advice and guidance for translator trainees with a large number of interesting and useful examples, which are more convincing than abstract theoretical arguments. The following excerpt is selected from Chapter 3 of Newmark's *Approaches to Translation*. In this chapter he postulates his two main methods of translation (i.e. semantic and communicative translation), and tries to apply them into different types of text.

Communicative and Semantic Translation

1. A translation must give the words of the original.
2. A translation must give the ideas of the original.
3. A translation should read like an original work.
4. A translation should read like a translation.
5. A translation should reflect the style of the original.
6. A translation should possess the style of the translation.
7. A translation should read as a contemporary of the original.
8. A translation should read as a contemporary of the translation.
9. A translation may add to or omit from the original.
10. A translation may never add to or omit from the original.
11. A translation of verse should be in prose.
12. A translation of verse should be in verse.

(*The Air of Translation*, T. H. Savory, Cape, 1968, p.54)

In the pre-linguistics period of writing on translation, which may be said to date from Cicero through St. Jerome, Luther, Dryden, Tytler, Herder, Goethe, Schleiermacher, Buber, Ortega y Gasset, not to say Savory, opinion swung between literal and free, faithful and beautiful, exact and natural translation, depending on whether the bias was to be in favour of the author or the reader, the source or the target language of the text. Up to the nineteenth century, literal translation represented a philological academic exercise from which the cultural reformers were trying to rescue literature. In the nineteenth century, a more scientific approach was brought to bear on translation, suggesting that certain types of texts must be accurately translated, while others should and could not be translated at all! Since the rise of modern linguistics (philology was becoming linguistics here in the late fifties), and anticipated by Tytler in 1790, Larbaud, Belloc, Knox and Rieu, the general emphasis, supported by communication-theorists as well as by non-literary translators, has been placed on the reader—on informing the reader effectively and appropriately, notably in Nida, Firth, Koller and the Leipzig School. In contrast, the brilliant essays of Benjamin, Valery and Nabokov (anticipated by Croce and Ortega y Gasset) advocating literal translation have appeared as isolated, paradoxical phenomena, relevant only to translating works of high literary culture. Koller (1972) has stated that the equivalent-effect principle of translation is tending to rule out all others, particularly the predominance of any formal elements such as word or structure.

The apparent triumph of the "consumer" is, I think, illusory. The conflict of loyalties, the gap between emphasis on source and target languages will always remain as the overriding problem in translation theory and practice. However, the gap could perhaps be narrowed if the previous terms were replaced as follows:

SOURCE LANGUAGE BIAS   TARGET LANGUAGE BIAS
LITERAL   FREE
FAITHFUL   IDIOMATIC
SEMANTIC / COMMUNICATIVE

Communicative translation attempts to produce on its readers an effect as close as possible to that obtained on the readers of the original. Semantic translation attempts to render, as closely as the semantic and syntactic structures of the second language allow, the exact contextual meaning of the original.

In theory, there are wide differences between the two methods. Communicative translation addresses itself solely to the second reader, who does not anticipate difficulties or obscurities, and would expect a generous transfer of foreign elements into his own culture as well as his language where necessary. But even here the translator still has to respect and work on the form of the source language text as the only material basis for his work. Semantic translation remains within the original culture and assists the reader only in its connotations if they constitute the essential human (non-ethnic) message of the text. One basic difference between the two methods is that where there is a conflict, the communicative must emphasize the "force" rather than the content of the message. Thus for "Bissige Hund" or "Chien mechant", the communicative translation "Beware of the dog!" is mandatory; the semantic translations ("dog that bite", "savage dog") would be more informative but less effective. Generally, a communicative translation is likely to be smoother, simpler, clearer, more direct, more conventional, conforming to a particular register of language, tending to under-translate, i. e. to use more generic, hold-all terms in difficult passages. A semantic translation tends to be more complex, more awkward, more detailed, more concentrated, and pursues the thought-processes rather than the intention of the transmitter. It tends to over-translate, to be more specific than the original, to include more meanings in its search for one nuance of meaning.

However, in communicative translation as in semantic translation, provided that equivalent-effect in secured, the literal word-for-word translation is not only the best, it is the only valid method of translation. There is no excuse for unnecessary "synonyms", let alone paraphrases, in any type of translation.

Conversely, both semantic translation and communicative translation comply with the usually accepted syntactic equivalents (Vinay and Darbelnet's "transpositions") for the two languages in question. Thus, by both methods, a sentence such as "Il traversa la Manche en nageant" would normally be translated as "He swam across the Channel". In semantic, but not communicative translation, any deviation from SL stylistic norms would be reflected in an equally wide deviation from the TL norms, but where such norms clash, the deviations are not easy to formulate, and the translator has to show a certain tension between the writer's manner and the compulsions of the target language. Thus when the writer uses long complex sentences in a language where the sentence in a "literary" (carefully worked) style is usually complex and longer than in the TL, the translator may reduce the sentences somewhat, compromising between the norms of the two languages and the writer. If in doubt, however, he should trust the writer, not the "language", which is a sum of abstractions …

A translation is always closer to the original than any intralingual rendering or paraphrase misnamed "translation" by George Steiner (1975), and therefore it is an indispensable tool for a semantician (semanticist) and now a philosopher. Communicative and semantic translation may well coincide—in particular, where the text conveys a general rather than a culturally, temporally and spatially bound message and where the matter is as important as the manner—notably then in the translation of the most important religious, philosophical, artistic and scientific texts, assuming second readers as informed and interested as the first. Further, there are often sections in one text that must be translated communicatively (e. g. non-lieu—"nonsuit"), and others semantically (e. g. a quotation from a speech). There is no one communicative nor one semantic method of translating a text—these are in fact widely overlapping bands of methods. A translation can be more, or less, semantic—more, or less, communicative—even a particular section or sentence can be treated more communicatively or less semantically. Thus in some passages, Q. Hoare and G. Nowell Smith (1971) state: "We feel it preferable to choose fidelity over good English, despite its awkwardness, in view of the importance of some concepts in Gramsci's work." Each method has a common basis in analytical or cognitive translation which is built up both proposition by proposition and word by word, denoting the empirical factual knowledge of the text, but finally respecting the convention of the target language provided that the thought-content of the text has been reproduced. The translation emerges in such a way that the exact meaning or function of the words only become apparent as they are used. The translator may have to make interim decisions without being able at the time to visualize the relation of the words with the end product. Communicative and semantic translation bifurcate at a later stage of analytical or cognitive translation which is a pre-translation procedure which may be performed on the source-language text to convert it into the source or the target language—the reluctant versions will be closer to each other than the original text and the final translation.

实践篇

第三章 会展实务翻译

学习目标

- 了解招展书的结构和内容
- 了解参展商手册的结构和内容
- 掌握会展名称的翻译方法
- 掌握会展名称和主题的翻译方法
- 掌握展品运输指南的翻译方法
- 掌握展位搭建指南的翻译方法

核心词汇

* 招展书(exhibition brochure)
* 参展商手册(exhibitor manual)
* 主办单位(organizer)
* 承办单位(co-hosted organizer)
* 展品范围(exhibition scope)
* 展馆平面图(floor plan)
* 招商宣传推广计划(investment promotion plan)
* 展会规则(rules & regulations of the exhibition)
* 运输指南(shipping guidelines)
* 搭建指南(construction directory)
* 正式度(degree of formality)
* 衔接(cohesion)

第一节　　招展书翻译

招展书是展会进行展位营销时的核心资料之一,也是目标参展商最初了解展会情况的主要信息来源。其主要内容包括:

(1) 展会介绍:展会名称、标志、主题、时间、地点、办展机构、展品范围、办展背景、特色、创新之处等。

(2) 以往展会回顾:往届参展商和专业观众数量、观众结构分析等。

(3) 市场状况介绍:行业状况、地区市场状况等。

(4) 展会招商和宣传推广计划:展会招商计划、宣传推广计划、相关活动计划、展会服务项目等。

(5) 参展办法:参展手续、付款方式、参展申请表和办展机构的联系办法等。

(6) 其他信息:参展费用、展馆图、展馆周边地区交通图、往届展会现场图片等。

一、招展书范例

(一) 展会介绍

2020世界智能网联汽车大会 & 第八届中国国际新能源和智能网联汽车展览会

新基建、新智联、新生活——开启汽车新时代
Newer Infrastructure · Smarter Connectivity · Better Life—Open a New Era of Vehicles

1. 主办单位

- 北京市人民政府(The People's Government of Beijing Municipality)
- 工业和信息化部(Ministry of Industry and Information Technology of the People's Republic of China)

- 公安部(Ministry of Public Security of the People's Republic of China)
- 交通运输部(Ministry of Transport of the People's Republic of China)
- 中国科学技术协会(China Association for Science and Technology)

2. 承办单位

- 工业和信息化部装备工业发展中心(Development Center of Equipment Industry, Ministry of Industry and Information of Technology PRC)
- 北京市经济和信息化局(Beijing Municipal Bureau of Economy and Information Technology)
- 中国电子信息产业发展研究院(China Center for Information Industry Development)
- 北京市顺义区人民政府(People's Government of Shunyi District, Beijing, China)
- 中国国际贸易促进委员会机械行业分会(China Council for the Promotion of International Trade Machinery Sub-Council)
- 中国电工技术学会(China Electrotechnical Society)

3. 展览执行单位

- 北京中汽四方会展有限公司(Beijing Auto Square Exhibition Co., Ltd.)

4. 展会简介

为促进节能与新能源汽车产业发展，贯彻落实国务院发布的《节能与新能源汽车产业发展规划(2012—2020年)》，积极推动科技进步，做好节能、环保、减排促进工作，进一步增强我国自主创新、自主开发、自主品牌和产业结构升级力度，加强国际交流与合作，推动节能与新能源汽车产业的快速发展，2013年10月17日—20日，在工业和信息化部等部委的支持下，首届"中国国际节能与新能源汽车展览会、节能与新能源汽车产业发展规划成果展览会、中国国际汽车新能源及技术应用展览会、中国国际纯电动车、混合动力车和燃料电池车及关键零部件技术交流展览会"(简称"中国国际节能与新能源汽车展"，英文简称IEEVChina)在北京国家会议中心隆重举行。

In order to promote the development of energy saving and new energy vehicle industry, implement the Energy-Saving and New Energy Development Plan for the Automobile Industry (2012 – 2020) issued by the State Council, actively promote technological progress, and accomplish the duties in promoting energy-saving environmental protection and emission reduction, and further strengthen the efforts in upgrading China's independent innovation, independent development, independent brand and industrial structure, strengthen international exchanges and cooperation, and promote the rapid development of the energy saving and new energy automobile industry, the First IEEVChina was held ceremoniously at China National Convention Center in Beijing, with the support of Ministry of Industry and Information Technology (MIIT) and other ministries on October 17th – 20th, 2013.

5. 展品范围

2020 中国国际工业博览会：新能源与智能网联汽车展

- 新能源汽车（乘用车、商用车、客车）
- 电动汽车关键零部件（电池、电机、电控）
- 充电基础设施及相关配套产品（充电机、充电桩、换电装置等）
- 氢燃料电池
- 智能网联汽车
- 智能网联核心技术
- 车体电子控制装置
- 车载电子装置
- 车载智能硬件
- 智能车载设备
- 车联网相关产品
- 智能出行

- New Energy Vehicle
- Key Parts of Electric Automobile (Battery / Motor / Electric Control)
- Charging Infrastructure with Related Products (Charging Machinery / Charging Pile / Charging Device)
- Hydrogen Fuel Cell
- Intelligent Network Vehicle
- Intelligent Network Core Technology
- Electronic Control Device
- Vehicle-Mounted Electronic Device
- Intelligent Hardware
- Intelligent Vehicle Equipment
- Car Networking with Related Products
- Intelligent Travel

（二）以往展会回顾

2019 中国国际工业博览会：新能源与智能网联汽车展

2019 展会回顾 Show Review	展示面积 / Exhibition Area 15 000 m²	参展企业 / Exhibitors 100+家	境外展商所占比例/ Proportion of Foreign Exhibitors 27%
	入场观众 / Visitors 193788人次	行业论坛 / Industrial Forums & Conferences 50+场	

观众分析 Visitors' Profile ▶▶▶

参观展会目的分析

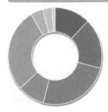

■ 采购 / Make Purchases	12.30%
■ 联络供应商和销售商 / Contact Existing Suppliers and Buyers	16.83%
■ 寻求特殊解决方案、创新技术 / Seek Solutions for Special Equipments	25.01%
■ 寻求并确定新的代理商、分销商及合作伙伴 / Identify New Agents/Distributors/Partners	9.27%
■ 收集和了解市场信息 / Gather and Know Market Information	28.80%
■ 参加会议 / Attend Forum/Conference	4.24%
■ 评估参展可能性 / Assess the Possibility of Participation	3.19%
■ 其他 / Others	1.09%

观众业务领域分析

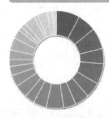

■ 整车制造 / Vehicle Manufacturing	20.71%
■ 动力驱动系统 / Power-Driven System	16.08%
■ 智能互联技术 / Smart Networking Technology	18.23%
■ 车载网络技术 / Technology on Vehicle	13.09%
■ 先进驾驶辅助技术 / Advanced Driving AIDS	17.87%
■ 车载智能硬件 / Intelligent Hardware Used on Vehicles	13.36%
■ 车载电子装置 / Electronic Devices Used on Vehicles	12.66%
■ 人机界面技术 / Interface Technology on Human Machine	10.89%
■ 高精度地图与定位技术 / Map and Position Technology with High Precision	15.56%
■ 交通大数据处理与分析 / Traffic Big Data in Processing and Analysis	11.67%
■ 充电基础设施 / Charging Infrastructure Facility	8.71%
■ 电力电工设备 / Electric Power Equipment	11.48%
■ 机械制造 / Machinery Manufacturing	9.72%
■ 机器人 / Robotics	8.05%
■ 工业自动化 / Industrial Automation	5.88%
■ 机床及相关行业 / Machine Tool and Related Industry	8.37%
■ 物流运输 / Logistics Transportation	10.64%
■ 市政建设 / Municipal Construction	7.72%
■ 公共交通 / Public Transportation	3.26%
■ 环保装备 / Environmental Protection Equipment	4.65%
■ 汽车节能技术 / Automobile Energy Saving Technology	9.54%
■ 模具制造 / Mould Manufacturing	3.17%
■ 通信技术/运营/服务 / Communication Technology/Operation/Service	8.57%
■ 计算机软/硬件 / Computer Software/Hardware	5.04%
■ 半导体照明及应用 / Semiconductor Lighting and Application	3.51%

(三)市场状况介绍

2022第十届中国国际管材展览会

1. 中国:钢管生产大国

2019年我国钢管产量8417.6万吨,其中焊管产量5619.2万吨,无缝管产量2798.4万吨。2019年钢管表观消费量7620.51万吨,其中焊管表观消费量5243.19万吨,无缝管表观消费量2377.32万吨;我国钢管行业进入深化结构调整、转型升级、环保生产、提质增效时期。

In 2019, China's steel pipe output was 84.176 million tons, of which 56.192 million tons were welded pipes and 27.984 million tons were seamless pipes. The apparent consumption of steel pipes in 2019 was 76.2051 million tons, of which 52.4319 million tons were welded pipes and 23.7732 million tons were seamless pipes. China's steel pipe industry has entered a period of in-depth structural adjustments and is undergoing transformations and upgradation towards environmentally friendly production, and quality and efficiency improvement.

2. 下游行业需求和商机

近年来钢管主要下游行业只有汽车产量略有下降,而天然气、原油、原油加工、管网建设、页岩气、发电量、房地产、煤燃、煤层气、机械制造等钢管主要下游均有不同的增长,这将给钢管行业带来利好,也为钢管行业2020年之后平稳运行提供了保证。

In recent years, major industries such as natural gas, crude oil and processing, pipeline network construction, shale gas, power generation, real estate, coal, coalbed methane, and machinery manufacturing have shown growth at different levels. This will bring huge benefits to the steel pipe industry and also provide a guarantee for the smooth operation of the steel pipe industry after 2020.

3. 管网建设

2020年,中国新建成油气管道里程约5081千米,油气管道总里程累计达到14.4万千米。2020—2030年是中国能源消费与碳排放达峰阶段,据预计,到2030年天然气需求量将达到5260亿立方米,到2035年左右需求将达到峰值6500亿立方米。这将加快油气管网等基础设施的建设。

In 2020, China's newly built oil and gas pipelines had a mileage of approximately 5,081 kilometers, and the total mileage of oil and gas pipelines reached 144,000 kilometers. China's energy consumption and carbon emissions are scheduled to peak during 2020−2030 period. It is estimated that natural gas demand will reach 526 billion cubic meters by 2030 and 650 billion cubic meters by 2035. This will speed up the construction of infrastructure such as oil and gas pipeline networks.

（四）展会招商和宣传推广计划

2022 第十届中国国际管材展览会
丰富的宣传渠道，助您获得更多流量
VARIOUS ADVERTISING TOOLS HELP YOU GET MORE EXPOSURE

为达到更多的宣传效益，接触更多的潜在买家，主办方提供展商与展品名单，为全球买家不断优化寻找供应商及产品的功能，促成高效的供需对接。

In order to help you achieve better promotion results and reach more potential buyers, the organizers provide exhibitor and product list, and continuously optimize the supply and demand search functions for global buyers.

与70余家优质的中外管材行业媒体合作，创新宣传。2020年首次推出VR云展，让展会的宣传效益触及展馆以外的全球买家，突破地域限制。

We have cooperated with more than 70 high-quality domestic and overseas tube industry media to promote the event in innovative ways. During the pandemic in 2020, the VR exhibition was launched for the first time, allowing the promotion of the exhibition to reach global buyers outside the exhibition hall, breaking through the geographical restrictions.

按照参展商需要量身定制推广服务（现场广告、特色赞助、同期活动合作、线上推广、印刷媒体等），提供优质高效的宣传工具，让参展商随时随地和全球潜在买家联系。

Customized advertising services, high-quality and efficient tools such as on-site advertising, featured sponsorship, concurrent event cooperation, online promotion, print media, etc. are provided according to exhibitors' needs, allowing exhibitors to contact potential buyers around the world anytime, anywhere.

（五）参展办法

2020 中国国际工业博览会：新能源与智能网联汽车展

A 室内光地
18平方米起租，参展商须自行承担展台搭建、装饰等相关费用
Raw Space
· Stand area (min. 18 sqm)

B 标准展台
9平方米（3米×3米）
· 一张洽谈桌
· 四把折椅
· 一个220V/800W电源插座
· 两个射灯
· 参展商公司中英文名称楣板
· 展位内满铺地毯

· Stand area (min. 9 sqm)
· Back walls and side walls (white)
· 1 reception desk
· 4 chairs
· 1 electric power point
· 2 spotlights
· 1 company sign (English/Chinese)
· Carpeting

（六）其他信息

1. 展区设置

2022 第十届中国国际管材展览会

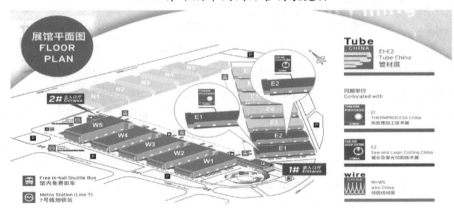

2. 参展费用

2020 中国国际工业博览会：新能源与智能网联汽车展

二、招展书翻译实践

（一）会展名称翻译

会展名称最突出的语言特点是其标签性,一般由名词性短语表达,通过用 congress, conference, forum, meeting, summit, symposium, assembly, workshop, seminar, session, meet, colloquium, ceremony, festival, day, contest, open, championship, competition, show, display, exhibition, fair, mart, expo 等名词来限定活动的主题、主办机构、参加者、举办时间和地点、顺序、目标等。

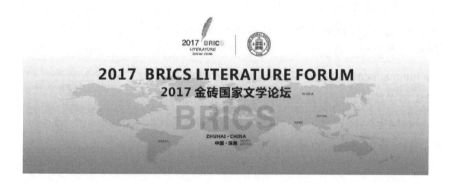

1. 年份

会展名称中涉及的数字主要是年份和活动举办的届数和次序。年份的数字汉译英时一般采取后置的排列方式,重点在于突出会议的主题。这些会展多是定期、定年举办的。

- 博鳌亚洲论坛2021年年会

Boao Forum for Asia Annual Conference 2021

- 2021全球人工智能大会

World Artificial Intelligence Conference 2021

但对于个别会展、赛事、节庆活动的名称翻译,为了突出年份概念,也可以做前置处理。

- 2019年世界杯特殊奥林匹克运动会签约仪式

2019 Special Olympics World Games Agreement Signing Ceremony

- 公共外交国际论坛（2020）暨第三届外交官论坛

2020 International Forum on Public Diplomacy & 3rd Diplomats Forum

2. 序数词

序数词既可以是词汇形式,也可以是数字加后缀,后者使用频率更高;罗马数字一般只用在诸如奥运会这类历史悠久的会展、赛事、节庆活动中。

- 第十届国际互联网大会

The Tenth International World Wide Web Conference

- 第四届世界休闲博览会
The 4th World Leisure Expo
- 第29届奥林匹克运动会组织委员会成立大会
Inaugural Ceremony of Beijing Organizing Committee for the Games of the XXIX Olympiad

3. 国名、地名位置

国名、地名翻译时在会展、赛事、节庆活动中的位置有前置和后置之分。国内举办的活动多数喜欢将本地的地名前置,国外在中国各地举办的会展、赛事、节庆活动基本都是将地名后置。

- 北京·香港经济合作研讨洽谈会
Beijing·Hong Kong Economic Co-Operation Symposium
- 2019北京国际旅游文化节
Beijing International Cultural Tourism Festival 2019
- 2019年中国亚洲杯足球赛倒计时100天主题活动
100 DAYS COUNTDOWN TO ASIAN CUP CHINA 2019
- 第二十一届中国杭州西湖博览会
The 21st West Lake International Expo Hangzhou China

4. 字母大小写

如果参展受众中国外人士居多,可以采用全大写形式,习惯上容易接受;否则,只实词首字母大写(含六个字母及以上虚词)即可。

- 第七届中国非物质文化遗产博览会
THE SEVENTH CHINA INTANGIBLE CULTURAL HERITAGE EXPO
- 奥运经济市场推介会
Market Promotion Conference on Beijing Olympic Economy

5. 缩略语的使用

国内会展名称较长,而国外会展名称相对较短,出现差异的原因是缩略语的使用。

- 国际奥委会全球合作伙伴签约仪式
IOC WORLDWIDE PARTNER SIGNING CEREMONY
- 亚太经合组织工商咨询理事会暨新闻发布会
APEC BUSINESS ADVISORY COUNCIL & PRESS CONFERENCE
- 翻译教育发展国际研讨会
CUITI FORUM

6. 冠名翻译

体育比赛、学术会议、活动演出等经常会得到一些企业的资助,资助的回报形式就是冠名。国内许多活动、赛事冠名都会出现在具体赛事、活动名之前,如"2019上海劳力士大师赛"（ROLEX SHANGHAI MASTERS 2019），其中的"劳力士"作为上海大师赛的主要赞助商，是瑞士著名钟表品牌，翻译时也是将品牌名放在赛事之前。这里需要说明的是，如果是独家赞助，展示时也可以表述为"×××杯（××× CUP）"。

7. 专业领域表述惯例

专业领域会展的名称准确性至关重要，需要严格按照该专业领域的表述惯例进行翻译。

- 数控机床与金属加工展

Metalworking and CNC Machine Tool Show

- 空中客车 A320 系列飞机天津总装线合资企业合同签字仪式

THE JOINT VENTURE CONTRACT FOR THE AIRBUS A320 FAMILY FINAL ASSEMBLY LINE IN TIANJIN SIGNATURE CEREMONY

- 荷兰银行（中国）有限公司正式成立新闻发布会

ABN AMRO (China) Co., Ltd. Press Conference

8. 变译

所谓变译，就是"译者根据特定条件下特定读者的特殊需要采用增、减、编、述、缩、并、改等变通的手段摄取原文中心内容或部分内容的翻译活动"。这是一种较灵活的翻译方法，采取的策略是纽马克的交际翻译。

- 中国商务旅行论坛媒体预告会

China Business Travel Forum Announcement Press Conference

"媒体预告会"并没有被硬译成 advance notice 或 advancement 一类的表述，而是以 Announcement Press Conference 对应。

- 第四届中国上海国际青年钢琴比赛

The 4th China Shanghai International Piano Competition

译文中并没有出现原文中的"青年"二字，这可能是因为这个比赛的参加者均为青年选手，是众所周知的事情，英文行文就不必刻意强调"青年"一词。

- 中国国际高新技术成果交易会

China High-Tech Fair

译文通过变译，省略了"技术成果"，不仅简明流畅，而且很好地达到了交际效果。

9. 约定俗成表达方式

- 上海浦东嘉里中心奠基动工典礼

Kerry Centre, Pudong Shanghai Ground Breaking Ceremony

- UPS 浦东机场国际航空转动中心动工仪式

UPS Shanghai International Air Hub Groundbreaking Ceremony

- 可口可乐中国总部新址及全球创新与技术中心奠基典礼

The Ground Breaking Ceremony of COCA-COLA China Headquarters and Global Innovation & Technology Center

凡是"动工仪式""奠基仪式",其英文表述一般都固定为 groundbreaking ceremony, cornerstone ceremony 等。

10. 简洁精练

这是会展名称翻译的最高境界,真正达到交际翻译的传神境界。

- 英国证券与投资协会中国办事处开业典礼

SII China Office Launch

- 中国首架自主知识产权喷气支线客机总装下线仪式

ARJ21—700 Roll-Out

- 第二届北京国际书法双年展

The Second Beijing International Calligraphy Biennale

以上三个例子堪称删繁就简的典范,不仅简短而且充分达意,给人一种文字的灵动感、美感,堪称会展名称翻译的经典。

(二)会展主题翻译

会展主题有时单独出现,有时和名称一起出现,翻译时多采用名称性短语,按原顺序翻译。

1. 会展名称和主题单独出现

- 中埃/中非学者研讨会

——互利共赢的中埃/中非关系

Seminar on China-Ethiopia and China-Africa Relationship

in a Mutually Beneficial and Win-Win Manner

- 第十七届中国会展经济国际合作论坛

新格局　新使命　新发展

THE 17TH CHINA EXPO FORUM FOR INTERNATIONAL COOPERATION

NEW PARADIGM　NEW MISSION　NEW DEVELOPMENT

- 2019年中国国际公共关系大会

中国公关业走进WTO

China International Public Relations Congress 2019

China PR Industry & WTO

- 不同国家,多样文化,一条生命之河——血液

第九届志愿无偿献血者招募国际大会

"Many countries, many cultures, one river … blood!"

The 9th International Colloquium on Recruitment of Voluntary, Non-Remunerated Blood Donors

2. 会展名称和主题一起出现

- 第四届相约北京联欢活动新闻发布会

THE FOURTH MEET IN BEIJING ARTS FESTIVAL PRESS CONFERENCE

(三) 会展名称/主题翻译中的介词使用

会展名称/主题翻译中常用介词有 on, of, for 等,各自聚焦不同。on 表示会展就某个主题而展开,of 表示为隶属某个机构的活动,而 for 则表示是为了某个主题而举办的活动。在一些场合,这三个介词可以互换。

1. on

- 亚洲普惠金融生态建设与数字化发展圆桌会

Roundtable on Ecosystem Building and Digital Development of Financial Inclusion in Asia

- 第二届中译外高层论坛暨"翻译文化终身成就奖"表彰大会

2nd Forum on Translation from Chinese into Foreign Languages & Award Ceremony for Lifetime Achievement in Translation

- 中国国际社会公共安全产品博览会

China International Exhibition on Public Safety and Security

2. for

- 中国国际贸易投资洽谈会

China International Fair for Investment & Trade

- 中外会展项目合作洽谈会

The Expo Project Fair for International Cooperation

- 国际汽车修理装备工具配件展览会

The International Exhibition for Auto Repair Equipment, Tools, Parts and Accessories

3. of

- 德国斯图加特国际复合材料及生产机械工业贸易展览会

International Trade Exhibition of Composite Materials and Production Machinery Industry in Stuttgart, Germany

- 南京国际新药发明科技年会

BITs Annual Congress of International Drug Discovery Science and Technology (IDDST) in Nanjing, China

- 北京知识产权保护状况新闻发布会

Press Conference of Beijing Intellectual Property Protection

(四) 会展组织机构名称翻译

国外会展组织机构十分简单,一般只有主办机构(organizer/producer)与赞助商

(sponsor/supporter)两种机构,主办方一般为民间企业或行业协会。国内会展组织机构普遍非常复杂,除主办方外,还有协办方、承办方等,甚至还有特别授权、成员单位、支持单位、指导单位、战略联盟等,而且其中含有许多政府机构。常见的会展组织机构名称中英文对照见表3.1:

表3.1 常见的会展组织机构名称中英文对照表

中文	英文
主办单位/商	host/organizer
协办单位/商	co-organizer
承办单位/商	organizer/undertaker/contractor
赞助单位/商	sponsor
冠名单位/商	title sponsor
支持单位/商	supporter
指导单位	supporter/co-sponsor
授权单位	supporter/co-sponsor
指定网站	official website
参展单位/商	exhibitor

(五)招展书正文翻译

根据莱斯的文本类型理论,招展书兼具信息、表情、感染三种功能,其中以信息、感染为主,相对应的翻译方法就是直译、仿译和编译。与此类似,在纽马克的文本类型分类中,招展书同时具有信息、表达和呼唤功能,其中以信息、呼唤功能为主,相对应的翻译方法就是语义翻译(表达类文本)与交际翻译(信息、呼唤类文本)共存。翻译过程中需要先对文本进行细致的文本分类,再辅以相对应的翻译方法,如直译、意译、编译、仿译等,最终达到有效的翻译目的。

例1 为促进节能与新能源汽车产业发展,贯彻落实国务院发布的《节能与新能源汽车产业发展规划(2012—2020年)》,积极推动科技进步,做好节能、环保、减排促进工作,进一步增强我国自主创新、自主开发、自主品牌和产业结构升级力度,加强国际交流与合作,推动节能与新能源汽车产业的快速发展,2013年10月17—20日,在工业和信息化部等部委的支持下,首届"中国国际节能与新能源汽车展览会、节能与新能源汽车产业发展规划成果展览会、中国国际汽车新能源及技术应用展览会、中国国际纯电动车、混合动力车和燃料电池车及关键零部件技术交流展览会"(简称"中国国际节能与新能源汽车展",英文简称IEEVChina)在北京国家会议中心隆重举行。

译文:In order to promote the development of energy saving and new energy vehicle industry, implement the *Energy-Saving and New Energy Development Plan for the Automobile Industry (2012 - 2020)* issued by the State Council, actively promote technological progress, and accomplish the duties in promoting energy-saving environmental protection and emission reduction, and further strengthen the efforts in upgrading China's independent innovation, independent development, independent brand and industrial structure, strengthen international exchanges and cooperation, and promote the rapid development of the energy saving and new energy automobile industry, the First IEEVChina was held ceremoniously at China National Convention Center in Beijing, with the support of Ministry of Industry and Information Technology (MIIT) and other ministries on October 17th –20th, 2013.

原文为"2020世界智能网联汽车大会 & 第八届中国国际新能源和智能网联汽车展览会"招展书的简介部分,前半部分介绍会展的背景,为表达型文本,后半部分是会展的基本信息,包括会展时间、地点、名称等,为信息型文本。有鉴于此,翻译时前半部分应该采用仿译,而后半部分应该采用减译。具体而言,译文的前半部分基本按照原文语序与逻辑进行翻译,而后半部分为了符合目标语习惯,使译文更加简洁易懂,采用了交际翻译的方法,即将画线部分减译为the First IEEVChina,极大地降低文本信息的接受难度,达到了很好的交际效果。

例2

展会优势

● 政府支持

在四川省政府和省经信办分别颁布《中国制造2025四川行动计划》(2015年)和《四川省推进智能制造发展的实施意见》(2017年)的政策背景下,四川省加快推进先进制造强省建设,正在培育一批百亿元企业、千亿元产业、万亿元集群。

● 区位优势

成都市作为西部制造业的龙头城市,位于成德绵经济圈核心区,交通便利,可辐射中西部通达全国。

● 资源整合

联合四川省及周边30余家行业协会,整合100000＋专业观众资源,实现精准邀约。

译文:

Exhibition Advantages

● Government Support

In the background of Sichuan's policies, the government promotes the building of manufacturing advanced province. Meanwhile, the government is cultivating a group of enterprise groups with total assets of over ten billion, one hundred billion and one trillion yuan.

● Region Advantages

As the capital city, Chengdu is the leading city of western manufacturing industry. It is located in the center of Chengdu-Deyang-Mianyang economic zone, so it has the advantage of convenient transportation which can reach the middle west of China.

- Resources Integration

We combine the province with more than 30 industry associations, and integrate more than 100,000 professional audience resources. We could provide accurate offer and <u>match the clients with enterprises</u>.

原文为"2021中国国际工业博览会:数控机床与金属加工展(MWCS)"招展书的"展会优势"部分内容,属于信息型文本,关注的焦点是信息传达的真实性。按照纽马克的交际翻译策略,译文在内容上应忠实传递源语信息,在形式上应遵循目的语习惯,便于读者更透彻、直观地接收源语信息。因此,原文画线部分在译文中采用了减译的方法,因为这些信息只会增加读者阅读的难度,减译便于读者理解文本。同时,为了更准确地帮助读者接收信息,译文画线部分 total assets, match the clients with enterprises 通过增译添加了原文中"无此形,但有其义"的信息;通过换译"龙头""辐射"为 leading, reach,方便读者进一步理解源语信息。

例3 作为我国政府首次批准举办的<u>世界级智能网联汽车大会,全球最大规模</u>以新能源和智能网联汽车为主国的国际展会,展览会对于落实"2025年我国智能网联汽车进入世界前列"目标、促进新能源和智能网联汽车产业的发展具有重要推动作用,大会积极引领未来出行方式的变革,打造节能与新能源汽车、智能网联汽车领域<u>规模最大</u>、<u>规格最高</u>、智能网联化元素<u>最丰富</u>的<u>国际化</u>、<u>专业</u>、高端会展平台,展示国内外新能源和智能网联汽车企业<u>良好形象</u>,加强新能源和智能网联汽车企业的<u>品牌化意识</u>,宣传推广<u>新产品和新技术</u>,推动<u>技术创新和跨界融合</u>,促进国内国际企业、人才及行业交流与合作,探索<u>新生态</u>、<u>新标准</u>、<u>新模式</u>。

译文:As the only world-class professional conference which is approved by the Chinese government for the first time, also the world's largest international exhibition with the theme of new energy and intelligent connected vehicles, IEEVChina plays an important role in the implementation of the goal of "China's Intelligent Connected Vehicles Entering the Forefront of the World in 2025" and promoting the development of China's new energy and intelligent connected automobile industry. The conference actively creates a leading way of future mobility, along with the conference created as the international & professional exhibition platform with a <u>large scale</u>, <u>high specification and rich</u> intelligent network elements in the field of energy-saving, new-energy and intelligent connected vehicles. It promotes not only new products and technologies, technological innovation and cross-border integration, but also the networking and cooperation between domestic and international enterprises. It explores new ecology, new standards, and new models.

原文选自"2020世界智能网联汽车大会 & 第八届中国国际新能源和智能网联汽车展

览会"招展书的简介部分,以呼唤型文本为主,以信息型文本为辅。如上所述,呼唤型文本关注的焦点是信息的传递效果和读者的情感呼应。其目的在于"唤起"读者去"思考"、去"感受"、去"行动"。原文通过大量的主观性描述,即划线的形容词和名词短语,给读者一种"领先、高端"的印象,从而激起他们参会的共鸣。因此,为实现此文本的"呼唤"功能,译文应顺从读者的欣赏习惯与心理感受,尽量使用其所熟悉的语言表达形式以获得预期的效果。在具体的翻译过程中,译文就信息功能而言主要采用直译的方法对原文内容进行了忠实的传递;而在呼唤功能层面上,考虑到中西文化及语言表述方式的差异,进行了一些变译,如"规模最大、规格最高""最丰富"由最高级转译成了原级 large scale, high specification 和 rich,符合西方客观的逻辑思维;对"高端""良好形象""品牌化意识"等抽象性较强的词汇也通过减译进行了弱化,因为这些词的含义其实都已融入上下文中,没有必要硬译出来。通过上述处理,读者在理解原文的同时,参会的意愿会极大地激发出来,这也达到了"呼唤"的目的。

第二节　参展商手册翻译

参展商手册(Exhibitor Manual)又称参展信息手册、参展指南或参展说明书。一般来说,主要包含以下八方面内容:

(1) 前言(Preface):主要是对参展商参加本届会展表示欢迎,同时说明手册编制的原则、目的等。

(2) 展览场地基本情况(About the Venue):包括展馆及展区平面图、展馆的交通图、展览场地的基本技术数据等。

(3) 展会信息(About the Exhibition):包括展会的名称、举办地点、展览时间、办展机构,展会指定承建商、指定运输代理、指定旅游代理、指定接待酒店等。

(4) 展会规则(Rules & Regulations of the Exhibition):包括展会有关证件使用和管理的规定、展会现场保安和保险的规定、展位清洁的规定、物品储藏的规定、现场使用水电的注意事项、现场展品销售的规定、消防规定、知识产权保护规定、现场展品演示的注意事项等。

(5) 展品运输指南(Shipping Guidelines):指对参展商及时安排展品等物品的运输有较大作用,对参展商将展品等物品运到展览现场所做的一些指引和说明,主要包括海外运输指南、国内运输指南等。

(6) 展位搭建指南(Construction Directory):指对会展展位搭建的一些基本要求和说明,主要包括标准展位说明、空地展位搭建说明等。

(7) 会展服务信息(Exhibition Service):指为了满足参展商及观众的会展期间工作和生活需要与会展前后旅游需求等做出的一些说明,主要包括会刊、广告发布、商务旅游、翻译服务、信息化配套服务、团膳外烩服务、金融服务、保险服务、航空服务、运输服务、商务中心等信息。另外，一些高规格的国际会展还提供线上服务、VR线上展示等服务内容。

(8) 相关表格(Forms)：指有关参展商在筹展和布展过程中需要使用的各种表格，主要包括展览表格和展位搭建表格两种。

一、参展商手册范例

本范例取自第四届中国国际进口博览会。

(一) 前言

• 前言

尊敬的参展商：

第三届中国国际进口博览会在新冠疫情全球蔓延的特殊时期如期举办，备受世界瞩目，取得丰硕成果。展会总展览面积近36万平方米，124个国家和地区的参展企业携大批新产品、新技术、新服务首发首展，百余场配套活动精彩纷呈，近40万名专业观众注册报名，全球媒体争相报道，是疫情防控常态化条件下我国举办的一场规模最大、线上线下结合的国际经贸盛会，安全、精彩、富有成效。

习近平主席在第三届中国国际进口博览会开幕式上通过视频发表主旨演讲，强调共同开放理念，传递出新时代中国与世界共享美好未来的积极信号，也为进博会的未来发展指明了方向。

2021年是"十四五"开局之年，中国踏上全面建设社会主义现代化国家的新征程。进入新发展阶段，进口博览会将全面贯彻新发展理念，成为助力构建新发展格局的有效载体。我们欢迎全球企业积极参加进口博览会，把握中国经济高质量发展重大机遇，深耕中国市场，促进国际合作，实现共赢发展。我们愿同大家一道，办好第四届中国国际进口博览会，进一步完善国际采购、投资促进、人文交流、开放合作"四大平台"功能，为推动世界经济复苏和发展、促进国际贸易繁荣和稳定、服务构建新发展格局做出积极的贡献。

诚挚感谢您参加中国国际进口博览会，我们在中国上海欢迎您的到来！

中国国际进口博览会

• Opening Remarks

Distinguished exhibitors,

The Third China International Import Expo (CIIE) was held on schedule in the special period when COVID-19 is raging globally, which has attracted worldwide attention and achieved fruitful results. With a total exhibition area of nearly 360,000 square meters, exhibitors from 124 countries and regions made their debut with a large number of new products, new technologies and new services. More than 100 supporting activities were unusually brilliant. Nearly 400,000 professional visitors registered and the global media rushed to cover the Expo, which was the largest international economic and trade event, both online and offline, held in China when prevention and control of the epidemic had become regular. It was safe, wonderful and fruitful.

President Xi Jinping delivered the keynote speech through video at the opening ceremony of the third CIIE, stressing the concept of common openness conveyed positive signals for China to share a better future with the world in the new era, and directed its way ahead.

The Year 2021 marks the start of the 14th "Five-Year Plan", when China embarks on a new journey of building a modern socialist country in an all-round way. Entering the new stage, CIIE will fully implement the new development concept and serve as effective carrier to build a new development pattern. We welcome global enterprises to actively participate in CIIE, seize the great opportunity of China's high-quality economic development, deeply engage in Chinese market, promote international cooperation and achieve win-win development. We are willing to work with you to successfully hold the 4th CIIE, improve the functions of the "four platforms" such as international procurement, investment promotion, people-to-people exchanges, and open cooperation, and make positive contributions to the recovery and development of the world economy, the prosperity and stability of international trade, and the establishment of a new development pattern.

We hereby sincerely thank you for your participation in the CIIE. Welcome and see you in Shanghai, China!

China International Import Expo (CIIE)

（二）展览场地基本情况

- 展馆介绍

（1）国家会展中心（上海）总建筑面积超150万平方米，集展览、会议、活动、商业、办公、酒店等多种业态为一体，是目前世界上在营的规模最大的会展综合体。主体建筑以伸展柔美的四叶幸运草为造型，采用轴线对称设计理念，设计中体现了诸多中国元素，是上海市的标志性建筑之一。

（2）国家会展中心（上海）可展览面积近60万平方米，包括近50万平方米的室内展厅和10万平方米的室外展场。综合体共17个展厅，包括15个单位面积为3万平方米的大展厅和2个单位面积为1万平方米的多功能展厅，货车均可直达。可全方位满足大中小型展会对展馆的使用需求。

- Venue Introduction

(1) With a total construction area of over 1.5 million square meters, the National Exhibition and Convention Center (Shanghai) integrates exhibition, conference, activity, business, office, hotel and other commercial activities, becoming the largest convention and exhibition complex in operation in the world. Moreover, by adopting the beautiful shape of a four-leaf clover and the design concept of axis symmetry, the main building becomes one of the landmarks in Shanghai.

(2) The National Exhibition and Convention Center (Shanghai) has an exhibition area of nearly 600,000 square meters, including nearly 500,000 square meters of indoor exhibition halls and 100,000 square meters of outdoor exhibition venues. Moreover, the complex has 17 exhibition halls, including 15 large ones with a unit area of 30,000 square meters and 2 multi-functional ones with a unit area of 10,000 square meters. These exhibition halls can be directly accessed by trucks. In this way, the it can comprehensively meet the requirements of large, medium and small exhibitions for exhibition halls.

(三) 展会信息

● 展会综合信息

1. 展会基本情况

1.1 展会名称

中国国际进口博览会

1.2 展会时间

2021年11月5日—10日

1.3 展会地点

国家会展中心(上海)

地址:上海市青浦区崧泽大道333号

1.4 主办单位

中华人民共和国商务部

上海市人民政府

1.5 合作单位

世界贸易组织、联合国开发计划署、联合国贸易和发展会议、联合国粮食及农业组织、联合国工业发展组织、国际贸易中心等国际组织

1.6 承办单位

中国国际进口博览局

国家会展中心(上海)

1.7 论坛

论坛名称:虹桥国际经济论坛

举办时间:2021年11月5日

举办地点:国家会展中心(上海)

主办单位:中华人民共和国商务部、上海市人民政府

承办单位:中国国际进口博览局、国家会展中心(上海)

1.8 展会布局

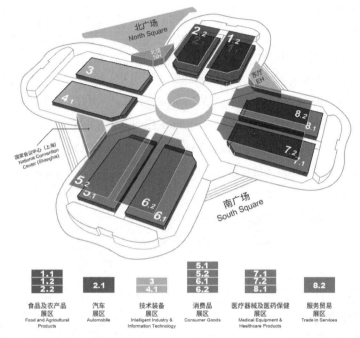

1.9 展会官方平台

官方网站:www.ciie.org

- General Information of the Expo

1. Basic Information

1.1 Name of the Expo

China International Import Expo (CIIE)

1.2 Time

November 5 −10, 2021

1.3 Venue

National Exhibition and Convention Center (Shanghai) (NECC)

Address:No. 333, Songze Avenue, Qingpu District, Shanghai

1.4 Hosts

Ministry of Commerce of the People's Republic of China

Shanghai Municipal People's Government

1.5 Supporters

The World Trade Organization (WTO)

The United Nations Development Programme (UNDP)

United Nations Conference on Trade and Development (UNCTAD)

Food and Agriculture Organization of the United Nations (FAO)

United Nations Industrial Development Organization (UNIDO)

International Trade Centre (ITC) and other international organizations

1.6 Organizers

China International Import Expo Bureau

National Exhibition and Convention Center (Shanghai)

1.7 Forum

Name: Hongqiao International Economic Forum

Date: November 5, 2021

Venue: National Exhibition and Lonvention Center (Shanghai)

Hosts: Ministry of Commerce of the People's Republic of China; Shanghai Municipal People's Government

Organizers: China International Import Expo Bureau; National Exhibition and Convention Center (Shanghai)

1.8 Expo Layout

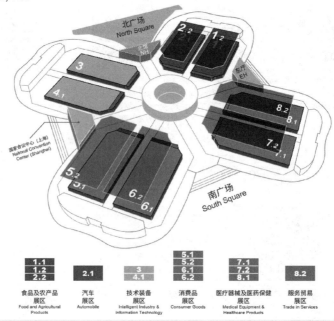

1.9 Official Platform of CIIE

Offcial Website: www.ciie.org

 Official APP

 Official Public Account of WeChat

 Official Microblog

 LinkedIn

Facebook

 Twitter

 Instagram

 YouTube

(四)展会规则

• 展会规定

本《展会规定》中,"主办单位"为中华人民共和国商务部、上海市人民政府,"承办单位"为中国国际进口博览局、国家会展中心(上海)。

1. 总则

1.1 根据中华人民共和国法律法规、上海市人民政府及各有关机构的相关规定,本《展会规定》对包括但不仅限于安全生产、消防安全、证件管理等相关条款及要求作出了全新的修订,请参展商、搭建商及服务商严格遵守。

1.2 本《展会规定》是承办单位与参展商之间签订的《参展合同》不可分割的组成部分;参展商、搭建商及服务商须遵守本《展会规定》,包括由承办单位推出的任何修订文本。

1.3 请参展商仔细阅读本《参展商手册》中有关安全生产、消防安全、文明参展等规定。如有任何不明或疑问,可在展会筹备阶段或展会现场向承办单位、展会指定服务商进行咨询。

1.4 参展商、搭建商及服务商在本届展会期间必须严格遵守承办单位印发或通知的各项规定及要求,包括《参展商手册》《展前通知》《进馆须知》《安全须知》《现场通告》等。

• Rules and Regulations

In these Rules and Regulations, the "Hosts" refer to the Ministry of Commerce of the People's Republic of China and Shanghai Municipal People's Government, and the "Organizers" refer to China International Import Expo Bureau and National Exhibition and Convention Center (Shanghai) Co., Ltd.

1. General Rules

1.1 According to the laws and regulations of the People's Republic of China, the relevant provisions of Shanghai Municipal People's Government and other relevant authorities, the relevant terms, conditions and requirements on/for, among others, production safety, fire control safety and credential management, have been revised in these Rules and Regulations for the exhibitors, the constructors and the service providers to comply with.

1.2 These Rules and Regulations constitute an integral part of the Exhibition Contract concluded by and between the Organizers and the exhibitors. The exhibitors, the constructors and the service providers are required to comply with these Rules and Regulations, including any revision hereto released by the Organizers.

1.3 The exhibitors should read the provisions concerning production safety, fire control safety and civilized participation in the Expo in the Exhibitor's Manual. In case of any questions or doubts, please consult the Organizers and CIIE's designated service providers during the preparation stage or at the Expo site.

1.4 The exhibitors, the constructors and the service providers shall strictly comply with all rules, regulations and requirements issued or circulated by the Organizers during the Expo, including the Exhibitor's Manual, Pre-Expo Notice to Exhibitors, Entrance Instructions, Safety Instructions, and Expo Announcements.

（五）展位搭建指南

3. 标准展台

3.1 标准展台展商须知

（1）标准展台的展商须填写展台楣板信息表，请在2021年9月25日之前回传至展会主场搭建商；不得私自遮盖、修改楣板。具体请详见附表12：《标准展台楣板信息表》。

（2）其他内容具体请详见**附件5**：《标准展台展商须知》。

3.2 展台尺寸

标摊尺寸：2970 mm × 2970 mm，总高度4000 mm，围板高度为2500 mm，楣板最低点距地面距离为2450 mm，楣板高度450 mm（含框架），楣板长度1800 mm（含框架）。

3.3 基本配置

1张方桌、4张折叠椅、1个地柜（1000 mm ×500 mm ×500 mm）、一个玻璃展柜（1000 mm ×500 mm ×2000 mm）、1张接待台（1000 mm ×500 mm ×750 mm）、3个层板（服装类将3个层板更换为2440 mm ×950 mm 的槽板以及16个挂钩）、4个LED 射灯、1个500W 插座（中国标准）、2个垃圾桶。

3. Standard Booth

3.1 Instructions to Exhibitors of Standard Booths

（1）Exhibitors of standard booths must mail the completed information sheet of the booth lintel board to the official constructor before September 25, 2021. Covering or modifying the lintel board without permission is not allowed. For more information, please refer to **Form 12**: **Standard Booth Fascia Board Information Form.**

（2）For more information, please refer to **Appendix 5**: **Notice to Exhibitors with Standard Booths.**

3.2 Exhibition Booth Size

The dimension of the standard booth is 2,970 mm × 2,970 mm × 4,000 mm. The hoarding of the standard booth is 2,500 mm high. The lintel board of the standard booth is 1,800 mm long (including the frame) and 450 mm high (including the frame) with a clearance of 2,450 mm from the floor.

3.3 Necessary Facilities

The necessary facilities include one square table, four foldable chairs, one floor cabinet (with a dimension of 1,000 mm × 500 mm × 500 mm), one glass showcase (with a dimension of 1,000 mm × 500 mm × 2,000 mm), one reception desk (with a dimension of 1,000 mm × 500 mm × 750 mm), three laminated boards (or one slot board of 2,440 mm × 950 mm and 16 hooks for garment exhibition booth), four LED spotlights, one 500 W socket (in Chinese standard) and two trash cans.

(六) 展品运输指南

- 展品运输

1. 运输服务及约定

欢迎参加中国国际进口博览会,承办单位指定了七家主场运输服务商,提供展品的境内外运输服务,包括业务承揽、方案制订、展品清关、运输、仓储和现场服务等。同时,承办单位推荐中国远洋海运集团有限公司作为国际段运输服务商,提供展品的海洋运输服务。为确保展会的顺利举办,请参展商依照本《展品运输》的有关约定做出安排,并在展品发运前及时与主场运输服务商对接,建立联系。

2. 运输服务商联系方式

2.1 指定主场运输服务商

上海国际展览运输有限公司 SHANGHAI EXPOTRANS LTD.			
负责区域 1.1H/2.1H			
公司地址:上海市静安区安远路555号8楼			
联系人	电话	手机	邮箱
李炯桢(Luke Li)	86-21-67008××	86-18021009××	01transporter@ciie.org
刘娴(Angela Liu)	86-21-67008××	86-13701755××	01transporter@ciie.org

- Shipping Guidelines

1. Shipping Services and Agreement

Welcome to the China International Import Expo. The Organizers have designated seven official forwarders to provide shipping services inside and outside China for the exhibition items, including undertaking of business, plan formulation, customs clearance, shipment, storage, and on-site exhibition-related services. In the meantime, the Organizers recommend China COSCO

Shipping Corporation Limited as the provider of shipping services for the exhibition items. To ensure a successful exhibition, exhibitors are suggested to arrange their shipments according to the provisions in the Shipping Guidelines and timely reach out and contact their official forwarders before the shipment of their exhibition items.

2. Contact Information of Freight Forwarders

2.1 Designated Official Forwarders

SHANGHAI EXPOTRANS LTD.			
Responsible Area: 1.1H/2.1H			
Address: 8/F, NO.555 AN YUAN ROAD, SHANGHAI 200040, CHINA			
Contacts	Tel	Mobile	E-mail
Luke Li	86-21-67008××	86-18021009×××	01transporter@ciie.org
Angela Liu	86-21-67008×××	86-13701755×××	01transporter@ciie.org

（七）会展服务信息

7. 金融服务

中国银行作为中华人民共和国商务部授予的"中国国际进口博览会战略合作伙伴"及"中国国际进口博览会银行类综合服务支持企业"，为进口博览会提供涵盖展前、展中、展后的全方位金融服务。

具体服务内容详见**附件15**，或联系如下服务团队：

联系人：刘晓红女士

电话：86-21-69721×××

手机：86-13818179×××

邮箱：liuxhlw_sh@bank-of-china.com

7. Financial Service

As the only official "Comprehensive Banking Enterprise" of CIIE by the Ministry of Commerce in China and one of the strategic partners and financial service providers of the event, Bank of China provides comprehensive financial services covering pre-exhibition, in-exhibition and post-exhibition for CIIE. Please refer to **Appendix 15** for specific service contents, or contact the following service teams:

Contact: Ms. Liu Xiaohong

Tel: 86-21-69721×××

Mobile: 86-13818179×××

E-mail: liuxhlw_sh@bank-of-china.com

（八）相关表格

表单回传截止日期：2021-10-10

附表 2：《展台内现场活动申请表》			
参展单位：		展台号：	
所属国家：		面积：_____ m²	
展台负责人：		座机：	
移动电话：		邮箱：	
活动（安全）负责人：		座机：	
移动电话：		邮箱：	
现场活动（仅限 11 月 5 日 14:00 之后至 11 月 10 日）			
活动名称：			
举办时间	11 月_____日—11 月_____日_____点至_____点		
活动内容简介	简述活动议程、时间安排等；如有表演，简述表演节目、时间安排		
预估总人数	_____人	社会名流	□是　□否
演职人员总人数	_____人	主流明星	□是　□否
活动嘉宾总人数	_____人	现场模特	□是　□否
活动形式		□开放式　　□邀请式	
是否有领导参加活动 （国内为部级及以上，国外为同等级别）		□是　　□否	
现场是否有安保方案和措施（如有，附后）		□是　　□否	

Please return this form by Oct. 10, 2021

Form 2：Application for Activity within Booth			
Exhibitor：		Booth No.：	
Country：		Area：_____ m²	
Person in Charge of the Booth：		Tel：	
Mobile：		E-mail：	
Person in Charge of the Activity（Safety）：		Tel：	
Mobile：		E-mail：	
On-site Activities（limited from 14:00 Nov. 5 to Nov. 10）			
Activity Name：			
Time	_____:_____ - _____:_____ Nov. _____ to Nov. _____		

(continuous)

Brief Introduction	Briefly describe the event agenda and schedule, etc. If there is a performance, briefly describe the performance program and schedule.			
Estimated Total Number of Persons	_____	Are there any celebrities?	☐ Yes	☐ No
Total Number of Performers	_____	Are there any stars?	☐ Yes	☐ No
Total Number of Guests	_____	Are there any models?	☐ Yes	☐ No
Activity Form		☐ Open Type ☐ Invitation		
Are there any leaders to participate in the activity? (Ministerial level leaders or above at home and the same level from abroad)		☐ Yes ☐ No		
Are there any on-site security plans and measures? (If yes, please attach it to this form)		☐ Yes ☐ No		

二、参展商手册翻译实践

(一) 展品运输指南翻译

正常国外展品运输流程如下:

备齐所需单证,备齐展品、打包(为展品投保)

安排运输(木质包装须在装运港口做熏蒸处理,并在外包装箱加施专用标识)

从所在地海关出关、在展览所在地海关入关安检

运至展馆、布展(若需要散发宣传品,则须将样本报海关审查)

Prepare the necessary documents, pack the exhibits (insurance for the exhibits)

Arrange the transportation (Wood packaging shall be fumigated at the port of shipment and pasted with special marks on the outer packing boxes)

Customs clearance at the exhibits local place and customs clearance security at the exhibition destination

Transport to the exhibition hall and arrange the exhibition (If some propaganda materials are to be distributed, the sample must be examined by the customs)

⇩	⇩
展出(申报展品的处理方式,若需回运,则填写《回运展品委托书》等表格)	Move-in (Report how to handle the exhibits, fill in the form of "power of attorney for returned exhibits" if return shipment is required)
⇩	⇩
撤展	Move-out
⇩	⇩
回运、转展、留购、散发或放弃	Return, transfer, purchase, distribute, or abandon

与会展合同和规章相类似,展品运输指南也属于信息类文本,但其实施的功能是告知,而不是前者的指令。因此,翻译时在语言层面上与前者相比,既有相同的特点,又有不同的一面。下面将从语言的三个层面(词法、句法和篇章)对此进行阐述。

1. 词法

著名语言学家马丁·朱斯(Martin Joos)按照语言使用的正式程度,提出五种语体:庄重体(frozen style)、正式体(formal style)、商议体(consultative style)、随便体(casual style)、亲密体(intimate style)(Joos,1962:28-61)。根据此分类,展品运输指南文本属于商议体。因此,从词法的角度来看,运输指南文本使用专业术语、书面语等正式程度较高词汇的频率会很高,而古语词、外来词、同义词连用和词项重复的表述则相对会比较少。

(1) 专业术语

例1 所有海运货物请以集装箱整箱发运。对于散货拼箱货物,由于船公司或港口代理不一定能在短时间内卸载(有时会超过4周),可能导致我们无法及时将展品运送至展会。

译文:For sea-freight shipment, only FULL CONTAINER LOAD (FCL) is recommended. For Less Than Container Load (LCL) shipment, exhibitors have to bear the risk that the shipping line / port operator may not debark your container within a short period (sometimes may be more than 4 weeks) which may endanger our on-time pick up / delivery to the fair.

译文中的 FCL 和 LCL 为海运行业的专业术语,类似术语在展品运输指南中经常出现。

(2) 书面语

例2 因为展商未遵守发运指示而产生的所有问题和相关的额外费用,由展商来承担。

译文:If Exhibitors do not consign their shipment strictly in accordance with the above consignment instructions, they must bear all the responsibilities and extra expense arising therefrom.

译文中的 consign, in accordance with, bear all the responsibilities 皆为书面语,而 therefrom 为古语词。

2. 句法

(1) should 和 will

作为情态动词,should 表示制约性的程度比 shall 要弱,多用于商贸实体行为,比较符合展品运输指南的主观指令功能;与此相类似,will 在展品运输指南中的强制程度也比较弱,更多的是对客观条件的假设,或对未来行为的预设。

例3 所有展台内使用或展示的展品、物料及装修须做好防火措施,并符合相关安全防火及建筑规定。

译文:For all the exhibits displayed, materials and decoration, exhibitors **should** make the fire prevention measures and comply with the relevant fire safety and building regulations.

例4

请注意:

● 受海关申报系统限制,一张海运单或空运单包含的展品不可超过50项,如有超过,请拆分提单。

● 所有空运货物必须有分单数据,请以"主运单＋分运单"形式发货。

● 不同展馆的展品不建议合拼一张提单。

译文:

Notes:

● Due to the limits of the customs declaration system, each sea or air waybill **should** not contain more than 50 items. If there are more than 50 items, please split the bill.

● All air cargo **should** have bill-splitting data, please ship it in the form of master air waybill plus house air waybill.

● Exhibition items to be consigned to different exhibition halls **should** not be included in one bill.

例5 超过截止申请日期,所有展具租赁价格增加30%,现场租赁、增加、移位或取消增加50%费用。

译文:After the deadline, all lease prices increase 30%, 50% increment **will** be charged on-site.

例6

3.5 晚到附加费

● 如展品于指定日期之后到达,主场运输服务商将收取基本运输费百分之三十(30%)的晚到附加费(冷藏冷冻品、生鲜和易腐品等特殊展品除外)。

● 对于晚到展品,主场运输服务商会尽全力将展品运至展台,但是不承担因展品未能准时运抵展台所带来的一切损失。

● 即使不能如期送货至展台,主场运输服务商亦会收取晚到附加费。

译文:

3.5 Additional Costs for Late Arrival

● In case the exhibition items arrive after the deadline, a 30% of freight **will** be charged additionally by the designated official forwarders. (Except for special exhibits such as refrigerated and frozen products, fresh and perishable products). (条件假设)

● For late arrivals, the designated official forwarders **will** try their best to convey the exhibits to the corresponding booths as appropriately as possible but not bear any losses caused by the failure to meet the deadline thereof. (行为预设)

● Even if the late arrivals are not delivered as scheduled, the additional costs **will** still be charged. (条件假设)

(2)被动语态

被动语态能较好地凸显信息焦点,强调客观事实,同时又能使表达委婉、中肯的语气,在指南类的文本中有大量运用。

例7 除上述唛头张贴要求外,还应根据展品特性进行以下相应标注:

● 易碎的物品,应在每个面上张贴"易碎"标记;

● 不可倾倒的物品,应至少在2个面上张贴"向上"标记;

● 不可置于室外的物品,应至少在2个面上张贴"雨伞"标记;

● 采用吊装的物品,应在相应位置注明"吊索"标记;

● 其他标记按照国际惯例使用。

译文:In addition to the above-mentioned mark requirements, the following corresponding marks should **be made** in light of the characteristics of the exhibits:

● For fragile items, a "Fragile" mark should **be marked** on each side;

● Items that shall not be tilted should **be marked** with "Up" on at least 2 sides;

● Items that shall not be placed outdoors should **be marked** with "umbrellas" on at least 2 sides;

● Items to be hoisted should **be marked** with a "sling" icon at the corresponding position;

● Other marks shall apply in accordance with international practices. (凸显信息焦点)

例8 建议您为您的进口展品的全程投保一切险。为便于查询及索赔,敬请您在参加展会期间携带保险合同书副本。

译文:It **is suggested** that you insure your exhibits for all risks (in the whole process of the Fair), and you **are requested** to bring copies of insurance policy to the fair for inspection and claim purposes.(表达委婉语气)

(3)因果从句和目的从句

相对而言,展品运输指南文本存在一定的主观性,所表现出来的语言特征就是使用因果从句(一般由 as 引导)和目的从句(一般由 in order to 引导),这与以客观性为主的会展规定(合同)文本常用条件从句存在较大的差异。

例9 因在长途运输途中展品会被承运方频繁装卸,并且会被多次置于露天场所或展览中心的露天仓库,所以包装箱应坚固耐用,以避免损坏或雨浸,尤其必须适用于展览会结束后重新包装和回运。

译文:**As** all packages of exhibits will be frequently loaded and unloaded during transportation, unpack for the fair and repack for the return movement, storage in open-air or will be placed outdoors, please ensure that your exhibits are packed in strong, water-proof wooden cases which are strong enough to protect the exhibits from damage and rain.

例10 由于海关要求运输代理对每件展品负责,因此如果没有通过我公司向海关做事先安排,参展商不被允许在展会开幕前、展会期间及结束后将任何展品带出展览中心。

译文:**As** the customs requires the official forwarders to be responsible for every exhibit, exhibitors will not be allowed either to take any of their exhibits out of the exhibition site before, during and after the exhibition without prior arrangement with the customs through us. We shall not be responsible for any confiscation and fines arising therefrom.

例11 为了避免展品因含有受中国海关管制的物品而被扣留,我们强烈建议参展商在发运展品前将展品清单电邮至主场运输服务商确认。

译文:**In order to** avoid the holding by Chinese customs because of controlled items included in the exhibition items, we strongly recommend that exhibitors e-mail the list of exhibits to the official forwarders for confirmation before the exhibits are shipped.

例12 在展会闭幕的当天,主场运输服务商会将空箱送还各展台并协助参展商包装。为了确保撤展顺利进行,持有超重或者超限展品的参展商可能要在隔天完成展品的重装。主场运输服务商会通知参展商确切的安排。

译文:On the CIIE's closing day, the official forwarders will return empty packages to exhibitors and help pack the goods. **In order to** ensure the smooth process of moving out, those exhibitors with overweight or oversize items are allowed to repack their goods the next day. The official forwarder will inform such exhibitors of the exact arrangements.

3. 篇章

展品运输指南是帮助参展商了解展会物流运输服务和注意事项的重要文件,它的篇章结构要素一般包括指定承运商的联系方式、货运途径、收货人信息(用于接管展品)、运输时间安排表(列有各项运输环节的最后期限)、所需交付的文件列表(如装运文件、报关所需文件、报关所需单证等)、唛头和包装要求、收费标准、保险及其他注意事项等。而且,为了与国际接轨,中文文本与英文文本结构基本对等,翻译时无须做大的改动。

(1) 指定承运商的联系方式(Contact Details of the Official Freight Forwarder)

展览主办单位已委任×××公司作为此展之海外运输及现场操作总代理。如有需要请联系:(略)

The organizer has appointed *** Co. as the overseas official freight Forwarder and on-site contractor for the captioned fair. All inquiries please contact:(OMITTED)

(2) 货运途径(Shipping Routing)

本届广交会接受以下进口展品货运途径:

The following transportation options are available for the exhibits of this Canton Fair:

● 将展品由境外通过海运整箱集装箱方式发运到广州港口。

Direct sea freight in full container from overseas to Guangzhou port.

……

(3) 收货人信息(Consignee)

从海外直达 A _____(港口名)或 B _____(机场名)的展品,收货人必须为 _____。

For shipment sent to A _____ (name of a port) or B _____ (name of an airport) directly, consignee's name must be: _____.

(4) 运输时间安排表(Shipping Deadline)

展品直达中国 A _____(港口名)或 B _____(机场名)。

Shipment of direct arrival at A _____ (name of a port) or B _____ (name of an airport) in China.

● 海运(Seafreight)

海运到达 A _____(港口名)

Latest arrival at A _____ (name of a port)

● 空运(Airfreight)

空运到达 B _____(机场名)

Latest arrival at _____ (name of an airport)

3）入馆日期(Move-in Date)

4）出馆日期(Move-out Date)

（5）所需交付的文件(Required Documents)

展商需要及时将以下用于报关的文件提供给我公司：

All exhibitors are required to submit the following documents for customs clearance timely.

- 2份正本海运提单或1份空运提单复印件

2 original bills of lading (B/L) for Ocean Freight or 1 copy of AWB for airfreight

- 暂准进口展览品报关清单（一箱一单）

Declaration Form for Temporary Import (one page for each package)

……

（6）唛头和包装要求(Case Marketing & Packing Requirement)

包装箱外三面必须清楚写上以下唛头：

For the outside marking of all packages, please clearly mark at least 3 sides as follows.

_____（展会名称）

展商：××××

展厅/展位号：××××

箱号：××××

毛重：××××（千克）

尺寸：长×宽×高（厘米）

_____ (name of exhibition)

Exhibitor：××××

Hall / Stand No.：××××

Case No.：××××

Gross Weight：××××(kg)

Dimension：L×W×H (cm)

（7）服务及收费标准(Service & Rates for Handling)

- 来程展品服务及费率(Inbound Movement Services and Tariff)

展会开幕前，将抵达A_____（港口名）或B_____（机场名）的展品从港口或机场的货物储存地运输到展馆现场存储场地，掏箱，分拣，搬运到展台，协助展商开箱和展品就位（不含组装），将空包装箱和包装材料运送到（露天）仓库。（仓储费另计）

For exhibits arrival directly at A _____ (name of a port) or B _____ (name of an airport), transportation from terminal to the storage area of the fair site, sorting and delivery to fair booth, assisting exhibitors in unpacking and positioning the heavy exhibits (assembling excluded), customs clearance on a temporary basis, removing empty cases and packing materials on the site storage place (outdoors). Storage charges are EXCLUDED.

抵达 A _____（港口名）的海运展品×××美元/立方米(最低 3 立方米/单)

By sea arrival at A _____ (name of a port) USD＊＊＊/ CBM（min. 3 cbm / consignment）

……

2）回程展品服务及费率(Outbound Movement Services and Tariff)

……

3）展品现场进出馆服务及费率(Move-In and Move-Out Service on Fair-Site)

……

（8）保险(Insurance)

- 不提供保险服务(Without Insurance Service)

运输费率不包括保险费,所有由我公司操作的展品风险由参展商自行承担。因此,所有参展商需要为他们的展品购买包括展览期间的全程保险,并将保险单的副本带到展览会备用。

As the official tariff is complied on the volume or weight basis and have now correlation with the value of exhibits, naturally no insurance has been covered in our charges and all work is undertaken by us at owners' risk. Therefore, all exhibitors are requested to have their exhibits fully insured for the whole in/out journey and the exhibition period. A copy of the insurance policy should be brought to the fair in case of any necessary survey.

2）提供代买保险服务(Providing Insurance Services)

建议您为您的进口展品的全程投保一切险。为便于查询及索赔,敬请您在参加展会期间携带保险合同书副本。

You are suggested to insure your exhibits for all risks (including during the course of the Fair), you are requested to bring copies of insurance policy to the fair for inspection and claim purposes.

进口展区展品承运商均能提供代办进口展品保险的有偿服务。

Exhibits transporter of international pavilion is ready to provide insurance services for import exhibits with certain charge.

……

（9）其他说明(Others)

展品包装的拆、装及展品交付 Unpacking, Repacking and Delivery of Exhibits

根据参展商做的标记或他们授权的代理的指示,我公司将展品送至展台,负责拆箱、重新包装和清关。建议展商派专人于进出馆期间在现场负责监督展品就位、拆箱和重新包装。

We will deliver exhibits to stands, assist unpacking and repacking and customs clearance against signature of exhibitors or their authorized agents. It is highly recommended that exhibitors arrange for their representatives to be present onsite during move-in and move-out period to supervise positioning, unpacking and repacking of exhibits, as the on-site operations will be carried out at exhibitors' risk.

……

（二）展位搭建指南翻译

参展商手册中的展位搭建指南内容主要包括指定主场搭建商信息、标准展台说明、特装展台设计及搭建规定、配套设施租赁以及搭建相关要求。从文本类型理论的角度来看，展位搭建指南也属于信息类文本，但实现的告知和指令功能各半。因此，在实施交际翻译的过程中，所选择的翻译方法既有会展合同与规章翻译的一面，也有展品运输指南翻译的一面。从告知功能来看，展位搭建指南要强于会展合同与规章文本，但弱于展品运输指南；与此相反，从指令功能来看，展位搭建指南要弱于会展合同与规章文本，但强于展品运输指南。另外，从语用学的视角考虑，展位搭建指南的决定方为主办方或协办方，而展品运输指南的决定方为第三方服务商，语旨内容不同，也会影响语式。

为了平衡信息类文本的告知功能和指令功能，介于正式体与商议体之间的展位搭建指南文本会采用专业术语、书面语等正式程度较高的词汇表达，而古语词、外来词、同义词连用和词项重复等表述出现的频率会较低。

例13　基本配置：1张方桌、4张折叠椅、1个地柜（1000 mm×500 mm×500 mm）、一个玻璃展柜（1000 mm×500 mm×2000 mm）、1张接待台（1000 mm×500 mm×750 mm）、3个层板（服装类将3个层板更换为2440 mm×950 mm的槽板以及16个挂钩）、4个LED射灯、1个500W插座（中国标准）、2个垃圾桶。

译文：Necessary facilities: The necessary facilities include one square table, four foldable chairs, one floor cabinet (with a dimension of 1,000 mm×500 mm×500 mm), one glass showcase (with a dimension of 1,000 mm×500 mm×2,000 mm), one reception desk (with a dimension of 1,000 mm×500 mm×750 mm), three **laminated boards** (or one **slot board** of 2,440 mm×950 mm and 16 hooks for garment exhibition booth), four **LED spotlights**, one 500 W socket (in Chinese standard) and two trash cans. （专业术语）

例14　参展商与特装施工服务商（含展会推荐的或通过审核的特装施工服务商）之间的任何约定或安排纯属双方之间达成的协议，由双方遵照执行。

译文：Any agreement or arrangement between exhibitors and special exhibition booth constructors (including those recommended or approved by the organizer) **is deemed** as an agreement reached and to be fulfilled by both parties. （书面语）

例15　施工或筹展完毕后，所有施工工具、施工余料、包装材料及辅料等均应于展馆封馆前清理出展馆外,不应存放于展位内或展位背面(侧面)的空间内。

译文:All constructional tools, surplus constructional and packing materials and accessories shall be cleared out of the exhibition hall **prior to** closure and subsequent to completion of construction works. The **aforesaid** items shall not be stored in the stand or any spaces behind (or beside) the stand. (书面语、词项重复)

在句法层面上,相较于会展合同与规章(详见第七章)和展品运输指南,展位搭建指南在祈使句与条件句翻译上显得更灵活、更多样化,详见表3.2。

表 3.2 不同的句法特征

表征	会展合同与规章	展位搭建指南	展品运输指南
祈使句语言表征	shall, may	shall, may, will	should, will
条件句语言表征	in case, in the event that	in case, if, should(句首)	in case, if, should(句首)

1. 祈使句翻译

在正式的语言环境中,祈使句一般表达叮嘱、劝告、希望、禁止、请求、命令等语气。中英文在表示禁止、要求或者命令上都是一样的,倾向于委婉表达。参展商手册的主要目的是向参展商传达参展的注意事项,其中不乏明令禁止或强烈不建议的行为。根据表3.1,展位搭建指南翻译时可以通过 shall, may, will 等情态动词表达不同的语气。

例 16 展台电箱分照明箱和动力箱,参展商在向展会主场搭建商申请时应注明电箱种类。申请动力箱时,须在 2021 年 9 月 25 日之前向展会主场搭建商提交申请。

译文:The exhibitor **shall** specify the type of electricity box (lighting box or power box) in the application. The application for renting a power box **shall** be submitted to the official constructor before September 25, 2021.

例 17 如参展商对压缩空气有特殊要求或超过 1.6 m³/min 的,建议参展商自带空压机并在 2021 年 9 月 25 日之前向展会主场搭建商提交申请。

译文:Any exhibitor **may** apply to the official constructor for bringing its own air compressor before September 25, 2021 if it needs a special air compressor or its compressor measures higher than 1.6 m³/min in capacity.

例 18 为确保展台用电安全,防止电气火灾事故发生,由服务商统一提供带电监控的展台电箱租赁服务(展台搭建商不再自带电箱),并负责该电箱的拆装工作。

译文:In order to ensure electrical safety and prevent the risk of electrical fire, the service provider **will** lease electricity boxes with power monitors and complete assembly and disassembly (i.e. it is not necessary for booth constructors to bring their own electricity boxes).

2. 条件句翻译

例19 另在接到申请通过通知后15日内,由参展商或其自带的特装施工服务商向承办单位交纳30万元(人民币)履约保证金(如无违约,展会结束后将无息退还)。

译文:In addition, within 15 days after receiving the notice of approval of the application, the exhibitor or its own special exhibition booth constructor shall pay a performance bond of RMB 300,000 to the exhibition organizer (which will be refunded without interest at the end of the exhibition **in case** of no default during the exhibition).

例20 结构中如有玻璃装饰或搭建的展台,必须确保施工及安装牢固,并在可视的高度设有醒目标识,以防造成人员伤亡。

译文:Exhibitors must ensure that their installations are secure enough, and there are bold signs at visible heights to prevent personal injury or death, especially **if** there are any booths with glass in the structure.

例21 施工如需临时用电,应按临时用电规定要求执行。

译文:**Should** there be any temporary power supply during the construction, the organizing committee shall support in accordance with the provisions of temporary electricity requirements.

在某些情况下,展位搭建指南翻译为更好地实施交际翻译的策略,符合英语表达习惯,以实现"以最佳关联方式传达给译文读者",条件句可以用 when, where 等时间或地点副词所引导的状语从句来引导。

例22 如需加班施工,应提前申请。

译文:**When** there is any overtime work needed, the construction party shall file an application in advance.

韩礼德(Halliday)于1962年首次提出衔接(cohesion)概念,并将其定义为"存在篇章内部,使之成为语篇的意义关系"。之后在他与哈桑(Hasan)合著的《英语的衔接》(*Cohesion in English*)(1976)一书中把衔接的手段分成五类:照应(reference)、替代(substitution)、省略(ellipsis)、连接(conjunction)、词汇衔接(lexical cohesion),其中前四种属于语法手段(grammatical device),后一种属于词汇手段(lexical device)。语法衔接主要指用连词、副词或词组将两个命题连接起来。由于汉语是意合的语言,内容可以用来表达逻辑,不需要关联词。而作为形合语言的英语则恰恰与之相反,往往需要借助表示逻辑关系的副词、连词等功能词来表达内容。因此,展位搭建指南翻译需要通过意会汉语的真正含义,用语法衔接的手段让目标语读者理解内容,从而达到交际翻译的目的。

考虑到展位搭建指南属于信息文本,同时兼具告知和指令功能,语言要求简洁易懂,但不能出现歧义现象。在实际使用过程中,在篇章层面上除了连接手段外,较少运用其他三种语法衔接手段。

例 23 展会倡导绿色环保理念，特制定了《绿色中国国际进口博览会标准》，本标准包含了绿色展台、绿色运营、绿色物流、绿色餐饮 4 个方面。其中，绿色展台从绿色设计、绿色选材、绿色安全施工 3 个阶段制定了相关标准，请参展商和搭建商积极响应，按绿色标准实施。

译文：In order to promote the concept of environment protection, the organizer has formulated the *Criteria for Green China International Import Expo*, which includes the provisions on environment-friendly exhibition booths, operation, logistics and catering service. **In particular**, applicable standards are formulated for environment-friendly exhibition booths including their design, material selection and safe operation. Exhibitors and exhibition booth constructors are required to comply with the standards.

例 24 展位电路设计单项回路不得超过 2000 W，若超过 2000 W，应采用三项电源设计，平衡分配用电负荷。

译文：The single loop circuit of the booth shall be under 2,000 W. **If not**, a three phase supply design should be adopted to balance the distribution of electricity.（省略）

例 24 原文中后一个短句是对前一个短句的否定补充情况说明。译文采用 if not 这一否定条件句式简写形式，符合英语的表达习惯。同时为达到简洁的目的，第一个短句反说正译，将"不得超过"译为 under，为下个短句的否定提供条件。

综上所述，参展商手册中的会展合同与规章、展品运输指南、展位搭建指南的所属文本类型皆为信息类，实现的功能依次为指令，以告知为主、以指令为辅，指令与告知兼顾，语篇衔接手段强度依次为弱、较弱、较弱，所运用的翻译策略都为交际翻译，具体翻译技巧灵活度依次为弱、较弱、较弱，详见表 3.3。

表 3.3 参展商手册文本及其翻译

文本	文本类型	实现功能	翻译表征（英语）			翻译策略	翻译技巧灵活度
			词法	句法	篇章		
会展合同与规章	信息型	指令	专业术语、书面语、古语词、外来词、同义词连用和词项重复等	祈使句（shall, may）、条件句（in case, in the event that）、被动句、长句、专用表达等	衔接手段强度弱	交际翻译	弱
展品运输指南	信息型	以告知为主，以指令为辅	专业术语、书面语	祈使句（should, will）、条件句（in case, if, should）、被动句、因果句、目的句等	衔接手段强度较弱	交际翻译	较弱
展位搭建指南	信息型	指令与告知兼顾	专业术语、书面语	祈使句（shall, may, will）、条件句（in case, if, should）、被动句等	衔接手段强度较弱	交际翻译	较弱

思考题

1. 如何结合文本类型确定招展书和参展商手册的翻译策略？
2. 翻译以下会展名称。
   （1）北京"两区"建设国际合作暨投资北京峰会企业供需洽谈对接会
   （2）中国国际进口博览会签约仪式
   （3）澳大利亚全国农业日
   （4）"萨马兰奇杯"国际青少年冰雪外语知识大赛云启动仪式
   （5）"江苏优品·畅行全球"线上对接会
   （6）大连市科技金融对接发布会
   （7）Korea International Fishing Show
   （8）International Trade Fair for Retail Promotions and Imports（IAW）
   （9）Franchise International Malaysia（FIM）
   （10）International Broadcasting Convention（IBC）
3. 翻译以下句子。

（1）The 1st China International Small and Medium Enterprises Fair（CISMEF）was held from the 18th to the 22nd October, 2004 in Guangzhou, which had achieved a great success. With 1,860 standard booths and 1,950 SMEs from 30 provincial delegations including Hong Kong, Macao, the fair had more than 118,000 attendances（consisting of 46,000 domestic buyers and 5,600 foreign buyers）. The intent-contracts in this fair reached 32 billion yuan.

（2）As all packages of exhibits will be frequently loaded and unloaded during transportation unpack for the fair and repack for the return movement, storage in open-air or will be placed outdoors, please ensure that your exhibits are packed in strong, water-proof wooden cases which are strong enough to protect the exhibits from damage and rain.

（3）For the weight of single piece of exhibits over 1,000 kgs, please also clearly mark the exterior of the case with "Center of Gravity", "Front Side and Back Side", "Lifting Point". For any Fragile and Up-Right Position items, please also label or mark the exterior of the box. Other markings should conform to the International Rules and Regulations Governing Packing Signs and Symbols.

（4）For safety reasons, ALL electrical installation work connecting to the main at the exhibition venue MUST be carried out SOLELY by the Official Standfitting Contractor. If the electric power needed exceed the range provided in the order form, exhibitors must contact official contractor DIRECTLY for special arrangements before the deadline of order submission.

（5）Before lighting and electricity is supplied for individual booth, exhibitors who need preceding electricity supply for test running should contact the Official Standfitting Contractor for prior arrangement. Availability of such supply is subjected to extra cost and the possibility of technical arrangement.

（6）危险品、冷藏品或贵重展品加收100%来回程基本运费。

（7）根据操作要求,对展品在集装箱内进行绑扎、加固或衬垫(包括普通集装箱、框架箱和开顶箱),由此产生的相关费用实报实销。

（8）所有于展台内使用或展示之展品、物料及装修材料,必须做好防火措施,并符合所有适用之防火及建筑条例。

（9）参展商须自行安排清理包装物料、纸箱、空盒、空箱、建筑废料等,并承担所有相关费用。

（10）请注意电力申请表格中的电源均不可合并使用,如"300安培电源×2个≠600安培"。

4．翻译以下段落。

（1）

会展综合体介绍

国家会展中心(上海)总建筑面积超过150万平方米,包括展馆、会议中心、商业广场、办公楼和一家高端酒店,集展览、会议、活动、商业、办公、酒店等多种业态为一体,是目前世界上最大的会展综合体。

国家会展中心(上海)位于上海虹桥商务区核心区,与虹桥交通枢纽的直线距离仅1.5千米,通过地铁与虹桥高铁站、虹桥机场紧密相连。周边高速公路网络四通八达,2小时内可到达长三角各重要城市,交通十分便利。

• 展览场馆:国家会展中心(上海)可展览面积共计近60万平方米,其中室内展厅总面积近50万平方米,北广场室外展场10万平方米,货车可直达各个室内展厅。

• 会议中心:国家会议中心(上海)是中国国际进口博览会开幕式、虹桥国际经济论坛举办地,是由78个大中小型会议室组成、共5.6万平方米面积的国际化现代会议设施"群落"。

（2）

---

9. 参展商的通行

9.1 只有在参展商足额付清展位费后,组展单位才会授予参展商每9平方米展位3张免费的参展商证。除此之外,参展商要求的任何额外的证件按照当届《进口展参展手册》的有关规定办理。

10. 展位搭建

10.1 境外参展商在筹展时间进馆布展前,必须向组展单位和组展单位现场管理人员出示所有展品的海关清单、ATA单证册等原件,并提交相关复印件后,方能进馆布展。

如未能按要求提供相关文档,组展单位有权阻止参展商进馆布展,损失一概由参展商承担。

10.2 所有升级标摊由组展单位指定的主场承建商搭建,光地展位由参展商自行委托经组展单位推荐的施工单位或参展商自带的并经组展单位认可的施工单位搭建。

10.3 如参展商自行委托施工单位搭建展位,则参展商对展位设计、搭建和相关的安全、防火工作负全责,并有义务确保展位搭建工作符合当届《进口展参展手册》列明的一切操作要求和技术要求以及政府部门的相关法规规定。

5. 修改以下译文。

原文:

一、标准展位
广交会提供统一模式的标展展位。

基本配置

如图例所示(略)

包括:三面围板、一块楣板、地毯、射灯4个、日光灯1个、洽谈桌1张、椅子4把、矿泉水一箱(一箱24瓶,"三千尺"配水质量监督电话:0086-20-86676702)、电话机一部。

展位尺寸

2970 mm×2970 mm,围板高度为2500 mm,楣板最低点距地面距离为2200 mm。

搭建规范

1. 展位内配置的射灯、日光管均按以上图例标注的位置搭装。
2. 转角位展位只搭两面展板,面向通道的两面不搭展板。

译文:

Item 1　Standard Stands

The Canton Fair provides standard stands of unified pattern.

Basic equipment

As is shown in the picture.

Including:Three-side walls, one fascia board, one carpet, four spotlights, one F/L light, one aluminum table, four chairs, and one box of mineral water (24 bottles in one case, Quality Supervisory Telephone of SQC mineral water:0086 – 20 – 86676702), and one telephone.

Stand Dimension

2,970 mm×2,970 mm, height of walls:2,500 mm, distance between the nadir point of fascia board and floor:2,200 mm

Setting-Up Specifications

(1) The spotlight and the F/L light shall be installed at the positions indicated in the above picture.

(2) For stands located at corners, panels will only be set up at two sides of the stands with other two sides facing the aisle open.

展会知识产权保护办法

第一章 总则

第一条 为加强展会期间知识产权保护,维护会展业秩序,推动会展业的健康发展,根据《中华人民共和国对外贸易法》《中华人民共和国专利法》《中华人民共和国商标法》《中华人民共和国著作权法》及相关行政法规等制定本办法。

第二条 本办法适用于在中华人民共和国境内举办的各类经济技术贸易展览会、展销会、博览会、交易会、展示会等活动中有关专利、商标、版权的保护。

第三条 展会管理部门应加强对展会期间知识产权保护的协调、监督、检查,维护展会的正常交易秩序。

第四条 展会主办方应当依法维护知识产权权利人的合法权益。展会主办方在招商招展时应加强对参展方有关知识产权的保护和对参展项目(包括展品、展板及相关宣传资料等)的知识产权状况的审查。在展会期间,展会主办方应当积极配合知识产权行政管理部门的知识产权保护工作。

展会主办方可通过与参展方签订参展期间知识产权保护条款或合同的形式,加强展会知识产权保护工作。

第五条 参展方应当合法参展,不得侵犯他人知识产权,并应对知识产权行政管理部门或司法部门的调查予以配合。

第二章 投诉处理

第六条 展会时间在三天以上(含三天),展会管理部门认为有必要的,展会主办方应在展会期间设立知识产权投诉机构。设立投诉机构的,展会举办地知识产权行政管理部门应当派员进驻,并依法对侵权案件进行处理。

未设立投诉机构的,展会举办地知识产权行政管理部门应当加强对展会知识产权保护的指导、监督和有关案件的处理,展会主办方应当将展会举办地的相关知识产权行政管理部门的联系人、联系方式等在展会场馆的显著位置予以公示。

第七条 展会知识产权投诉机构应由展会主办方、展会管理部门、专利、商标、版权等知识产权行政管理部门的人员组成,其职责包括:

(一)接受知识产权权利人的投诉,暂停涉嫌侵犯知识产权的展品在展会期间展出;

（二）将有关投诉材料移交相关知识产权行政管理部门；

（三）协调和督促投诉的处理；

（四）对展会知识产权保护信息进行统计和分析；

（五）其他相关事项。

第八条　知识产权权利人可以向展会知识产权投诉机构投诉，也可直接向知识产权行政管理部门投诉。权利人向投诉机构投诉的，应当提交以下材料：

（一）合法有效的知识产权权属证明：涉及专利的，应当提交专利证书、专利公告文本、专利权人的身份证明、专利法律状态证明；涉及商标的，应当提交商标注册证明文件，并由投诉人签章确认商标权利人身份证明；涉及著作权的，应当提交著作权权利证明、著作权人身份证明。

（二）涉嫌侵权当事人的基本信息。

（三）涉嫌侵权的理由和证据。

（四）委托代理人投诉的，应提交授权委托书。

第九条　不符合本办法第八条规定的，展会知识产权投诉机构应当及时通知投诉人或者请求人补充有关材料。未予补充的，不予接受。

第十条　投诉人提交虚假投诉材料或其他因投诉不实给被投诉人带来损失的，应当承担相应法律责任。

第十一条　展会知识产权投诉机构在收到符合本办法第八条规定的投诉材料后，应于24小时内将其移交有关知识产权行政管理部门。

第十二条　地方知识产权行政管理部门受理投诉或者处理请求的，应当通知展会主办方，并及时通知被投诉人或者被请求人。

第十三条　在处理侵犯知识产权的投诉或者请求程序中，地方知识产权行政管理部门可以根据展会的展期指定被投诉人或者被请求人的答辩期限。

第十四条　被投诉人或者被请求人提交答辩书后，除非有必要作进一步调查，地方知识产权行政管理部门应当及时作出决定并送交双方当事人。被投诉人或者被请求人逾期未提交答辩书的，不影响地方知识产权行政管理部门作出决定。

第十五条　展会结束后，相关知识产权行政管理部门应当及时将有关处理结果通告展会主办方。展会主办方应当做好展会知识产权保护的统计分析工作，并将有关情况及时报展会管理部门。

第三章　展会期间专利保护

第十六条　展会投诉机构需要地方知识产权局协助的，地方知识产权局应当积极配合，参与展会知识产权保护工作。地方知识产权局在展会期间的工作可以包括：

（一）接受展会投诉机构移交的关于涉嫌侵犯专利权的投诉，依照专利法律法规的有关规定进行处理。

（二）受理展出项目涉嫌侵犯专利权的专利侵权纠纷处理请求，依照专利法第五十七

条的规定进行处理。

（三）受理展出项目涉嫌假冒他人专利和冒充专利的举报，或者依职权查处展出项目中假冒他人专利和冒充专利的行为，依据专利法第五十八条和第五十九条的规定进行处罚。

第十七条 有下列情形之一的，地方知识产权局对侵犯专利权的投诉或者处理请求不予受理：

（一）投诉人或者请求人已经向人民法院提起专利侵权诉讼的；

（二）专利权正处于无效宣告请求程序之中的；

（三）专利权存在权属纠纷，正处于人民法院的审理程序或者管理专利工作的部门的调解程序之中的；

（四）专利权已经终止，专利权人正在办理权利恢复的。

第十八条 地方知识产权局在通知被投诉人或者被请求人时，可以即行调查取证，查阅、复制与案件有关的文件，询问当事人，采用拍照、摄像等方式进行现场勘验，也可以抽样取证。地方知识产权局收集证据应当制作笔录，由承办人员、被调查取证的当事人签名盖章。被调查取证的当事人拒绝签名盖章的，应当在笔录上注明原因；有其他人在现场的，也可同时由其他人签名。

第四章 展会期间商标保护

第十九条 展会投诉机构需要地方工商行政管理部门协助的，地方工商行政管理部门应当积极配合，参与展会知识产权保护工作。地方工商行政管理部门在展会期间的工作可以包括：

（一）接受展会投诉机构移交的关于涉嫌侵犯商标权的投诉，依照商标法律法规的有关规定进行处理；

（二）受理符合商标法第五十二条规定的侵犯商标专用权的投诉；

（三）依职权查处商标违法案件。

第二十条 有下列情形之一的，地方工商行政管理部门对侵犯商标专用权的投诉或者处理请求不予受理：

（一）投诉人或者请求人已经向人民法院提起商标侵权诉讼的；

（二）商标权已经无效或者被撤销的。

第二十一条 地方工商行政管理部门决定受理后，可以根据商标法律法规等相关规定进行调查和处理。

第五章 展会期间著作权保护

第二十二条 展会投诉机构需要地方著作权行政管理部门协助的，地方著作权行政管理部门应当积极配合，参与展会知识产权保护工作。地方著作权行政管理部门在展会期间的工作可以包括：

（一）接受展会投诉机构移交的关于涉嫌侵犯著作权的投诉，依照著作权法律法规的有关规定进行处理；

（二）受理符合著作权法第四十七条规定的侵犯著作权的投诉，根据著作权法的有关规定进行处罚。

第二十三条　地方著作权行政管理部门在受理投诉或请求后，可以采取以下手段收集证据：

（一）查阅、复制与涉嫌侵权行为有关的文件档案、账簿和其他书面材料；

（二）对涉嫌侵权复制品进行抽样取证；

（三）对涉嫌侵权复制品进行登记保存。

第六章　法律责任

第二十四条　对涉嫌侵犯知识产权的投诉，地方知识产权行政管理部门认定侵权成立的，应会同会展管理部门依法对参展方进行处理。

第二十五条　对涉嫌侵犯发明或者实用新型专利权的处理请求，地方知识产权局认定侵权成立的，应当依据专利法第十一条第一款关于禁止许诺销售行为的规定以及专利法第五十七条关于责令侵权人立即停止侵权行为的规定作出处理决定，责令被请求人从展会上撤出侵权展品，销毁介绍侵权展品的宣传材料，更换介绍侵权项目的展板。

对涉嫌侵犯外观设计专利权的处理请求，被请求人在展会上销售其展品，地方知识产权局认定侵权成立的，应当依据专利法第十一条第二款关于禁止销售行为的规定以及第五十七条关于责令侵权人立即停止侵权行为的规定作出处理决定，责令被请求人从展会上撤出侵权展品。

第二十六条　在展会期间假冒他人专利或以非专利产品冒充专利产品，以非专利方法冒充专利方法的，地方知识产权局应当依据专利法第五十八条和第五十九条规定进行处罚。

第二十七条　对有关商标案件的处理请求，地方工商行政管理部门认定侵权成立的，应当根据《商标法》《商标法实施条例》等相关规定进行处罚。

第二十八条　对侵犯著作权及相关权利的处理请求，地方著作权行政管理部门认定侵权成立的，应当根据著作权法第四十七条的规定进行处罚，没收、销毁侵权展品及介绍侵权展品的宣传材料，更换介绍展出项目的展板。

第二十九条　经调查，被投诉或者被请求的展出项目已经由人民法院或者知识产权行政管理部门作出判定侵权成立的判决或者决定并发生法律效力的，地方知识产权行政管理部门可以直接作出第二十六条、第二十七条、第二十八条和第二十九条所述的处理决定。

第三十条　请求人除请求制止被请求人的侵权展出行为之外，还请求制止同一被请求人的其他侵犯知识产权行为的，地方知识产权行政管理部门对发生在其管辖地域之内的涉嫌侵权行为，可以依照相关知识产权法律法规以及规章的规定进行处理。

第三十一条　参展方侵权成立的，展会管理部门可依法对有关参展方予以公告；参展方连续两次以上侵权行为成立的，展会主办方应禁止有关参展方参加下一届展会。

第三十二条 主办方对展会知识产权保护不力的,展会管理部门应对主办方给予警告,并视情节依法对其再次举办相关展会的申请不予批准。

第七章 附则

第三十三条 展会结束时案件尚未处理完毕的,案件的有关事实和证据可经展会主办方确认,由展会举办地知识产权行政管理部门在15个工作日内移交有管辖权的知识产权行政管理部门依法处理。

第三十四条 本办法中的知识产权行政管理部门是指专利、商标和版权行政管理部门;本办法中的展会管理部门是指展会的审批或者登记部门。

第三十五条 本办法自2006年3月1日起实施。

——http://www.mofcom.gov.cn/article/swfg/swfgbh/201101/20110107352022.shtml

第四章　会展申请报告翻译

学习目标

- 知晓会展申请报告的交际主体与媒介
- 了解会展申请报告的篇章布局
- 熟悉英文会展申请报告的语言特征
- 掌握会展申请报告的翻译方法

核心词汇

* 注册申请书（application for registration）
* 申办报告（candidature file）
* 标准模板（standard template）
* 序言（preamble）
* 承诺/保证（commitment/covenant/guarantee）
* 法律地位（legal status）
* 总体构想（general concept）
* 场地规划（site planning）
* 配套设施（supporting facilities）
* 财务计划（financial program）
* 媒体服务（media services）
* 市场开发（marketing）
* 《国际展览会公约》（Convention Relating to International Exhibitions）

第四章 会展申请报告翻译

第一节 会展申请报告篇章布局

大型国际会展活动的筹备委员会在立项策划及可行性研究的基础上向主管国际组织(BIE、ICO 等)的权力机构提交正式申请报告,这是候选城市参与赢取举办权的起始环节,其细节要求通常由相应国际组织的法律文件明确规定。作为结构最完整、内容最丰富的正式文案,世界博览会和奥林匹克运动会的申请报告最具代表性,其翻译质量更是意义重大。

世博会申请文件的正式名称为注册或认可申请书(Application for Registration or Recognition)①,依据是《国际展览会公约》(Convention Relating to International Exhibitions)第Ⅲ部分(Registration)第 6 章第 1 条规定:

The Government of a Contracting Party in whose territory an exhibition coming within the scope of the Convention is planned (hereinafter referred to as "the inviting Government") shall send to the Bureau an application for registration or recognition indicating the laws, regulations or financial measures it proposes to make for the exhibition.

申请承办奥运会的正式文件名称则是申办报告(Candidature File)②,正如《2008 年奥林匹克运动会候选城市手册》(*Manual for Candidate Cities for the Games of the XXIX Olympiad 2008*)第二部分——申办报告所指出的:

... the practical foundation on which a candidature is built: the Candidature File, which represents a city's "master plan" for organising the Olympic Games.

It is very important to remember that the replies given by the Candidate Cities in their file represent a commitment by the Candidature Committee in the event that the city in question is elected to host the Olympic Games.

由于世博会和奥运会申请报告主题鲜明,内容具有强烈的法定性和官方色彩,其篇章布局不仅规范、清晰,而且"格式化"特征明显。

一、中国 2010 年上海世界博览会注册报告

《注册展览会程序与日期规则》第Ⅱ部分(Registration)第 1 条(Application for Registration) A 款第 2 段规定:

---

① 依据 BIE 的规定,世界博览会分为两类,即注册类博览会(registered international exhibition)和认可类博览会(recognized international exhibition)。详情参阅《国际展览会公约》第二部分——组织国际展览会的总则(General Conditions Governing the Organisation of International Exhibitions)。

② 该手册是由国际奥林匹克委员会依据《奥林匹克宪章》(Olympic Charter)制作的正式文件。为确定各届奥运会的举办城市,IOC 每次都会制定并颁布类似指导性文件,帮助候选城市完成申办程序。

The application for registration must indicate:

a) the pertinent legislative and financial measures and the legal status of the organisers;

b) the title and preliminary plan relating to the theme (choice, definition development, applications) and to the congresses and symposiums contributing to their diffusion, as well as whether it is intended to associate these activities with a wider international campaign having the support, for instance, of the United Nations system;

c) the Exhibition's duration;

d) the classification summarising Exhibition activities;

e) the site area of the Exhibition showing if appropriate any off-site zoning proposals for the location of parking facilities, entertainment areas and the like associated with the exposition;

f) the financial program;

g) a preliminary promotional program for the Exhibition at both national and international level;

h) the preliminary program for the site's re-utilisation;

i) the preliminary commercialisation program.

因此，中国2010年上海世界博览会注册报告的篇章结构如下：

序言(Preamble)
1. 相关法律和财政措施以及组织机构的法律地位(The Pertinent Legislative and Financial Measures and the Legal Status of the Organizer)
2. 名称、主题与持续时间(Title, Theme and Duration of the Exposition)
3. 上海世博会主题深化与园区内活动分类和介绍(Theme Development and the Classification of Exhibition Activities)
4. 世博会场地规划(The Planning of the Exhibition Site)
5. 财务计划(Financial Program)
6. 沟通与推介计划(Domestic and International Communication & Promotion)
7. 后续利用的初步计划(Preliminary After-Use Plan)
8. 初步商业化运作计划(Preliminary Commercial Operation Program)
9. 法律附件(Legal Documents)

二、北京2008年奥林匹克运动会申办报告

根据IOC制定的指导性文件《2008年奥林匹克运动会候选城市手册》第Ⅱ部分(Candidate File)第2.2.2节(Volumes and Themes)有关申办报告内容的规定，北京2008年奥林匹克运动会申办报告基本按照此要求布局：

- 第一卷(Volume Ⅰ)

序言(Preface)

LETTER OF SUPPORT BY PRESIDENT JIANG ZEMIN

LETTER OF SUPPORT BY PREMIER ZHU RONGJI

LETTRE FROM LIU QI, MAYOR OF BEIJING

LETTRE FROM YUAN WEIMIN, PRESIDENT OF COC

导言

一、国家、地区及候选城市特点

二、法律

三、海关和入境手续

四、环境保护与气象

五、财政

六、市场开发

INTRODUCTION

THEME 1   NATIONAL, REGIONAL AND CANDIDATE CITY CHARACTERISTICS

THEME 2   LEGAL ASPECTS

THEME 3   CUSTOMS AND IMMIGRATION FORMALITIES

THEME 4   ENVIRONMENTAL PROTECTION AND METEOROLOGY

THEME 5   FINANCE

THEME 6   MARKETING

- 第二卷(Volume Ⅱ)

导言

七、比赛项目总体构想

八、比赛项目

九、残疾人奥运会

十、奥运村

INTRODUCTION

THEME 7   GENERAL SPORTS CONCEPT

THEME 8   SPORTS

THEME 9   PARALYMPIC GAMES

THEME 10   OLYMPIC VILLAGE

- 第三卷(Volume Ⅲ)

导言

十一、医疗和卫生服务
十二、安全保卫
十三、住宿
十四、交通
十五、技术
十六、新闻宣传与媒体服务
十七、奥林匹克主义与文化
十八、保证书
结束语
INTRODUCTION
THEME 11　MEDICAL/HEALTH SERVICES
THEME 12　SECURITY
THEME 13　ACCOMMODATION
THEME 14　TRANSPORT
THEME 15　TECHNOLOGY
THEME 16　COMMUNICATIONS AND MEDIA SERVICES
THEME 17　OLYMPISM AND CULTURE
THEME 18　GUARANTEES
CONCLUSION

鉴于《中国2010年上海世界博览会注册报告》和《北京2008年奥林匹克运动会申办报告》这两个文本具有很好的代表性,本章以其为例,从文本类型理论视角对其进行分析,进而讨论申请报告翻译的策略与技巧。

第二节　英文会展申请报告语言特征

英文会展申请报告作为最典型的会展前文案,具有鲜明的语言特色——格式布局具有较强的规范性,内容上主客观相结合,遣词造句追求严谨和可读性。

一、规范性

所谓规范性,是指英文会展申请报告在格式布局方面必须遵循特定的规范,其中既包括相关国际组织的强制性要求,也包括约定俗成的语言使用习惯,而后者正是本小节要说明的。

英文会展申请报告属于正式文体,故必须遵循英语正式文体的格式要求。

(一) 格式

段落采用齐头格式,即首行无缩进,段落之间以空行标志分段,这不同于汉语书写中惯用的首行缩进格式。同时,对齐方式采用左对齐格式,这不同于汉语书写中惯用的两端对齐格式。

(二) 布局

对于相关国际组织没有明确规定的英文会展申请报告而言,文案布局至少须满足一般英文报告的惯常要求。尽管功能不同的报告形式与篇幅大相径庭,但标准模板通常由以下几部分构成:Cover, Contents Page, Foreword, Executive Summary, Main Body, Glossary, Appendices (Shevlin, 2005: 55 – 61)。

1. 封面(Cover)

按照惯例,3页以上的报告都应添加封面,使报告显得更为正式。封面上只需写明报告题目及撰写者名称即可,不标注页码。题目字体必须较大,名称字体则可略微缩小。请注意不要全部大写,也不使用下划线。

2. 目录(Contents Page)

目录的作用体现在凸显专业性、可读性、条理性、覆盖面。

3. 前言(Foreword)

前言亦可被视为权威人士对报告的支持(endorsement)和赞同(approval)。撰写前言的意图在于说服读者确信报告值得认真对待。通过介绍撰写者、品评方法或解释主题的重要性,提出报告的中心思想(central message)或建议(recommendation)。

4. 概览(Executive Summary)

概览的内容通常包括以下两项:报告的主要内容和报告的结论或建议。

5. 正文(Main Body)

报告正文展现的是读者作决定所需了解的一切信息。

6. 术语表(Glossary)

涉及专业术语的报告应在正文后列术语表,详述报告中相关术语的明确定义。

7. 附录(Appendices)

附录部分包括所有重要的详细资料和原始数据,通常以罗马数字(Roman numeral)编号排列,添注描述性的标题(descriptive title)更有助于读者理解。

二、主客观描述的结合

（一）客观性

1. 极少使用第一人称

英文会展申请报告的客观性首先反映在第一人称代词的出现频率偏低，即使在陈述有关自身的信息时，也很少使用 we 等代词，而是代之以全名、缩写等自称。如此措辞，目的在于提高文本的说服力和可信度，传递给读者近似中立的错觉。

BOCOG will be an independent, legal entity and, as such, will have the right to exercise legal authority and the right of jurisdiction in civil affairs. **BOCOG** will also be legally responsible for civil obligations and liabilities in accordance with the law.

—2.2.2 Organizing Committee of the Olympic Games

2. 大量使用专业术语

考虑到目标读者均为相关领域专家，术语的使用不仅不会妨碍信息接收者的理解，反而能凸显文本的专业性。而且，客观的专业术语相比于带有主观色彩的日常表述，更符合申请报告这种文本的文体要求。

The current Chinese industrial and commercial tax regime (excluding **tariffs** and **agricultural tax**) comprises 17 specific taxes. Of these, the following taxes would apply for the hosting of the Olympic Games in Beijing:

- business tax;
- value-added tax (VAT);
- consumer tax;
- corporate income tax;
- individual income tax;
- vehicle and road tax; and
- stamp duty.

—5.4.1 Taxes

Beijing's medical service is a leader in Asia and is at the level of world's best practice in such fields as **neurosurgery, heart surgery, sport medicine, ophthalmology and preventive medicine**. Beijing's hospitals are equipped with highly specialised diagnostic and therapeutic equipment. For example, in the area of medical imaging, this includes **PET, MRI, CT, diagnostic ultrasound and nuclear radiology**.

—11.1.2 Beijing's Medical System

3. 大量使用被动语态

英文会展申请报告注重客观描述的另一特征就是大量使用被动语态,不仅能将动作抽象为客观状态,还能紧扣主题展开事实陈述。

The public **shall be encouraged** to use fewer private cars and enjoy an environment-friendly life style. Primary and secondary school children **shall be given** advice to use recycled paper and be friendly to wildlife. Energy-efficient and water-saving facilities **are required** at hotels, restaurants and stores. The use of disposable products **shall be restricted**, while facilities using ozone-depleting substances **shall be** strictly **prohibited**.

——4.3 Environmental Management for the Game

During the Games, airport operations **will be adjusted** to ensure that members of the Olympic Family **are processed** quickly and efficiently. Dedicated Olympic Passageway for the entry of the Olympic Family and dedicated ground transport operations which **will be separated** from the rest of the airport operation.

——14.1 Airport Data (2000 and 2008)

(二)主观性

最能体现英文会展申请报告主观性的语言特征是频繁使用带有主观评价色彩的修饰语,这一特色在北京奥运会申办报告中彰显无遗。

The Olympic Village will provide every resident with a **friendly, caring** atmosphere, and a **comfortable, stimulating** lifestyle. There will be **ample** opportunity for relaxation, leisure/recreational activities as well as a **full** range of quality services. Residents will also be able to participate in activities that promote cultural understanding in line with the spirit of Olympism. It is intended that the athletes and other residents have a **happy, exciting** and **unforgettable** experience.

——10.2.1 Characteristics

该文本通过黑体标注的具有主观评价色彩的修饰语,从侧面烘托相关的各项客观事实,从而实现主客观描述的完美结合。

三、严谨性

英文会展申请报告作为有法律效力的正式文案,典型语言特征表现为关键术语的统一性及引述的精确性。

(一)关键术语的统一性

对于具有特定含义的关键术语,保持用法的前后统一是英文会展申请报告的一条基本准则,否则会降低文本的权威性,并引起读者的歧义理解。

  10.9 Financial **Guarantee** for the Olympic Village
  The Beijing Municipal Finance Bureau will finance the initial expenses of the project in the period before the delivery strategy is confirmed. The city of Beijing has **guaranteed** to underwrite the construction of the Olympic Village. In order to ensure that the Olympic Village is constructed as a technologically advanced model of environmentally sustainable urban development, the Beijing Municipal Government will provide certain financial subsidies, mainly in the form of preferential and favorable conditions for the provision of land and land use. (For specifics of the financial guarantee, see Theme 18)
  10.10 **Guarantee** of Owner of Existing Buildings and Infrastructures
  All of the buildings and facilities in the Olympic Village will be new, and no existing facilities will be used.

  报告中通过法律术语 guarantee 表述政府部门以及相关组织团体依据 IOC 的要求作出的具有法律效力的承诺。

(二) 引述的准确性

  准确引述既是客观描述事实的重要方法,也在一定程度上体现了文本的权威性。就会展申请报告而言,引述较多出现在会展场地、住宿、交通、财政等领域。

  The headquarters staff and the guests of the IFs, whose sports are included in the program of the Summer Olympic Games, will be accommodated in 1 five-star hotel, 1 four-star hotel and 1 three-star hotel, which are 1 kilometre away from the IOC headquarters hotel, and 1 three-star hotel in the vicinity of the aquatic sports sites, offering a total of 950 rooms for them to choose from. The headquarters hotel for sailing competitions will be the five-star Shangri-la Hotel in Qingdao.
  There will be 2,150 rooms for NOC guests at 7 three-star to five-star hotels located in the famous Wangfujing Commercial District within 1 kilometre of the IOC headquarters hotel.
  In accordance with the requirements of the IFs, 7 hotels near the competition venues will serve as the Judges and Referees' Village, providing a total of 2,090 rooms.
  For "As" officials, 860 rooms of various grades have been obtained in areas around the Olympic Village.
  During the Olympic Games, over 93,000 rooms at student apartments and other accommodation facilities will be provided for the volunteers and BOCOG staff members, which will fully meet their accommodation demands.

—13.3.1 Number of Rooms Obtained

  上述文本就奥运会的住宿接待能力进行了分门别类和详尽、细致的介绍,以此表明申办城市的信心和实力。

四、可读性

可读性也是英文会展申请报告的重要语言特征,围绕单纯主题紧密展开的简短段落以及广泛使用的分项列表句式,都有助于提升读者的阅读舒适度,减轻他们理解上的负担。

(一)段落主题的单纯性

英文会展申请报告特别注重保持段落篇幅简短、主题单纯,在确保衔接顺畅及逻辑连贯性的基础上提升文本的可读性。

Beijing Municipality has three levels of administration: city, districts and counties, and townships. Beijing currently has 18 districts and counties.

The Beijing Municipal People's Congress is a state power at the local level, which is popularly elected. It exercises the following powers: deciding on the plan of economic construction and social development for Beijing; electing, appointing and removing from office leaders of municipal administrative, judicial, and law enforcement bodies. The Congress and its Standing Committee can formulate and promulgate local laws within the framework of the Constitution, the State laws and administrative regulations.

The Beijing Municipal Government led by the Mayor is Beijing's local government authority. It exercises the powers of government, provides a full range of services to the people of Beijing, and implements resolutions of the Beijing Municipal People's Congress.

—1.1 Political Institution

所引文本阐述主题为北京的行政机构和权力机构及其权力的行使。第一自然段介绍行政机构,第二自然段介绍权力机构及其权力的行使,第三自然段介绍权力行使的主体。尽管整体内容不复杂,但英文表述还是将其划分为三个自然段,目的当然是使各小节的信息更为单纯、句与句的衔接更为流畅,从而提升整体可读性。

(二)分项列表句式

使用分项列表句式是英文会展申请报告的另一可读性特征,由此大量复杂的平行结构得以清晰地表述,主要由名词短语、述宾短语和主谓短语构成。

The forecast budget for the Beijing 2008 Olympic Games has been prepared on the basis of a conservative forecast of receipts and a realistic forecast of expenditure. The process of preparing this budget has included:

- consultation with the Governments of China, Beijing Municipality and other relevant local areas;
- consultation with experts both nationally and internationally for each budget item;
- detailed review and analysis of the budgets of previous games, particularly Sydney;

- consultation with the IOC and COC; and
- comprehensive review of the budget process by Arthur Andersen and Bovis Lend Lease who have specialist knowledge relating to the Sydney.

从上文的结构可以看出,通过分项列表句式(名词短语),把复杂的预算准备工作清晰地呈现给评委,而且逻辑紧密、可读性非常强。

第三节　会展申请报告翻译实践

奥运会申办报告和世博会注册申请书都是具有法律效力的纲领性规划文案,语言表达主要以客观描述为主,并适时配合申办者的主观评价。值得注意的是,此类申请报告构成一个复杂的综合体,在文本功能上存在混合的可能性,即在具备信息功能的同时还兼具表达和呼唤功能,翻译时只有做到灵活、有效,才能达到最好的效果。

一、信息类文本翻译

根据文本类型理论,信息类文本可以采用交际翻译策略进行翻译,通过欠额翻译的方式,通顺、清晰地传递源语信息。由于更注重目标语文化和表达效果,译文一般显得地道、流畅。

(一) 计量单位翻译

根据2005年颁布的《翻译服务译文质量要求》(GB/T 19682—2005),计量单位翻译"一般沿用原文计量单位,必要时可换算为国际标准计量单位,或按顾客和翻译服务方约定。计量单位及其表达符号的使用应前后一致""时间、货币、计量单位等符号可直接引用原文符号,或符合目标语言相关标准和惯用译法,或按双方约定。数学、物理、化学等基础学科符号和其他技术领域专业符号一般采用相关标准和学科通用表达符号"。

鉴于申请报告的正式文本特性和信息功能,计量单位翻译尽量采用国际标准计量单位,在准确传递源语信息的基础上提升译文的可读性。以下两个实例摘自2024年巴黎夏季奥林匹克运动会申请报告。

例1

47. GENEROUS ROOM SIZES EXCEEDING REQUIREMENTS

Residential accommodation within the Village will be provided in bright, ultramodern accommodation built with athletes in mind. With an average floor area in a double room at 14.5 m^2, room sizes in the Olympic Village will considerably exceed IOC guidelines and provide the extra space and privacy athletes really need. No room which accommodates two athletes will be smaller than 12 m², Single rooms are similarly generous in their proportions. The average floor area of a single room is 11 m², varying from 9.6 m² to 12 m² wall-to-wall.

Room type	Olympic Games			Paralympic Games		
	Minimum floor area/m²	Maximum floor area/m²	Average floor area/m²	Minimum floor area/m²	Maximum floor area/m²	Average floor area/m²
Single rooms	9.6 m²	12 m²	11 m²	9.6 m²	12 m²	11.5 m²
Double rooms	12 m²	17 m²	14.5 m²	12 m²	17 m²	14.5 m²

48. AMPLE ROOMS FOR ATHLETES AND OFFICIALS

The Village will have abundant accommodations built for athletes and future residents of this important community. With large rooms and supporting services and infrastructure, Paris 2024 can also guarantee that Football and Sailing athletes will have a home in the Olympic Village at the conclusion of their competitions so that they can enjoy the same Games experience and explore the wonders of Paris during the Games.

Please refer to Table 48.

Table 48　Village Number of Rooms and Beds

Type of Rooms	Olympic Games		Paralympic Games		
	Number of Rooms	Number of Beds	Number of Rooms	% of Rooms Wheelchair Accessible	Number of Beds
Single Rooms	2,900 (29%)	2,900	4,060 (62%)	100%	4,060
Double Rooms	7,080 (71%)	14,160	2,490 (38%)	100%	4,980
Total	9,980	17,060	6,550	100%	9,040

译文：

47. 高标准住宿

奥运村将为运动员提供采光充足、高度现代化的住宿环境。奥运村的房间面积将远超国际奥委会的要求，为运动员提供真正需要的额外空间和私密环境。双人间的平均面积达14.5 m²，最小面积不小于12 m²。单人间面积同样宽敞，从9.6 m²到12 m²不等，平均面积为11 m²。

房型	奥运会			残奥会		
	最小面积/m²	最大面积/m²	平均面积/m²	最小面积/m²	最大面积/m²	平均面积/m²
单人间	9.6 m²	12 m²	11 m²	9.6 m²	12 m²	11.5 m²
双人间	12 m²	17 m²	14.5 m²	12 m²	17 m²	14.5 m²

48. 运动员/官员客房充裕

奥运村将修建大量住所，供运动员和嘉宾使用。宽敞的房间、一流的配套服务和基础设施能确保足球和帆船运动员在比赛结束后感受到奥运村"家"的感觉，他们既可以享受2024年巴黎奥运体验，又可以在奥运期间游览巴黎名胜。

参阅表48。

表48 奥运村房间数与床位数

房型	奥运会		残奥会		
	房间数	床位数	房间数	无障碍设施比例	床位数
单人间	2900（29%）	2900	4060（62%）	100%	4060
双人间	7080（71%）	14160	2490（38%）	100%	4980
总计	9980	17060	6550	100%	9040

例2

- Conservative currency and exchange rate assumptions

The exchange rate utilised in the OCOG budget projections is 88 euro cents per US dollar (EUR 0.88 = USD 1.00). This rate was based on average weekly exchange rates over the past two years (mid-2014 to mid-2016), thus taking into account the most recent fluctuations in exchange markets.

- Currency exchange rates

	2014–2015	2015–2016	Average (OCOG Budget Rate)
1 EUR =	USD 1.16	USD 1.11	USD 1.14
1 USD =	EUR 0.86	EUR 0.90	EUR 0.88

Source – Bloomberg

Given the difficulty in making long-term predictions regarding currency exchange rates, Paris 2024 has already identified optimal hedging strategies and accounted for their related costs in the OCOG budget. Further, the OCOG will work to minimise currency risk through a series of measures in its contractual agreements and cash flow management.

- Stable inflation

The inflation rate in France has been stable over the long-term.

The budgeted inflation rate for the OCOG is assumed at 1.4% per year. This conservative approach is based on the overall long-term stability in inflation experienced in France, and more specifically from the average experience over the past ten years. The chart below indicates a peak annual inflation rate of 2.8% and an average rate of just 1.3%; thus the budgeted inflation rate adopted is appropriate and conservative based on recent experience and the gradual return of sustained economic growth worldwide.

- French inflation rates (2006 −2015)

	Inflation/%									
2006	2007	2008	2009	2010	2011	2012	2013	2014	2015	
1.6	1.5	2.8	0.1	1.5	2.1	2.0	0.9	0.5	0.0	
2006 / 2015 (10-year average)										
1.3										

Source-National Institute of Statistics and Economic Studies (INSEE)

The OCOG will work to minimise inflation risk through initiatives such as early procurement of large expenditure items, free access to the largest economy in the world via the EU market in order to increase competitive pricing and strong internal financial discipline.

译文：
- 货币与汇率预计

基于过去两年(2014年年中至2016年年中)的周平均汇率，加之近期外汇市场的波动，奥组委预计奥运会期间美元对欧元的汇率为0.88(0.88欧元=1美元)。

- 货币汇率

货币	2014—2015	2015—2016	平均值(奥组委预算)
1欧元	1.16美元	1.11美元	1.14美元
1美元	0.86欧元	0.90欧元	0.88欧元
数据来源：彭博			

鉴于对货币汇率做出长期预测相对困难，巴黎奥组委制定了最优对冲策略，将奥运会涉及的开销纳入预算范围。此外，在合同协议和现金流管理方面，奥组委将采取一系列措施，尽可能地降低货币风险。

- 通胀稳定

法国通货膨胀率将长期稳定。

由于法国通货膨胀长期稳定，奥组委根据过去十年的平均通胀率，保守估计预算中通胀率为每年1.4%。如下表所示，法国年通胀率峰值为2.8%，年平均通胀率仅为1.3%。故基于全球经济持续增长回升的趋势和近年数据，预算的通货膨胀率相对合理和保守。

- 法国通货膨胀率(2006—2015)

	通胀率/%									
2006	2007	2008	2009	2010	2011	2012	2013	2014	2015	
1.6	1.5	2.8	0.1	1.5	2.1	2.0	0.9	0.5	0.0	
2006/2015(近十年平均值)										
1.3										
数据来源：法国国家统计局(INSEE)										

为尽可能降低通货膨胀风险,奥组委将采取一些新举措,例如提早采购大额支出项目,通过欧盟市场自由进入全球最大经济体,以提升价格竞争力,加强内部金融规则。

例1和例2在翻译计量单位 m^2、EUR 和 USD 时,采用直接引用原文符号(例1中的 m^2)和符合目标语言(例2中的"欧元"和"美元")的惯用译法。

(二)专业术语翻译

会展申请文案中介绍配套服务信息的文本特征之一是遣词造句时大量使用有关会展服务项目及其设施的专业术语。一些常见的专业术语,如安保领域通用的监控系统名称"周界警戒系统"(perimeter alarm system)、"实时图像监控系统"(real-time video monitoring system)、"移动图像传输系统"(mobile video transmission system)、"安全监视系统"(security monitoring system)、"证件注册管理和电子查验系统"(accreditation management and electronic verification system)等,都具有鲜明的行业特征,频现于各类会展场地安保企划文案。

专业术语的优势在于能以最为直观的方式向相关领域专家展示场地服务的高度专业性,因此在翻译过程中我们应尽量将之转换成目标语的通用行业术语,否则易使目标语读者产生误解。

例3

北京市有健全的医疗急救网络。120电话紧急通信系统可24小时直接与北京急救中心联络。覆盖全市的急救站点、综合性医院以及大部分专科医院都可以为市民提供急救服务。全市现有急救车1600辆,配备现代化的通信和急救设备。

——《北京2008年奥运会申办报告》主题第11.1.2节

译文:

Beijing has an efficient medical <u>emergency services</u> network. The emergency number 120 provides immediate access on a 24-hour basis to the Beijing <u>First-Aid</u> Centre, which coordinates emergency stations strategically located to cover the entire city as well as general hospitals and most specialised hospitals. At present, the City has a fleet of 1,600 ambulances, each carrying modern communications and <u>emergency care</u> equipment.

例4

奥运会道路系统将设有奥运专用车道,其核心是利用奥林匹克交通环,主要由两条城市快速环路(四环路和五环路的一部分)以及主干线和联络线组成(见图14-1)。85%的比赛场馆在奥林匹克交通环沿线,且各场馆均有两条以上的交通路线与奥林匹克公园连接。在保证安全的前提下,高峰时间的行车速度可达每小时60千米以上。

——《北京2008年奥运会申办报告》主题第14.3节

译文：

The Olympic Route Network will provide dedicated lanes for Olympic transport. At its core will be the Olympic Traffic Ring. It comprises part of two expressways (See Map 14-1), the 4th and 5th ring roads, together with trunk roads and connecting roads. 85% of the competition venues will be located along the Olympic Traffic Ring and all venues will have at least 2 routes available to the Olympic Green. These routes will allow safe access at the speed of no less than 60 km per hour even in rush hours.

例 3 和例 4 在翻译医疗和道路配套信息时使用了该领域通行的相关术语，如 emergency services, First-Aid, emergency care, dedicated lanes, expressways, ring roads, trunk roads, connecting roads 等，对目标语读者而言，不仅专业，而且通俗易懂。

二、表达类文本翻译

与信息类文本翻译不同，表达类文本往往更注重表达效果，采用的多为语义翻译策略，通过超额翻译的方式，准确传递源语信息，帮助目标语读者理解，形式上可能会出现笨拙的"翻译腔"，可读性有待进一步提升。

会展申请报告的序言部分带有一定的文学色彩，在一定程度上反映了申请方的审美情趣，具体体现在多样化的修辞手法，如上海世界博览会注册申请书的序言部分，就采用了设问和排比两种修辞方法进行"自问自答"和层层推进。同时，英语亦有修辞性设问和排比的表现手法，且其形式与功能与汉语相一致，考虑到其隶属表达类文本，翻译时建议采用语义翻译的策略。

例 5

中国将在 2010 年上海世博会上为世界人民奉献什么？毫无疑问，中国人民将为五湖四海的宾客奉上一届成功、精彩、难忘的盛会。

中国 2010 年上海世博会将是一次探讨新世纪人类城市生活的伟大盛会。21 世纪是城市发展的重要时期，预计到 2010 年，全球总人口中的 55% 将居住在城市……

中国 2010 年上海世博会将是一曲以"创新"和"融合"为主旋律的交响乐。创新是世博会亘古不变的灵魂；跨文化的碰撞和融合则是世博会一如既往的使命……

中国 2010 年上海世博会将是世界各国人民的一次伟大聚会……

中国 2010 年上海世博会还将成为人类文明的一次精彩对话……

——《中国 2010 年上海世博会注册申请书》序言

参考译文：

Then what will Expo 2010 Shanghai China deliver to the world? There is no doubt that the Chinese people will present to the world a successful, splendid and unforgettable exposition.

Expo 2010 Shanghai China will be a great event to explore the full potentials of urban life in the 21st century, a significant period in urban evolution. It is expected that 55 percent of the world population will be living in cities by the year 2010 …

Expo 2010 Shanghai China will prove a symphony with the main melody of innovation and harmony. Innovation constitutes the immortal soul of world expositions while cross-cultural interaction and harmony rernain their invariable mission …

Expo 2010 Shanghai China will also be a grand international gathering …

In addition, Expo 2010 Shanghai China will offer a wonderful opportunity for cross-culture dialogues …

如例5所示,如果英语、汉语的修辞形式与功能类似,语义翻译的效果一般来说就会比较理想。译文中的设问和排比不仅不违和,而且直白明了。

另外,申报书的会展组织机构陈述部分,往往会采用分项列举的形式来逐一说明机构的构成与责任权力。作为较典型的表达类文本,该部分内容强调原作者的权威和可信度,翻译时基本要求采用"字面"翻译,即语义翻译。

例6

北京奥申委的执行机构是执行委员会,下设:

- 办公室
- 研究室
- 对外联络部
- 新闻宣传部
- 体育部
- 工程规划部
- 财务部
- 技术部
- 环境生态部

——《北京2008年奥运会申办报告》主题第2.2.1节

译文:

The Executive Committee is the executive body of BOBICO, with the following departments under its control:

- General Office
- Research & Analysis
- External Relations
- Press & Publicity
- Sports & Venues
- Construction & Project Planning

- Finance & Marketing
- Technology
- Environment & Ecosystem

例7

组委会的主要职责：协调相关法律法规、规章及政策的拟定和实施工作，协调、推动各地区和中央有关部门的参展事务，推动落实中国政府邀请各国政府和有关国际组织参展，就上海世博会筹备、举办过程中的重大事宜作出决议、决定，确定世博会政府总代表。组委会的日常联络和协调工作由中国国际贸易促进会承担。

参考译文：

It (the National Organizing Committee) is mainly responsible for：

- <u>Coordinating</u> the drafting and implementation of relative laws, regulations, rules and policies；
- <u>Coordinating and facilitating</u> the participation in the Expo of various regional governments and relevant central government departments；
- <u>Facilitating</u> the issuance of invitations by the Chinese Government to the governments of various countries and to international organizations to participate in the Expo；
- <u>Making</u> decisions on major matters during the preparation and staging of the Expo；
- <u>Appointing</u> a Commissioner General of the Exposition to represent the Chinese Government.

The daily routine of its communication and coordination rests with China Council for the Promotion of International Trade (hereinafter referred to as the "CCPIT").

例6对北京奥申委执行委员会的构成进行了阐述，是对官方权威性的说明，原文与译文都采用国际通用的列表句式，所运用的翻译策略为语义翻译，这对于目标语读者而言，可读性更强，阅读体验更好。例7中在采用上述翻译思路的基础上，针对汉语的段落式表述，译文采取更简洁、易懂的列表句式，更符合目标语读者的阅读期待。

三、呼唤类文本翻译

呼唤类文本的目的是"号召读者去行动、去思考、去感受"，特别强调可读性，译者可以充分发挥目标语的优势，不拘泥于原文的表达方式，所采用的翻译策略是交际翻译，常用的翻译方法是等效再创作。会展申报报告的宣传推广和市场营销部分作为具有呼唤类属性的文本，翻译时需要注重文本功能的实现，而非形式的对等。

例8

……向本地消费者灌输世博会是"一辈子难得一次的机会""不容错过，也不要让你的孩子错过""每个人都受欢迎"等信息。

——《中国2010年上海世博会注册申请书》第6.3.4节

译文1：

Enthuse the local market that this is a "once in a lifetime opportunity", "everyone is invited", and "Do not miss out, or let your children miss out".

本例引述了上海世博会组委会广泛宣传的口号,包括"一辈子难得一次的机会""不容错过,也不要让你的孩子错过""每个人都受欢迎"。译文1通过语义翻译忠实地将原文内容进行传递,但其实现的功能仅为信息传递,"共鸣"效果不明显。

译文2：

Inspire the local market that Expo 2010 will offer an opportunity "Once in a lifetime" where "Everyone is invited", so "Don't miss out, nor let your children miss out".

译文3：

Give local customers the spiel：Expo 2010 will offer a "Once in a lifetime opportunity", "Everyone is invited", "Don't miss out", and "Don't let your kids miss out".

译文2为我们提供了另外一个富有创意的思路——挖掘此类引语之间的逻辑关系,并直接以此类引语发挥句子功能,译文3中的 give ... the spiel 乃模仿美国市场营销员用语,使读者的共鸣感更强烈。

例9

黄浦江是上海的"母亲河",又是中国民族工业的发祥地之一。黄浦江两岸地区保留着上海城市发展的历史轨迹,老城厢、外滩、陆家嘴等重要城市空间是上海城市发展的历史缩影。上海世博会场地具有丰富历史内涵和突出景观价值,能够充分地体现"城市,让生活更美好"的主题。

——《中国2010年上海世博会注册申请书》第4.1.1节

译文：

The Huangpu River is not only the "Mother River" of Shanghai, but also a birthplace of the national industry of China. The area along the River testifies to the evolution of Shanghai, for it is dotted with the old city quarters, the Bund, the Lujiazui area and other important places which epitomize the history of Shanghai's growth. Boasting rich historical contents and outstanding tourist attractions, the site for Expo 2010 lend itself to the sufficient presentation of "Better City, Better Life".

例9为上海世博会场地选址的首项理由——有利于体现会展主题。原文围绕该场地的独特地理要素"黄浦江"展开,通过描述其历史内涵与景观价值,得出世博会选址"能够充分地体现"主题的合理结论。其中,第二句是揭示黄浦江两岸地区人文优势的核心,翻译时需要注意的是,译者想要提升选址理由的可信度,就需要对"老城厢、外滩、陆家嘴等"是黄浦江沿岸的"重要城市空间"进行前置知识的匹配，即帮助读者了解这些名胜景观的具体方位。因此，译文应当明示原文隐含的"黄浦江两岸"与上述城市空间之间的地理关系，实现更理想的告知功能，在形式上需要作出调整，等效再创作的翻译方法更合理、有效。

思考题

1. 英文会展申请报告的语言风格对译者处理中文文案是否起到借鉴作用？试以分项列表句式举例说明。

2. 如何结合文本类型确定符合会展申请报告的翻译策略？

3. 修改以下译文。

（1）北京，这座历史悠久、生机勃勃的城市，荣幸地有机会再次申办奥运会。

译文：Beijing, with its ancient past, dynamic present and exciting future, has the honour to present its second bid to host the Olympic Games.

（2）中国国务院相关部委和上海市政府也已分别签署了承诺函，积极支持上海世博会的举办。

译文：Meanwhile, messages of commitment from relevant ministries and commissions under the State Council and the Shanghai Municipal Government have been signed in support of the Expo.

（3）建立一个 BIE、世博会组织者和参展国的协调机制。

译文：To establish a mechanism framework between the BIE, the Organizer and participating countries.

（4）中国政府鼓励竞争、放松管制，已使用户获得了更好的服务、更低的价格，以及更先进的网络和设施。

译文：The Chinese Government encourages competition and deregulation. This has already resulted in improving customer service, lower pricing and more advanced networks and equipment.

（5）在尽可能多的赛事中安排足够的观众席位。

译文：As many events as possible will be allocated reasonable and fair proportion of public seats.

4. 翻译以下段落。

（1）The main dining hall will be located in the nave of the 220 mm × 24 m Cite du Cinema along with its connected patios. With a ceiling height of 18 m, the large nave has been brilliantly restored, celebrating the building's industrial heritage. The main dining hall, with seating for 5,000, is located 150 m across from the athlete transport mall on the east side of the Village.

（2）Directly connecting to 319 cities throughout the world, Paris-CDG is ranked among the world's top 10 airports in total passengers. It is located 12 km from the Main Media Centre and less than 20 km from the Olympic and Paralympic Village. By 2024, the number of boarding gates will grow from 226 to 259, increasing the airport's capacity by 19%. In addition to the existing suburban line RER B, access to the airport by public transport will be enhanced through the delivery of metro line 17, and most importantly, by the CDG Express, a direct and dedicated rail service which will connect the airport to the city centre within 20 minutes.

(3)

Venue Plan Concept: Infinite Excitement

The venue plan for the Olympic and Paralympic Games Tokyo 2020 consists predominantly of two thematic and operational zones: the "Heritage Zone" which houses several iconic venues used at the Tokyo 1964 Games and further sustains the enduring legacy of Tokyo 1964; and the "Tokyo Bay Zone" which serves as a model for innovative urban development and symbolises the exciting future of the city.

(4)

Severe Restrictions on Street Vending

The Road Traffic Law strictly controls street vending and action will be taken during the Games period to ensure street vending is controlled in accordance with the law.

Severe Restriction on Resale of Tickets

TOCOG will implement the official ticket resale programme under IOC guidelines and will strictly prohibit the resale of tickets outside the programme.

The resale of tickets to the general public in public areas is strictly prohibited under the ordinances of the respective Prefectural Governments.

(5) Municipal governments other than Tokyo that are involved in the Tokyo 2020 Games also strictly regulate advertising space through similar ordinances.

TOCOG will intensively monitor the use of outdoor, public transport, airport and other advertising space in the run up to and during the Games. Injunctions can be obtained immediately to protect all sponsors and licensees from rights infringements.

MANUAL FOR CANDIDATE CITIES FOR THE GAMES OF THE XXIX OLYMPIAD 2008

PART I: GUIDE

Introduction

As Candidate Cities, you are now in Phase II of the process to designate the Host City of the Games of the XXIX Olympiad in 2008.

The aim of this Manual is to guide you through the various steps of your candidature until the election of the Host City on 13th July 2001 during the 112th IOC Session in Moscow.

The Guide outlines what is required of a Candidate City as well as the procedures, rules and deadlines to be respected during Phase II. It also contains many useful recommendations and, along with the following documents, should be considered as essential reading for anyone connected with the preparation and promotion of a candidature for the Olympic Games:

- Candidature Procedure.
- Conditions Governing the Use of the Olympic Symbol by Candidate Cities for an Olympic Games.
- Code of Ethics.
- Undertaking.

(The text of the Undertaking appears in this Guide. The original document is annexed to the Manual and must be signed by the representatives of the Candidate City authorities and the NOC of the country, and submitted to the IOC with the Candidature File).

This Manual is subject to the provisions of the Olympic Charter and the Host City Contract. Should there be any conflict between, on the one hand, this Manual and, on the other hand, the Olympic Charter and/or the Host City Contract, the Olympic Charter and/or the Host City Contract shall prevail.

The contents of this Manual and its appendices represent the current position of the IOC on such matters. The IOC reserves the right to amend such guidelines and other directions. It is the responsibility of the City and the NOC to adapt to such amendments so that the Games will be organised in the best possible manner.

STAGES OF THE CANDIDATURE

1. Summary of Main Landmarks

The main landmarks of the candidature process are briefly summarised below:

- Information meeting between the IOC and the Candidate Cities (25th September 2000, Sydney).
- Signature of the Candidature Procedure.
- Creation of an emblem to represent your candidature.
- A single ten-minute presentation to the IOC Executive Board by a small delegation from the Candidate City. The aim of this presentation is to give the Candidate Cities the opportunity to introduce its management to the IOC

Executive Board (December 2000, Lausanne).
- Submission of the Candidature File and signature of the Undertaking.
- Deposit of $150,000—with the IOC at the time of submitting the Candidature File—to be returned with interest to those cities which have not been awarded the Games. Any outstanding costs by the Candidate Cities may be deducted from the deposit (e.g. registration of marks). In the event of a withdrawal of a Candidature, $25,000 of the deposit is non-refundable.
- Designation by the IOC Executive Board of the Candidate Cities which will be submitted to the IOC Session for the election of the Host City.
- Election of the Host City by the IOC Session.

2. Deadlines

Acceptance of Candidate Cities by the IOC Executive Board	28th –29th August 2000, Lausanne
Drawing of lots by the IOC Executive Board to determine the order of Candodate City presentations, etc.	13th September 2000, Sydney
Games of the XXVII Olympiad, 2000	15th September—1st October 2000, Sydney
Information meeting between the IOC and the Candidate Cities	25th September 2000, Sydney
Signature of the Candidature Procedure	6th September 2000
Ten-minute presentation to the IOC Executive Board	13th December 2000, Lausanne
Submission of Candidature File to the IOC	17th January 2001
Visits of the OIC Evaluation Commission to the Candidate Cities	mid-February to mid-April 2001
Report of IOC Evaluation Commission to the IOC Executive Board	mid-May 2001
Designation by the IOC Executive Board of Candidate Cities to be submitted to the IOC Session for election	
Election of the Host City of the Games of the XXIX Olympiad in 2008	13th July 2001 112th IOC Session, Moscow

3. Official Registration of the Candidature

The candidature becomes official when the Candidature Procedure has been signed by the Candidate City and its NOC, within the time limit established by the IOC.

4. Promotion Campaign

Once the candidature has been officially registered with the IOC, the promotion campaign may begin.

Consideration should be given to the creation of an emblem representing the candidature (consisting of the Olympic symbol—the five rings—and another element representing the candidature), following the provisions of the Olympic Charter and in accordance with the Conditions governing the use of the Olympic symbol by Candidate Cities for the Olympic Games. This emblem must be submitted to the IOC for approval. It may not be made public prior to IOC authorisation.

Candidate Cities must be cost conscious throughout the promotion campaign. The candidature will be under tough public scrutiny and, whilst all efforts to promote the project will be enthusiastically supported during the candidature, the post-election attitudes of the public, media, sponsors and supporters can be very critical and damaging. In this respect, it is essential to consider the value and target audience of any promotional activities, particularly those involving international travel, and to plan and budget accordingly in order to avoid unnecessary expenditure and criticism.

Maintaining objectivity throughout the promotion campaign is essential. Casual promises and unrealistic goals are very quickly seen through and can often damage the image of the candidature and its chances of success. For this reason, it is important to maintain coherence and harmony between the projects described in the Candidature File and those developed in the promotion campaign.

All the declarations, guarantees and agreements contained in the Candidature File have the force of obligations, as do all the other commitments made by the Candidate City, the NOC, the Candidature Committee, and all declarations made during official presentations.

5. Candidature File: Preparation and Presentation

The Candidature File, which consists of a compilation of the answers of the Candidate City to the IOC's Questionnaire in Part II, is one of the IOC's principal tools in evaluating a candidature and analysing its technical characteristics. The file must accurately reflect the current situation of the city and present its plans in a realistic manner.

The Candidature File must be presented in accordance with the Model Candidature File described at the end of this Manual. In order to facilitate the IOC's assessment of replies and to allow for an objective analysis, it is important that the order of questions is respected and that precise and concise answers are given.

Collaboration with your national sports federations and the International Federations is essential when preparing your Candidature File.

The Candidature File may not be distributed or made public until it has been submitted to the IOC, and the IOC's written authorisation has been obtained.

(1) **Delivery of the File to the IOC**

By the deadline of 17th January 2001, seventy (70) copies of the bilingual Candidature File (French and English) must be given to the IOC administration (for IOC internal use, members of the IOC Evaluation Commission and Executive Board and the Olympic Museum). They may be sent by post, or by special messenger, or they may be handed over personally. The IOC does not consider the personal delivery of the files to the IOC headquarters as an official occasion. As such, no ceremony will be arranged.

(2) **Study of the Candidature and Dispatching of the File**

The Candidature File is studied by the IOC to ensure that all the required information has been provided. The IOC may ask for any further information it deems necessary.

At the end of this process, the IOC gives its authorisation to the Candidate Cities to dispatch a copy of the file to the following persons or organisations:

- IOC members
- Honorary IOC members
- Each International Olympic Summer Sports Federation
- The Association of Summer Olympic International Federations (ASOIF)
- The Association of National Olympic Committees (ANOC)
- Each of the five NOC Continental Associations (ANOCA, PASO, OCA, EOC, ONOC)

Such Candidature Files must be identical in all aspects to the Candidature File approved by the IOC. The Candidature Files sent to the above persons/organisations must not contain any additional material to that approved by the IOC. A copy of any covering letter accompanying the file must be sent to the IOC.

Upon receipt of written authorisation from the IOC, the Candidate City is at liberty to release its Candidature File to the public and to the media.

6. Visit of the IOC Evaluation Commission

After receiving the Candidature File, the IOC co-ordinates the visits of an IOC Evaluation Commission to the Candidate Cities, as stipulated in bye-law to Rule 37 of the Olympic Charter. The Commission inspects the sites proposed for the Games and holds meetings with the Candidature Committee and experts on all aspects and themes of the candidature. At the end of the visits to all Candidate Cities, the Evaluation Commission issues a report.

7. Designation of Cities to Be Submitted to the IOC Session for Election

After examination of the report of the IOC Evaluation Commission, the IOC Executive Board will designate the cities which will proceed through to the vote at the IOC Session.

8. Election of the Host City

The Host City of the Games of the XXIX Olympiad in 2008 will be elected at the 112th IOC Session in Moscow. Each Candidate City will make a presentation to the IOC Session at which the vote will take place. The order of presentations is determined by the IOC by the drawing of lots. (See Candidature Procedure—Chapter 1—General Rules).

9. Preparing for the Potential Constitution of the Organising Committee for the Olympic Games

The Olympic Games are the exclusive property of the IOC which owns all rights and data relating thereto, in particular, and without limitation, all rights relating to their organisation, exploitation, broadcasting, recording, representation, reproduction, access and dissemination in any form and by any means or mechanism whatsoever, whether now existing or developed in the future. (Rule 11 of the Olympic Charter)

It is essential that the Candidature Committee plans for the constitution of an Organising Committee for the Olympic Games (OCOG) as it is the OCOG which is the main body responsible for organising the Olympic Games.

The Candidature Committee should ensure that all parties concerned in the preparation of the candidature are aware of this fact and that in the earliest stages of planning consideration is given to the persons who may form a potential Organising Committee, in the event that the city is elected to host the Games. It is important that there is some continuity between the Candidature Committee and an eventual Organising Committee.

Immediately after the announcement of the Host City, the Host City Contract is signed by the IOC, the Host City authorities, duly empowered by the city to make this commitment, and the NOC of the country in which the city is located. This contract specifies in detail the obligations incumbent upon the city chosen to organise the Olympic Games.

Within ten days of signing the contract, the elected city must increase the guarantee deposit (initially $150,000) to $1,000,000. This deposit must progressively be increased to a total of $5,000,000 from funds taken from the OCOG's revenue, including the sale of television rights and the marketing programme.

The Host City Contract will also contain a mechanism pursuant to which the IOC will have the right to withhold certain monies owing to OCOG pending resolution of any disputes involving the OCOG.

The OCOG must be constituted within <u>five months</u> of the date on which the Host City Contract is signed. The executive body of the OCOG must include: the IOC member(s) in the country, the President and Secretary General of the NOC, an athlete representative and at least one member representing and designated by the Host City. The executive body may also include representatives of public authorities and other leading figures. In order to ensure continuity, it would be appropriate for some members of the Candidature Committee to be members of the OCOG.

From the time of its constitution and until the time of its dissolution, the OCOG must conduct its activities in accordance with the Olympic Charter and the instructions of the IOC Executive Board. Moreover, it will be called upon to act in its capacity as party to the Host City Contract and will be jointly and severally liable, with the Host City and the NOC of the country, for realising the obligations contained in the Host City Contract and its annexes.

The OCOG must comply fully with the commitments and the promises made during the candidature phase, both in the technical file and the declarations and comments made by the Candidature Committee during its presentations to the Session and other Olympic meetings.

—https://library.olympics.com/

第五章 会展评估报告翻译

学习目标

- 知晓会展评估报告的信息来源和交际主体
- 了解会展评估报告的结构布局
- 了解英文会展评估报告的语言特征
- 掌握会展评估报告的翻译方法

核心词汇

* 评估报告（evaluation report）
* 营销报告（marketing report）
* 第三方评估机构（third-party evaluation agency）
* 数据指标（data indicator）
* 人气指数（popularity index）

第一节　会展评估概述

一、会展评估方法

会展评估报告是对会展工作、会展质量和会展效果进行系统、深入评价的过程。通过撰写会展评估报告可以更加深刻地了解会展环境，为此后会展工作提供经验和建议，提高会展的价值和服务质量。会展评估报告的主要信息来源包括：主办方自己的评估；参展者对主办方工作的评估（参展者对主办方一般都给予好的或较好的评价，如果有较低的评价，应当认真了解）；观众（包括现有客户和潜在客户）对主办方、展馆/展台的评价；专家对主办方、展馆/展台的评价;政府部门、新闻媒体对主办方、展馆/展台的评价。根据不同阶段的效果测评,进行汇总分析,对整个展览活动过程的效果进行总体评价。

会展评估一般采用定性与定量的方法。定性评估的内容包括:对展台的设计、展期宣传、展品、管理、工作态度、工作效率、服务意识、展览与其他营销方式的比较的评估;对市场潜力、趋势的评估等(有时也称作评估因素)。定量评估的内容包括接待客户情况、接待客户平均成本、成交情况、成交平均成本、成本效益比等(也常称作评估指数)。

定量指标主要集中在:

▲ 观众的数量

▲ 观众的质量

参观者质量与展出效率成正比,即参观者质量高,展出效率就高。参观者的质量通常体现在购买兴趣指数、购买影响指数和购买计划指数等方面。

▲ 观众的活动

平均参观展览时间,指参观者参观整个展览会所花费的时间,一般以小时表示,该指数与展览会效果成正比;平均参观展台时间,指参观者参观每个展台所花费的平均时间,一般以分钟表示。

▲ 展台效率

一种是工作人员接待目标观众的数量在目标观众总数中的比例,另一种是展台总开支除实际接待的目标观众数量之商,后一种方式也称作接触参观者平均成本。

▲ 成本效益比评估

成本效益也称作投资收益,评估因素比较多,范围比较广。一种典型的成本效益比是用开支比成交,另一种典型的成本效益比是用开支比建立新客户关系数。

▲ 成交评估

分为消费成交和贸易成交。

二、会展评估内容

一般而言,大型会展的评估包括以下内容:

1. 展台效果优异评估

如果展台接待了70%以上的潜在客户,而客户接触平均成本低于其他展台的平均值,其展台效果就是优异。

2. 成本效益比评估

这里的成本效益比内涵比较广,可以是此次展览的成本与效益相比,也可以是此次的成本与效益与前次或类似项目相比,还可以是展出的成本效益与其他营销方式相比。例如,如果展出开支为20万元,展出效益(展览成交额)为8000万元,那么成本效益比为1∶400。

3. 成交评估

该评估包括消费成交和贸易成交两种。对贸易性的展览会而言,成交评估是展会评估最重要的内容之一。成交评估的内容一般有：有无达到销售目标；成交额；成交笔数；意向成交额；实际成交额；与新客户成交额、与老客户成交额；展览期间成交额；预计后续成交额。

4. 接待客户评估

这也是商务会展最重要的评估内容之一，包括：

参观展台的观众数量。可以细分为接待参观者数、现有客户数和潜在客户数，其中潜在客户数是重点。

参观展台的观众质量。按照评估内容和标准分类统计观众的订货决定权、建议权、影响力、行业、区域等，然后根据统计情况将参观观众分为"极具价值""很有价值""一般价值""无价值"等。

接待客户的成本效益。计算方法是用展览总支出额除以所接待的客户数或者所建立的新客户关系数。

5. 调研评估

调研评估，即通过展出对市场和产品有无新的了解和认识、有无更明确的发展和努力方向等进行评估。

6. 竞争评估

竞争评估指对在展览工作方面和展览效果方面与竞争对手相比较的评估。

7. 宣传/公关评估

宣传/公关评估具体包括：宣传公关有无效果，效率、效益多大；是否需要增加投入提升展出者形象；形象对实际成交有多大作用。

会展评估是一个很复杂的体系，其中有些内容还具有一定的争议性，所以评估时应该根据实际情况审慎选择、谨慎操作。

第二节　会展评估报告文本分析

一、会展评估报告文本类型

会展评估报告的主题涉及面较广，大致可以分为三类：会展工作评估报告、会展质量评估报告和会展效果评估报告。会展工作评估报告主要反映工作质量、效率和成本效益；会展质量评估报告通过参展商数量质量及其参展时间、观展者数量质量及其观展时间、人流密度指数等方面数据的调研评估项目质量；会展效果评估报告针对的则是项目成果。无论评估报告的主题如何变化，文本一般都包括以下内容：评估的背景和目的；评估方法；评估结果；结论和建议。（王平辉，2008：193）

就会展评估报告的交际主体而言,信息发送者应为会展项目组织机构,当然也不排除与第三方机构合作或者直接委托第三方机构进行评估。与此相对应的是信息接收者,包括会展组织者(同时也是发送者)、会展主管部门、行业协会组织、会展参与者等,目的是通过科学的评估标准和客观结果来制定行业发展的规章制度、推广项目筹办的成功经验、塑造品牌优势及对参展与否做出理性的判断。因此,无论是从报告撰写者的意图,还是从其目标语读者的期待来看,客观的、专业的语言风格是评估类文本的固有要求。换言之,会展评估报告的基础是客观、真实的数据及其他佐证材料,而报告主体中所包含的全部价值判断都应当以相关数据及其他佐证材料为支撑。有鉴于此,会展评估类文本属于以信息传递为主要目的的典型文本(信息类文本),且只有尽可能科学、全面、客观、真实地保留原文内容,才能实现译文的预期功能,交际翻译是其最好的翻译策略。

二、会展评估报告结构布局和语言特征

(一)结构布局

英文会展评估报告除了具有独特的语言风格外,还具有完整的结构布局,一般包含标题、序言、目录、正文、署名等要素。

1. 标题

英文评估报告的标题必须说明报告针对的具体会展项目,且多以 Report 标识类型。若该报告的内容仅涵盖会展的某个特定领域,那么这也应构成标题不可或缺的成分,如 IOC Marketing Report Beijing 2022。

2. 序言

序言是评估报告正文前的概述部分,其内容通常包括活动的背景介绍、评估报告的宗旨等。值得注意的是,该部分内容也可能邀请特定权威人士撰写,如《2022 北京冬奥会市场营销报告》的序言就是由国际奥委会主席托马斯·巴赫(Thomas Bach)(图 5.1)、国际奥委会市场营销委员会主席吉里·凯瓦尔(Jiri Kejval)、北京冬奥组委主席蔡奇分别撰写的。

3. 目录

会展评估报告中篇幅较长的文本都应配置目录,以方便读者阅览。编撰目录的要求在于清晰,并与正文主体保持一致。图 5.2 为《2022 北京冬奥会市场营销报告》的目录,以供参考。

图 5.1　会展评估报告序言

CONTENTS

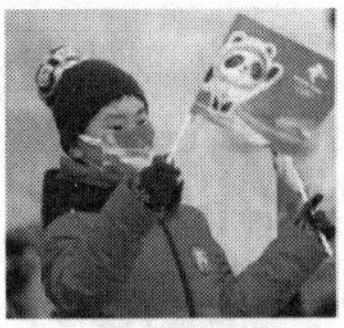
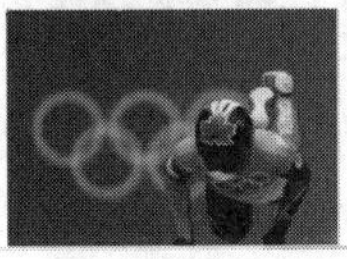

Forewords 4
Together for a Shared Future 10
Olympic Marketing Overview 20
Olympic Broadcasting 24
Olympic Partnerships 36
Fan Engagement 60
Licensing and Merchandising 70
The Olympic Brand 76
Acknowledgements 84

图 5.2　会展评估报告目录

4. 署名

公开发表的会展评估报告的署名部分有时会比较复杂，不但涉及文稿撰写、版面设计等，还需注明享有独立著作权的摄影人。另外，提供撰写者的相关联系信息也是较为通行的惯例，见《2022 北京冬奥会市场营销报告》的署名页（图 5.3）。

EDITORIAL, DESIGN AND PRODUCTION
IOC
Touchline

PHOTOGRAPHY
IOC Images
Beijing 2022
Getty Images

RESEARCH
Publicis Sport & Entertainment

International Olympic Committee
Maison Olympique, 1007 Lausanne, Switzerland
Tel: +41 (0) 21 621 6111
www.olympics.com/ioc

© This publication may not be reproduced, even in part, in any form, without the written permission of the IOC. All reproduction, translation and adaptation rights are reserved for all countries.

图 5.3　会展评估报告署名页

（二）语言特征

英文会展评估报告是以客观佐证材料立论并撰写的文本，因而其最鲜明的语言风格集中体现于大量的数据指标和引述。

1. 数据指标

在运用数据指标进行佐证的过程中，会展评估报告一般会采用以下两种方式：一是使用统计数据来佐证价值判断；二是通过图表注释展示统计数据。

统计数据的运用并非单纯地堆砌，而是为了支撑相关价值判断的合理性。以下文本中的数据统计就是为了说明2022年北京冬季奥运会赛事转播中传统电视与互联网数字平台观看量均创新高,在历届冬奥会中遥遥领先。

> Around the world, there were more hours of coverage made available to fans than at any previous Olympic Winter Games edition, including record coverage through digital platforms.
>
> This saw Beijing 2022 become the most digitally engaged Olympic Winter Games ever, with billions of engagements across digital platforms, including Olympic and Media Rights Holders' properties.
>
> In total, Beijing 2022 reached a global audience of more than two billion people, with viewers around the world consuming almost 12 billion hours of coverage across both linear TV and digital platforms. This equates to an average of 5.9 hours per viewer.
>
> But while digital viewing and consumption increased significantly—with the number of people watching digitally increasing by 123.5 per cent compared with the Olympic Winter Games PyeongChang 2018—linear TV remains the most dominant platform, accounting for 92 per cent of all broadcast hours consumed globally.

对于统计数据的展示,除文本外,会展评估报告还采用图表形式,并附有解释说明。图5.4是《2022北京冬奥会市场营销报告》"一起向未来"(Together for a Shared Future)部分中有关北京冬奥会的综合性数据。其中,不仅列举了参赛选手的男女人数,还包括赛事项目数量、参赛及获得奖牌的国家/地区奥委会数量、改造利用原有奥运会场馆数量等数据。图表配以文字说明不仅简单扼要,而且一目了然,目标语读者阅读体验感极佳。

2. 引述

引述也是英文会展评估报告的主要语言特色之一。通过引用相关人士的评论来说明活动的成效,这样的总结更为客观、更具说服力。例如,《2022北京冬奥会市场营销报告》"奥林匹克品牌"(The Olympic Brand)部分便有多处直接引述运动员、专业人士及官方人士的言论。

引述一:Just seeing the rings; it's something magical. You dream about this as a kid.

— Ireen Wust (NED), six-time Olympic gold medalist in speed skating

引述二:Our marketing and media rights partners are the pillars on which the Olympic Movement is funded, and we therefore need to ensure that their exclusive commercial rights are protected.

— Timo Lumme, Managing Director, IOC Television and Marketing Services

图5.4 图表形式展示统计数据

引述三：The emblems of Beijing 2022 combine Chinese culture, an international, modern style and winter sports together.

— Cai Qi, Beijing 2022 President

第三节　会展评估报告翻译实践

会展评估报告从文本类型来看，属于较典型的信息类文本，但兼具呼唤类文本的属性，翻译时主要采取交际翻译的策略，通过解释原文、调整文体、排除歧义，努力使译文对目标语读者所产生的效果与原文对源语读者所产生的效果相同。考虑到使用数据指标和引述为会展评估报告的语言特征，本小节主要讨论其在正文中的翻译，而标题与序言翻译可参阅本书第三章，不再赘述。

一、数据指标

数据指标是会展评估报告立论的基础，其重要性不言而喻。现以《第十六届中国国际高新技术成果交易会调研报告》第三部分"人气指数统计"和第五部分"专项调查结果"为例进行翻译讨论。

人气指数是会展区域人气旺盛的指标，为准确把握会展相关行业内在规律和发展趋势，更好发挥行业间联动发展提供决策依据。根据该调研报告，人气指数统计包括专业观众人气指数统计和采购商人气指数统计。其中，前者细分为专业观众人气构成情况（图5.5）、每日特邀团体观众人气指数（图5.6）、每日专业观众人气指数分布情况（图5.9）；后者包括采购商总人气构成情况（图5.7）和每日采购商人气指数分布情况（图5.8）。

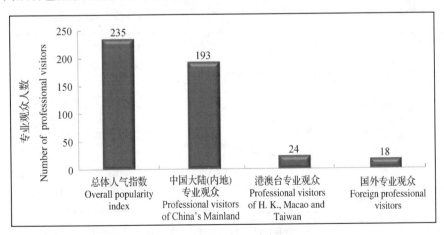

图5.5　专业观众人气构成情况

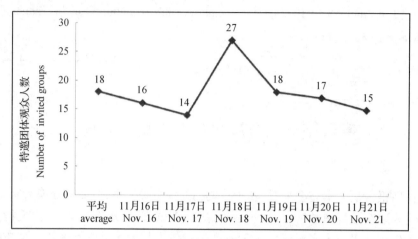

图 5.6 每日特邀团体观众人气指数

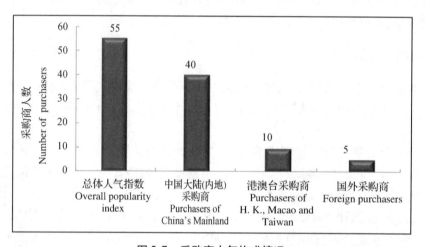

图 5.7 采购商人气构成情况

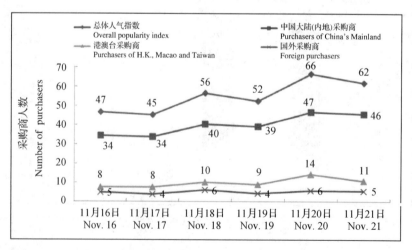

图 5.8 每日采购商人气指数分布情况

一般来说,会展评估报告中有两种运用数据指标方式,分别是文字描述和图表描述,而且二者总是前后出现、相辅相成。

例1

每日专业观众人气指数

在每日专业观众人气<u>指数分布</u>中,从11月16日—21日的<u>总体走势</u>情况来看,各类型专业观众的人气指数均是在前3天比较<u>平缓</u>,但在11月19日均出现大幅上升的趋势;在11月20日,则又出现略微回落的现象;在11月21日,则攀升到最高值,且后三天总体指数均高于前3天的指数。详见图5.9。

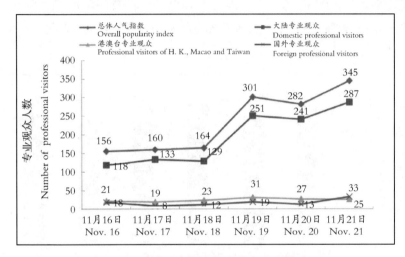

图5.9　每日专业观众人气指数分布情况

译文:

● The daily trade visitors' overall popularity index

In the daily distribution of professional visitor popularity index, from the overall trend of November 16 −21, the popularity index of all types of professional visitors <u>was</u> relatively flat in the first three days, but on November 19, there <u>was</u> a significant upward trend. On November 20, there <u>was</u> a slight decline while it <u>reached</u> the highest the next day. In general, the overall index in the last three days <u>was</u> higher than that in the previous three days. Details are as follows.

例1在阐释指标相关信息的基础上对具体会展活动中该项指标的概况进行了说明。从文本类型角度看,该文本为标准的信息类文本,可以采用目标语相关专业读者所接受的交际翻译策略进行翻译,要点如下:涉及数据指标针对的是已结束项目的具体开展情况,应翻译成过去时态;数据指标统计的相关专业通行语或术语,应确保译文的准确性与统一性(如 index,trend,flat,significant,slight,decline 等);句式采用英语常见的简单句和比较句(如 the overall index in the last three days was higher than that in the previous three days 等)。

例2

● 活动满意率情况

(1) 总体满意率

本届高交会活动总体满意率为100.00%。具体来看，super-super活动、项目配对洽谈活动和中国移动游戏资本峰会的满意率均为100.00%。由此可见，活动参与者认为本届高交会活动举办水平非常高。

(2) 各指标满意率结果

从活动各指标满意率来看，活动主题满意率为98.99%；活动形式满意率为98.99%；活动组织满意率为100.00%；嘉宾水平满意率为98.99%；现场氛围满意率为98.99%；活动收获满意率为97.98%。由此可见，活动各项指标满意率均较高，尤其活动组织得到活动参与者的高度评价。详见图5.10。

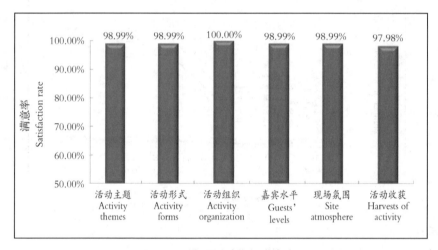

图5.10　主要活动指标满意率

译文：

● The satisfaction rate of activities

(1) Overall satisfaction rate

The overall satisfaction rate of the Fair is 100.00%. Specifically, the satisfaction rates of "Super-super", project pairing negotiation and China Mobile Game Capital Summit all reach 100.00%. It can be seen that the participants think highly of the activities.

(2) Satisfaction rate of each indicator

From the satisfaction rates of all indicators, activity themes, forms and organization reach 98.99%, 98.99% and 100.00% respectively; while the satisfaction rates of guest levels, site atmosphere and harvests of activity are 98.99%, 98.99% and 97.98% respectively. It can be seen that the satisfaction rates of the activities are high, and in particular the organization is highly recognized by the participants. Details are as follows.

与例1翻译要点类似,例2翻译要点包括:涉及数据指标的内涵及功能说明,翻译时采用现在时态;采用目标语读者习惯的省略句式,避免重复(… activity themes, forms and organization reach 98.99%, 98.99% and 100.00% respectively; while the satisfaction rates of guest levels, site atmosphere and harvests of activity are 98.99%, 98.99% and 97.98% respectively);主观的总结性评价可以适当进行语言形式转换,确保功能对等即可(It can be seen that the participants think highly of the activities. / … and in particular the organization is highly recognized by the participants.)。

二、引述

引述会展参与者的观点、意见及评论等,作为撰写者主观价值判断的客观基础,是评估类文本为提升语篇客观性而普遍采用的策略。引述的方式包括直接引语和间接引语。

直接引语翻译时一般应尊重原文与作者,采用交际翻译的策略,应引起注意的是标点符号的使用。被引用文献名及其撰写者的标注是元交际话语的表现形式之一。由于直接引语必须借助引号表明起始界限,如果对被引用的文献名也做同样处理,显然极易导致混淆,或至少不甚醒目。习惯上,在英语文本中,以斜体形式表示书名亦更为常见(Shevlin,2005:205)。此外还需注意撰写者英文名称引用的准确性。

另一方面,引号分单引号(single quotes)、双引号(double quotes)。汉语引用只用双引号;英式英语除报刊外,一般书籍中多用单引号;美式英语则更倾向于用双引号。同时需要说明的是,英文中的破折号长度仅为汉语破折号的一半,不要混淆。以下实例摘录自《第十六届中国国际高新技术成果交易会调研报告》第六部分"参展参会者评语摘录"。

例3

某国内参展商:本届高交会的整体环境和氛围都非常好,展会上有很多来自不同国家、不同行业的公司展示他们最新的产品和成果。

某国外参展商:高交会逐渐达到了一个国际化的水平,展览内容也在不断创新和发展,不断拉近与德国等国家展会的距离,向世界性展会迈进。

某国外投资商:每年高交会都会有很多行业的亮点,能够传达出很多行业相关信息,而且政府在为高交会服务方面也做得很好。

某国内专业观众:高交会在深圳属于最高层次的展会,每年都有不同的主题,对行业的引领作用是毋庸置疑的;如果要了解项目和行业最新情况和发展现状,一定要来高交会。

人民网:本届展会充分发挥高交会作为我国高新技术领域对外开放的重要窗口和平台作用,聚焦优质创新资源。

译文:

A domestic exhibitor: A positive environment and atmosphere has been created for the

China High-Tech Fair, in which companies from different countries and various industries have demonstrated their latest products and achievements.

A foreign exhibitor: The China Hi-Tech Fair has gradually reached the international level, keeping continuous innovation and development, and getting closer to the exhibition level of Germany and so on, and developed into an international exhibition.

A foreign investor: There are bright spots of a variety of industries showed on the China High-Tech Fair every year, which may convey information to the attendees. And the government has done this well too.

A domestic trade visitor: The China High-Tech Fair is known as one of the highest level exhibitions in Shenzhen, with a particular theme for every year. There is no doubt that it plays a critical role in the industries. It is the only place to help us better understand the latest information and development.

People.com.cn: China High-Tech Fair 2014 has fully played a role as the very important window and platform of China to promote the opening and cooperation in high and new technology areas, focusing on excellent innovation resources.

间接引语包括话题类间接引语（仅涉及主题，常见于概述部分）、内容类间接引语（引述讲话具体内容，常见于正文部分）和综合类间接引语（引述特定话题的具体内容，常见于概述、正文和结语部分）。

例4

从本届高交会评估结果来看，本届高交会获得了参展商、投资商、专业观众、普通观众的高度认可，所举办的论坛及活动也获得了参加者的高度评价，满意度得分再创新高，呈现出逐年上升的趋势。

译文：

The exhibitors, investors, trade visitors and public visitors give highly recognition of China High-Tech Fair 2014, as well as the forum and activities. The satisfaction reached a record high, indicating a rising trend.

思考题

1. 会展评估报告的语言特征如何影响翻译策略的使用？试举例说明。
2. 如何处理会展评估报告文本的信息性和意图性之间的关系？
3. 翻译以下段落。

(1)

第一部分　项目基本介绍

一、调研信息概要

（一）评估模块说明

本届高交会效果评估主要分为三个模块，具体包括高交会满意率及效果评估、专项调查（论坛及活动评价、信息发布活动评价）和人气指数统计。

（二）评估执行说明

本次评估计划完成样本 2600 份，实际完成样本 2836 份，经审核后有效样本为 2719 份，样本有效率为 95.87%。

二、主要分析方法

本届高交会满意度及效果评估的统计分析方法主要有五种，具体包括对比分析、频数分析、单因素方差分析、优先改进指数分析和结构方程分析。

三、问卷信度说明

本次评估经过统计，得出参展商问卷信度为 0.967，观众问卷信度为 0.912，投资商问卷信度为 0.730，论坛及活动问卷信度为 0.884，信息发布活动问卷信度为 0.887，表明评估结果非常可靠。

(2)

IT 展、节能环保展与新能源展展览效果满意率

由于该项调研主要从展览业务角度出发，独立设计指标，与总体满意率之间不存在直接对比意义。

（1）参展商满意率

从参展商满意率来看，IT 展参展商满意率为 95.82%，节能环保展与新能源展参展商满意率为 96.05%。从各指标满意率来看，IT 展的招展服务满意率最高，为 98.91%；节能环保展与新能源展的业界影响力满意率最高，为 99.25%。详见图 21。

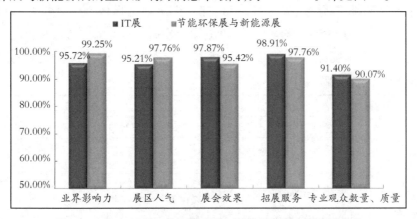

图 21　高交会 IT 展、节能环保展与新能源展展商指标满意率

（3）

Around the world, there were more hours of coverage made available to fans than at any previous Olympic Winter Games edition, including record coverage through digital platforms.

This saw Beijing 2022 become the most digitally engaged Olympic Winter Games ever, with billions of engagements across digital platforms, including Olympic and Media Rights Holders' properties.

In total, Beijing 2022 reached a global audience of more than two billion people, with viewers around the world consuming almost 12 billion hours of coverage across both linear TV and digital platforms. This equates to an average of 5.9 hours per viewer.

But while digital viewing and consumption increased significantly—with the number of people watching digitally increasing by 123.5 per cent compared with the Olympic Winter Games PyeongChang 2018—linear TV remains the most dominant platform, accounting for 92 per cent of all broadcast hours consumed globally.

会展评估报告基本结构

活动的会后评估是对于活动举办成效、问题的客观论述,能够全面地反映活动各项指标的完成情况。对于活动资金提供方而言,能够直观了解活动的成效;对于主办单位、承办单位而言,能够作为复盘的总结材料,找出问题,总结经验。

一、制定评估指标

针对会展策划阶段制定的各项指标或者上级单位要求的指标,对各项指标进行归类,按照重要程度分配不同权重。一般可分为一、二、三级指标,且各级指标的分数总和为100分。

以某活动为例,将国际性、专业性、成效性三个一级指标作为评估指标,权重分别为20％、45％、35％。以境外参会代表情况、权威评价等8个指标为二级指标,以国际嘉宾参会比例、各参与方满意度、合同签约数量等38个指标作为三级指标,并根据制定的各项指标写出具体分值和考核要点。

一级指标	二级指标	三级指标	指标释义
国际化 (20分)	境外参会 代表情况 (10分)	境外演讲嘉宾比例(3分)	境外演讲嘉宾数量占演讲嘉宾总数的比重
		境外参会代表国别数(3分)	境外参会代表(听众＋演讲嘉宾)来自的国家和地区数量
		大型商协会参会数(2分)	参会代表(听众＋演讲嘉宾)所属国际性、区域性及国家级商业组织或协会数量
		世界500强企业参会数(2分)	参会代表(听众＋演讲嘉宾)所属世界500强企业数量

续表

一级指标	二级指标	三级指标	指标释义
专业化(45分)	国际化服务水平(10分)	中外文标识系统(3分)	会场内外及周边是否拥有明确、清晰的中外文标识系统
		翻译服务配备(2分)	会议论坛现场的同声传译、交传翻译是否到位
		翻译服务质量(3分)	嘉宾对译员翻译的流畅性、准确性的评价
		服务人员外语能力(2分)	服务人员是否能用流畅外语进行沟通和服务
	组织策划能力(13分)	方案完整性(3分)	方案是否包含主题、规模、参会对象、议程、主承办及合作单位、预期成果等信息点,内容是否详细
		演讲嘉宾规格(3分)	邀请的演讲嘉宾是否具有行业代表性、权威性
		会议资料完备性(3分)	资料(日常安排、会务接待、与会细则、代表证、会议资料等)的完备性
		宣传渠道多样性(4分)	通过传统媒体、户外媒体、新媒体开展对外宣传工作的情况
	质量把控能力(12分)	演讲内容与论坛主题贴合度(4分)	演讲嘉宾的演讲内容与大会主题的贴合程度
		演讲内容的可操作性和前瞻性(4分)	演讲嘉宾演讲内容是否具有现实操作性和前瞻性
		会议流程把控(2分)	活动流程(演讲顺序、演讲时间)是否与会议议程相一致
		嘉宾风险规避(2分)	演讲嘉宾是否按时到场参会,有无嘉宾预备方案及是否出现重大错误
	配套设施与服务水平(20分)	设备设施水平(4分)	会场内外的设备设施:AV、声像设备;摄影摄像、速录、录音等记录设备;照明设备;贵宾室、休息室;安检设备、安全通道;医疗救护点
		线上展览搭建水平(4分)	包括线上展位的数量、质量等内容
		接待服务水平(3分)	嘉宾对主承办单位接待服务水平评价:交通、住宿、餐饮、签到、礼仪等
		信息化服务水平(3分)	参会代表对会议服务工作中新一代信息技术手段应用情况的评价,如微信、官网注册系统等
		安全应急服务水平(3分)	现场安全应急服务保障水平,包括安全应急预案制作、有无安全事故发生及安全事故处理是否得当
		专业咨询服务水平(3分)	专业咨询是否服务到位;嘉宾对专业咨询服务是否满意
成效性(35分)	项目管理能力(13分)	项目文档健全度(3分)	项目配套文档是否齐备
		项目文档质量(3分)	活动相关材料是否真实有效
		主题及议题设定的目标达成情况(4分)	议题是否紧扣论坛暨峰会办会目标及办会宗旨
		权威评价(3分)	参会相关领导、行业权威人士、主流媒体等对本活动的评价

续表

一级指标	二级指标	三级指标	指标释义
	预期成果设定上报情况(12分)	合同类签订任务数量和质量(2分)	合同类任务数量、合理性、任务质量评价
		协议类签订任务数量和质量(2分)	协议类任务数量、合理性、任务质量评价
		投资类签订任务数量和质量(2分)	投资类任务数量、合理性、任务质量评价
		线上展览平台(2分)	线上展览平台的搭建,包含平台的技术水平、观众体验等
		"华为云"线上直播平台(2分)	线上直播平台的稳定性、会议观看量
		其他各类成果签订任务数量和质量(2分)	成果类包括国内各省(自治区、直辖市)层面发布的各种政策报告、倡议书、行动宣言、签订的合作协议、备忘录等任务数量合理性和质量评价
	目标达成情况(10分)	合同类实际签订落实情况(2分)	合同类活动实际签订的合同数量、金额情况
		协议类实际签订落实情况(2分)	协议类活动实际签订的协议数量、金额情况
		投资类实际签订落实情况(2分)	投资类活动实际签订的协议数量、金额情况
		参会人员满意度(1分)	参会人员对活动举办的满意度
		线上会议观看量(2分)	线上会议观看量百分比
		下届参展、参会意向(1分)	下届参展参会意向百分比

二、评估方式

第三方机构根据指南制定评估指标、办法和步骤。评估须数据真实、评价客观。

三、评估方法

指标分析法、调研问卷法、层次分析法、对标分析法、德尔菲法、深度访谈法等。

四、评估结果

评估结果包括评估报告、指标评分、评分说明、意见建议等。

范例:

一、背景资料

(一)项目立意

(二)基本信息

1. 活动名称

2. 时间、地点

3. 主题

4．主办单位

（三）预期目标

1．层次高端

2．内容丰富

3．形式创新

4．宣传得力

5．成果落地

二、评估方式

（一）评估依据

（二）评估方法

（三）评估步骤

三、峰会亮点

（一）嘉宾层次规模高端

（二）国际舞台×××声音

（三）双线会展云集现场

（四）赋能产城融合发展

（五）助力投资成果落地

四、评估结论

（一）完成目标达到预期

1．国际化

2．专业化

3．成效性

（二）务实创新成效显著

（三）产城融合更为紧密

（四）社会各界反响较好

（五）组织高效保障完备

（六）媒体矩阵传播有力

（七）参与各方满意度高

五、待改进与建议

（一）建议提升市场化程度

（二）建议深化国际合作

（三）建议提升资源落地能力

（四）建议建立长效合作机制

（五）建议增加资源保障

——https://www.zhihu.com/question/281519656/answer/2340049388

会展评估报告内容

会展评估报告主要包括工作评估、会展质量评估以及会展效果评估三大方面。

会展评估报告一般由参展公司独立完成,或委托专业评估公司进行。会展活动涉及范围广泛、牵涉课题众多,因此评估内容也相对丰富,主要包括会展工作评估、会展质量评估以及会展效果评估三大方面。

（一）会展工作评估

会展工作评估的主要目的是了解工作的质量、效率和成本效益,具体内容包括:

1. 有关展出目标的评估

主要根据会展公司的经营方针和战略、目标是否合适进行评估。

2. 有关会展效率的评估

会展效率是会展整体工作的评估指数。评估的方法有两种:会展人员实际接待参观客户的数量在参观客户总数中的比例,参展总开支除以实际接待的参观客户数量之商。后一种方式也称为接触潜在客户的平均成本,是一个非常有价值的可以用货币值表示的评估指数。

3. 有关会展人员的评估

会展人员的表现包括工作态度、工作效果、团队精神等方面,这些不能直接衡量,一般是通过询问参加会展的观众来了解和统计。另一种方法是计算会展人员每小时接待观众的平均数。一般而言,如果会展活动的评估结果显示"差"的会展人员超过人员总数的6%,就应当采取措施提高会展人员素质。评估内容包括展品的选择是否合适、市场效果是否好、展品运输是否顺利、增加或减少某种展品的原因等。

4. 有关宣传工作的评估

评估内容包括宣传和公关工作的效率、宣传效果、是否比竞争对手吸引了更多的观众、资料散发数量等。对新闻媒体的报道也要收集、评估,包括刊载、播放次数、版面大小、时间长短、评价等。

5. 其他人员评估

其他人员评估内容包括会展人员组合安排是否合理,效率是否高,言谈、举止、态度是否合适,会展人员工作总时间是否适宜,会展人员工作轮班时间是否过长或过短等。

6. 有关设计工作的评估

定量的评估内容有展台设计的成本效率、展览和设施的功能效率等。定性的评估内容有公司形象如何、会展资料是否有助于展出、展台是否突出和易于识别等。

7. 有关管理工作的评估

评估包括会展筹备公司的质量和效率、会展管理的质量和效率,工作有无疏漏,尤其是培训等方面的工作。

8. 有关开支的评估

开支评估是计算参展成本的基础,但因会展活动具有很强的后期连贯性投资,隐性开支很大,所以清楚评估其开支比较困难。

9. 会展记忆率评估

会展记忆率是指参观客户在参加会展后8—10周仍能记住会展情况的比例,会展记忆率是能够反映整体参展工作效果的专业评估指数。

(二) 会展质量评估

参展公司要考核一个会展的质量,需要从会展的参展企业数量、售出面积等方面综合考虑。其中,有关参展企业的评估主要包括:

1. 参展企业数量。
2. 参展企业质量。参展企业质量与展出效率成正比。
3. 平均参观时间。指参观者参观整个会展所花费的时间,该指数与会展效果成正比。
4. 平均参展时间。指参展企业参加每次会展所花费的平均时间,该指数可以用来安排具体会展工作。
5. 人流密度指数。指会展的参观者的平均数量,一般情况下,综合性消费展参观人数比较多,专业性会展人数较少。

(三) 会展效果评估

有关会展效果评估的争议比较多,主要是对工作项目与工作成果之间关系的理解不同。要做好会展效果评估,同时不要将评估结果绝对化。会展效果评估的内容包括:

1. 参展效果优异评估

如果参展企业接待了70%以上的潜在客户,客户接触平均成本低于其他会展的平均值,会展效果就是优异的。

2. 成本效益比评估

成本效益也可以称作投资收益,评估因素比较多、范围广泛,可以用此次会展的成本与效益相比,用此次的成本与前次类似项目相比,用效益与前次或类似项目相比,也可以用展出成本效益与其他营销方式相比。一种典型的成本效益比是用展出开支比展览成交额,要注意这个成本不是产品成本而是展出成本。另一种典型的成本效益比是用开支比建立新客户关系数。由于贸易成交比较复杂,用展览开支比展览成交额所得结果不够正确,而与潜在客户建立关系是会展的直接结果,与客户建立关系意味着未来成交,因此可以把与潜在客户建立关系作为衡量会展投资收益的基础。

3. 成本利润评估

有一种评估观点是不仅要计算成本、计算成本效益,还应该计算成本利润。比如签订买卖合同,先用成本总开支除以成交笔数,得出每笔成交的平均成本,再用会展总开支除以成交总额,得出成交的成本效益,最后用成交总额减去会展总开支和产品总成本,得出利润,再用会展成本比利润,即成本利润。不同观点认为会展成交可以作为评估的内容,但是不能作为评估的主要内容。如果以建立新客户关系数为主要评估内容,则不存在利润。因此,不主张评估成本利润。

4．成交评估

成交评估分消费成交和贸易成交。消费性质的会展以直接销售为展出目的，因此可以用总支出额比总销售额，然后用预计的成本效益比与实际的成本效益比相比较，这种比较可以反映展出效率。贸易性质的会展以成交为最终目的，因此成交是最重要的评估内容之一，但也是会展评估矛盾的焦点之一。许多会展单位喜欢直接使用展出成本与展出成交额相比较的方法计算成交的成本效益。要注意这是一种不准确、不可靠的方法，因为有些成交确实通过会展达成，而有些成交却是不展出也能达成的，可能是会展之后达成的。因此，要慎重做评估并慎重使用评估结论。成交评估的内容一般有成交额、成交笔数、实际成交额、意向成交额、与新客户成交额、与老客户成交额、新产品成交额、老产品成交额、会展期间成交额、预计后续成交额等，这些数据可以交叉统计计算。

5．接待客户评估

这是贸易会展最重要的评估内容之一，主要包括：

（1）参加会展的观众数量，可以细分为接待参展企业数、现有客户数和潜在客户数。

（2）参加展览的观众质量，可以参照展览会组织者的评估内容标准分类，统计观众的订货决定权、建议权、影响力、行业地域等，并按自己的实际情况将参展企业分为"极具价值""很有价值""一般价值""无价值"四类。

（3）接待客户的成本效益，尤其是与新客户建立关系的成本效益，是最重要的评估内容，是此次展览与前次展览方式或与其他推销方式相比较的重要标准。计算方法是用展览总支出额除以接待的客户数或所建立的新客户关系数。

6．调研评估

通过展出对市场和产品有没有新的了解、有没有更明确的发展和努力方向等进行评估。

7．竞争评估

竞争评估指在展览工作方面和展览效果方面与竞争对手相比较的情况。

8．宣传、公关评估

这方面的评估比较困难，因为定性内容比较多、评估技术比较复杂。具体评估内容包括宣传、公关有无效果，效率、效益有多大，是否需要增加投入提升展览单位形象，形象与实际成交有多少关系等。

——http：//www.xdmice.com/Study/Study_list_336.html

第六章 会展功能性文案翻译

学习目标

- 了解会展致辞的篇章结构与功能目的
- 了解会展信函的结构内容与表述原则
- 了解会议背景板标语的语言特征与版面设计要素
- 知晓会议台签的摆放原则与功能特征
- 掌握会展功能性文案翻译方法

核心词汇

* 致辞（address）
* 开幕词（opening speech）
* 闭幕词（closing speech）
* 称呼（salutation）
* 邀请函（letter of invitation）
* 套译（equivalent translation）
* 支持信（endorsement）
* 担保信（guarantee）
* 申请函（application）
* 背景板标语（slogan of background board）

第一节　致辞翻译

致辞（address），亦作"致词"，原指用文字或语言向他人表达思想感情的一种方式，在商务会展语境中，特指在展会、会议或其他公众场合所发表的重要讲话。其内容涵盖甚广，主要包括开幕词（opening speech）、闭幕词（closing speech）、祝酒词（toast）、欢迎词（welcoming speech）、答谢词（thank-you speech）、欢送词（send-off speech）、告别词（farewell speech）等。

英汉致辞都是致辞者与听众交流感情的一种方式，在人际功能上存在着许多共性，但社会环境和传统文化的不同所带来的语言表达方式的差异也是客观存在的。

从人际功能来看，英汉致辞中的"给予"和"求取"角色表现得尤为明显。一方面，致辞者向听众提供某种信息，表明自己的态度和立场；另一方面，致辞者呼吁听众采取行动来支持自己的主张。因此，在致辞语篇中，陈述句一般占据主要地位，其次是祈使句，一般不使用疑问句。同时，为了更好地实现话语的人际意义功能，英汉致辞常使用某些对等的情态动词。例如，must 传达坚定的语气，用于强调义务和树立致辞者的权威；can 表示有能力做某事，用于强调目标的现实性；will 表达推测，用于激发听众的憧憬和希望。此外，英汉致辞中第一人称复数 we、our 的大量使用意味着致辞者将自己和听众置于同一立场，使听众感到亲近，更容易引发共鸣。

从行文结构来看，英汉致辞也基本类似，通常由称呼（salutation）、开篇（opening sentences）、正文（body）、结束语（closing sentences）等构成，表达时适当采用排比、引用、幽默等修辞手段。当然，这些相似之处是由相同的交际目的和活动背景决定的，它们具有一定的格式与规范，如英文称呼语基本限定在以下表述范围内：

▲ Dear Guests, Ladies and Gentlemen

▲ Excellencies, Ladies and Gentlemen

▲ Dear Ministers, Distinguished Guests, Ladies and Gentlemen

▲ Distinguished Guests and Delegates, Ladies and Gentlemen

▲ Honorable Chairman, Honorable Guests, Ladies and Gentlemen

▲ Excellency, Mr. Chairman, Dear Colleagues, Ladies and Gentlemen

▲ Mr. Chairman, Your Excellency, Distinguished Guests, Ladies and Gentlemen

▲ Honorable Minister Wan, Excellencies, Distinguished Participants

▲ Excellencies, Friends, Colleagues, Ladies and Gentlemen

▲ Honorable Ministers, Distinguished Guests and Participants

▲ Dear Colleagues, Ladies and Gentlemen

英汉开篇的表述也大致采用下述表达法:

▲ On behalf of …, I am delighted to welcome all of you to …

我谨代表……欢迎大家来到……

▲ I'm honored to have this opportunity to welcome all of you to …

我十分荣幸地欢迎大家来到……

▲ It is a great pleasure for me to welcome you all to … / It gives me great pleasure to welcome all of you to …

我非常高兴地欢迎各位出席……

▲ It is my pleasant duty to extend to you a cordial welcome on behalf of …

我谨代表……对各位的到来表示热烈欢迎……

▲ It is a real honor and privilege for us to welcome you to …

我们非常荣幸地欢迎大家出席……

▲ It is with a profound feeling of pleasure and privilege that, on behalf of …, I extend a hearty welcome to you all, especially to the distinguished guests from …

我代表……非常荣幸地欢迎大家的到来,尤其是来自……的贵宾们……

▲ As the chairperson of this symposium, I have the pleasure and honor of welcoming all of you to this international meeting.

作为本届研讨会的主席,我十分高兴和荣幸地欢迎各位出席今天的国际会议。

▲ May I welcome all of you to …

欢迎各位参加……

▲ On behalf of …, I bid a warm welcome to you all gathered here to participate …

我代表……对前来参加……的各位朋友表示热烈的欢迎……

▲ May I begin by welcoming you to …

首先,我对各位朋友的到来表示欢迎……

相较于人际功能与行文结构的类似,英汉致辞由于社会环境、风俗习惯、思维方式和价值取向的不同而在语言表达上呈现出一定的差异。例如,在欢迎词中,中文"一路辛苦了"作为开篇的问候语非常常见,但在英语中不能直译为 You must be very tired,这样会让远道而来的客人误以为自己一路颠簸、面容憔悴,这才导致主人语出此言。因此,比较妥帖的表达应为 How was your journey? 或者 Thank you for coming all the way。又如,在欢送词中,中国人常说"招待不周,敬请见谅"这样的客气话,如果直译为英语 Excuse me for not having served you very well,则不免让客人信以为真,产生误解,而用 We wish you have enjoyed the trip! 更能表达真实意图。

有鉴于此,英汉致辞的语言特点从宏观上看,表现为结构严谨、句法简明、层次清晰、表达易懂,同时礼仪规范、情感真挚,两种语言大致能做到对等;但从微观考虑,两者存在的差异在翻译时不容忽视。大体来说,致辞属于表达类文本,兼具呼唤功能,翻译时要遵循"作者第一"的原则,既要忠实于原作者要表达的思想内容,又要忠实于原作者的语言风格,所以常用的翻译方法是语义翻译或"字面"翻译。因此,汉英致辞翻译的原则可以参考以下三点:

1. 传递致辞人的情感

致辞是一种极富人情味的感情交流途径,致辞者运用通俗的言辞、动人的语调、专注的神情向听众阐明观点、传达信息,引起他们情感上的共鸣和心灵上的震撼,翻译致辞同样需要充满深情厚谊,从目的语中选择恰当的词汇和修辞手段再现原作的情感。例如,国际奥委会主席巴赫在2020东京奥运会开幕式上致辞时有这样一段话:

原文:This is the unifying power of sport. This is the message of solidarity, the message of peace and the message of resilience. This gives all of us hope for our further journey together.

译文:这就是体育的凝聚力。这是团结的信号、和平的信号和坚韧的信号。这让我们对接下来的奥运旅程充满了希望。

这是巴赫真情实感的表达,他希望能通过奥运会比赛使全世界人民团结在一起战胜疫情,这既是体育精神,也是全人类的希望。为了忠实地传达这种情感,译文采用了原文的排比句式,以增强语言气势,同时对关键词 unifying power, message, resilience, hope 的翻译也与这种情感交相呼应。

2. 保持原文的风格

由于致辞场合及致辞者性情的不同,致辞的语言风格也各异。有些人喜欢言简意赅,有些人习惯引经据典;有些人喜欢平铺直叙,有些人喜欢别开生面;有些人喜欢质朴的语言,有些人则偏爱华丽的辞藻。无论是哪一种风格,译者都要耐心琢磨、仔细体会、认真模仿,力求再现原作者的风格而不是展现自己的文风,只有这样才能较好地把握原文的主旨,让目的语读者领会原作的精髓。这也是进行表达型文本语义翻译时要遵守的基本原则。

3. 译文力求通俗易懂

一般来说,致辞者的目标听众来自社会各个阶层,优秀的致辞者会力求给他们留下清晰、完整、深刻的印象。因此,在翻译过程中要想致辞者之所想,尽量运用听众耳熟能详的词汇来表达,避免使用佶屈聱牙的偏词、怪词。例如,2011年国家主席胡锦涛出访美国的白宫致辞开篇就用到了"一元复始"这样一个极具中国特色文化内涵的成语。对于"一元复始,万象更新",在英文中很难找到现成的习语表达与之对应,因此译者直接将其译为 at the beginning of the year,虽然缺少了独特的文化韵味,但能被美国听众普遍接受。

一、开幕词翻译

开幕词是党和国家领导人或企事业单位领导人在会展或重大活动开始前所作的讲话,旨在阐明活动的重要意义和现实意义。开幕词篇幅通常比较短,致辞者开篇即切入正题,语言偏口语化且富有感情色彩,语气热情、慷慨。因此,在翻译时宜采用饱含感情的词汇、简明扼要的语言和短小精悍的句式。此外,英汉常用的起始语和预祝词也是必不可少的,如"宣布……开幕"(declare the opening of …)、"预祝……取得圆满成功"(I wish … a complete success)等。例如,2021年国家主席习近平在博鳌亚洲论坛年会上有以下的致辞:

- 原文:

> 尊敬的各位国家元首、政府首脑,
> 尊敬的各位国际组织负责人,
> 尊敬的各位博鳌亚洲论坛理事,
> 各位来宾,
> 女士们,先生们,朋友们:
> 　　"与君远相知,不道云海深。"很高兴出席博鳌亚洲论坛2021年年会,同大家在"云端"相聚。首先,我代表中国政府和中国人民,并以我个人的名义,对出席会议的线上线下所有嘉宾,表示热烈的欢迎!对各位新老朋友,表示诚挚的问候和美好的祝愿!
> 　　……
> 　　女士们、先生们、朋友们!
> 　　同舟共济扬帆起,乘风破浪万里航。尽管有时会遭遇惊涛骇浪和逆流险滩,但只要我们齐心协力、把准航向,人类社会发展的巨轮必将行稳致远,驶向更加美好的未来!
> 　　谢谢大家。

- 译文:

> Your Excellencies Heads of State and Government,
> Your Excellencies Heads of International Organizations,
> Your Excellencies Members of the Board of Directors of the Boao Forum for Asia,
> Distinguished Guests,
> Ladies and Gentlemen,
> Dear Friends,
> 　　"True friendship brings people close however far apart they may be." It gives me great pleasure to attend the Boao Forum for Asia Annual Conference 2021 and meet you all in this cloud meeting. Let me begin by extending, on behalf of the Chinese government and people and also in my own name, a warm welcome to all the guests participating both in person and online, and cordial greetings and best wishes to all friends old and new.
> 　　……
> 　　Ladies and Gentlemen, Friends,
> 　　"By setting sail together, we could ride the wind, break the waves, and brave the journey of ten thousand miles." We may at times encounter stormy waves and dangerous rapids, but as long as we pool our efforts and keep to the right direction, the giant vessel of human development will stay on an even keel and sail toward a bright future.
> 　　Thank you.

原文中的起始语和预祝词(下划线部分)翻译时采用了范式模板,同时对文中表达致辞人情感的文字进行了语义翻译,以传递准确的思想内容,如"与君远相知,不道云海深""同舟共济扬帆起,乘风破浪万里航""惊涛骇浪""逆流险滩""齐心协力""行稳致远"等。译文通过"很高兴出席""代表……表示热烈的欢迎""表示诚挚的问候和美好的祝愿""更加美好的未来"四个层次的推进,对原文内容与逻辑进行了忠实的表述和呈现,实现了表达类文本翻译的目的。

二、闭幕词翻译

闭幕词是会议的主要领导人代表会议举办单位在会议闭幕时的讲话,其内容一般是概述会议所完成的任务,对会议的成果做出评价,对会议的经验进行总结,对贯彻会议精神提出要求和希望,主要有以下四个特点:

1. 总结性

闭幕词是在会议或活动的闭幕式上使用的文本,要对会议内容、会议精神和进程进行简要的总结并做出恰当评价,肯定会议的重要成果,强调会议的主要意义和深远影响。

2. 概括性

闭幕词应对会议进展情况、完成的议题、取得的成果、提出的会议精神及会议意义等进行高度的语言概括。因此,闭幕词一般都短小精悍、逻辑清晰、语言简洁明快。

3. 号召性

为了激励参加会议的全体成员为实现会议提出的各项任务而奋斗,增强与会人员贯彻会议精神的决心和信心,闭幕词的行文充满热情,语言坚定有力,富有号召性和鼓动性。

4. 口语化

闭幕词要适合口头表达,写作时语言要通俗易懂、生动活泼。

相较于开幕词,闭幕词在文本属性上不仅有强烈的表达色彩,而且客观性更明显。翻译时基本采用与开幕词翻译相类似的方法——语义翻译,必要时也可以使用交际翻译。例如,第29届奥林匹克运动会组织委员会主席刘淇在北京奥运会闭幕式上有以下致辞。

• 原文:

尊敬的胡锦涛主席和夫人,
尊敬的罗格主任和夫人,
尊敬的各位来宾,
女士们、先生们、朋友们,

第29届奥林匹克运动会已经胜利地完成了各项任务,在北京奥运会即将落下帷幕的时刻,我谨代表北京奥组委向国际奥委会,向各国际单项体育组织、各国家和地区奥委会,向所有为本届奥运会作出贡献的朋友们表示衷心的感谢!

在过去的16天中,来自世界204个国家和地区的运动员弘扬奥林匹克精神,在公平的竞争环境中顽强拼搏,展示了高超的竞技水平和良好的竞赛风貌,创造了骄人的运动成绩,共打破38项世界纪录、85项奥运会纪录,当凯旋的号角吹响的时候,让我们向取得优异成绩的运动员表示热烈的祝贺!向所有参加比赛的运动健儿致以崇高的敬意。同时,也让我们向为此付出辛勤劳动的媒体记者和工作人员表示衷心的感谢!

"同一个世界,同一个梦想"。今天的世界需要相互理解、相互包容、相互合作、和谐发展。北京奥运会是世界对中国的信任,不同国家、地区,不同民族,不同文化的人们组成了团结友爱的奥林匹克大家庭,加深了了解,增进了友谊。

中国人民用满腔热情兑现了庄严的承诺,实现了"绿色奥运、科技奥运、人文奥运",留下了巨大而丰富的文化和体育遗产。

2008年北京奥运会是体育运动的盛会、和平的盛会、友谊的盛会。

朋友们,熊熊燃烧的奥运圣火即将熄灭,但中国人民拥抱世界的热情之火将永远燃烧。在这个时候,我们希望朋友们记住充满生机与活力的北京和各协办城市,记住钟情于奥林匹克运动的中国人民,记住永远微笑、甘于奉献的志愿者。让我们真诚地祝愿奥林匹克运动不断发展。

谢谢!

● 译文:

Respected President Hu Jintao and Mrs. Hu,

Respected IOC President Rogge and Mrs. Rogge,

Distinguished guests,

Ladies and gentlemen,

Dear friends,

The Games of the XXIX Olympiad is coming to a successful conclusion. At the moment the curtain is about to fall on the Beijing Olympic Games, please allow me, on behalf of BOCOG, to express my sincere gratitude to the IOC, IFs, NOCs, and all friends who have contributed to the success of this Olympic Games.

The past 16 days have witnessed superb athletic performances and sportsmanship. Athletes from 204 countries and regions have competed in the Games in the Olympic spirit. They have shown off their great perseverance, given their very best in a fair play environment, and achieved amazing results by breaking 38 world records and 85 Olympic records. Let us congratulate the athletes on their great achievements! Let us pay tribute to all those who have participated in the Games! Let us thank the media and all the staff who have worked so hard to make the Games such a great event!

"One World, One Dream". The world today is in need of mutual understanding, inclusiveness, cooperation and harmonious development. The Beijing Olympic Games is a testimony of the fact that the world has its trust rested upon China. Owing to the Games, people have been united as one Olympic family, regardless of their nationalities, ethnic origins and cultural backgrounds. Their understanding has been deepened and their friendship renewed.

The Chinese people, teeming with enthusiasm, have honored the commitments they solemnly made. They have realized the concepts of "Green Olympics, High-Tech Olympics and People's Olympics", leaving a huge and rich legacy both in culture and sport.

The Beijing 2008 Olympic Games is a grand celebration of sport, a grand celebration of peace and a grand celebration of friendship.

Dear friends, the Olympic flame atop the National Stadium will soon extinguish, and yet the Chinese people's enthusiasm in embracing the world will be ablaze forever. At this moment, we hope you will bear in mind the vigour and vitality of Beijing and the co-host cities, bear in mind the Chinese people who are deeply faithful to the Olympic Movement, and bear in mind the smile and dedication of the volunteers. We sincerely wish the Olympic Movement a sustainable development.

Thank you!

原文第一段宣布奥运会即将闭幕并表达对各参与方的感谢，第二、三、四、五段为奥运会赛事总结，第六段为奥运精神号召，逻辑清晰，内容规范。译文采取的策略基本以语义翻译为主，辅以交际翻译。首先，针对表达类文本的情感传递，对"衷心的""顽强""高超的""良好的""骄人的""优异""满腔热情""庄严的""巨大而丰富的""永远""真诚地"等主观性表述进行了"字面"翻译，致辞人的情感张力得到了丰富传送；其次，考虑到英语语言简约、客观的特点，对"当凯旋的号角吹响的时候"进行了淡化处理，没有进行形式上的翻译。另外"熊熊燃烧"翻译为 flame atop，客观地描述奥运圣火，更符合西方读者的语言习惯。通过这些语言处理，交际翻译得到了有效实施，更能激发起全世界人民对奥林匹克运动的热爱与"更快、更高、更强"奥林匹克精神的弘扬，以及对和平和友谊的希望，最终实现了闭幕词的交际功能。

第二节　信函翻译

会展信函不仅包括以招展、招商为目的撰写的邀请函,还包括申请函、支持函、担保函等功能性信函。前者的主体内容近似招展书、参展商手册等文案,后者的内容则更为独特,但总体来看,两者都同时具有信息、表达和呼唤功能,其中以信息和呼唤功能为主,翻译方法是语义翻译和交际翻译相结合。

一、邀请函翻译

会展邀请函一般包含以下内容。首先是会展概况,包括会展名称、内容、目的、特点与功能等,还有历届会展的情况以及所取得的成就。其次是组织机构,介绍主办方、协办方及赞助商等的实力。此外,还有会展的规模、布局、展位价格、申请参展的程序等。从文体上看,会展文本是一种商务文体。它具有传递信息及宣传劝导功能,需要想方设法地把参展的好处介绍出来,以吸引国外企业来参展或进行赞助,也就是以实现预期效果为目的。

会展邀请函属于比较拘谨、正式的公文体,行文端正,用字简练,一般遵守商务英语的写作原则,即"七 C"原则:correctness(正确)、conciseness(简练)、clearness(清楚)、completeness(完整)、concreteness(具体)、courtesy(礼貌)、consideration(体谅),表达上一般遵守以下三个原则。

1. 语气上礼貌且友好

虽然写信者必须陈述自己的观点、立场,但语气常显得很考虑对方、很尊敬对方,所以会经常使用一些第一人称、第二人称的代词,尽量多用一些直接和肯定的语气而避免使用否定句等,这都体现了其语言追求礼貌、尊敬的特点。例如,We sincerely invite global exhibitors, professional purchasers, professional visitors and other people from all walks of life to participate in the Exhibition to share development opportunities. 就要比 Global exhibitors, professional purchasers, professional visitors and other people from all walks of life are sincerely invited to participate in the Exhibition to share development opportunities. 显得亲切、有礼貌。

2. 选词上力求准确清楚,避免陈词、长词及词义重复

会展邀请函必须准确清楚地表达所要传递的信息,谨慎使用夸张、比喻等手法,尽量避免使用模棱两可的词语,以免产生不必要的争议,因为会展邀请函通常作为确定有关当事人权利和义务的依据。

原文:经过八年的发展,高交会以其"国家级、国际性、高水平、大规模、讲实效、专业化、不落幕"的特点,成为目前中国规模最大、最具影响力的科技类会展,有"中国科技第一展"之称。

译文：Since 1999, China Hi-Tech Fair (CHTF) has been staged successfully for 8 consecutive years, with the distinct "state-level, international, high standard, large scale, practical, professional and all-year-round" identities. CHTF is the largest and most influential hi-tech trade show in China, as well as a Chinese exhibition brand with considerable international influence. It is known as "the No. 1 hi-tech trade show in China".

在诸如以上会展的邀请函中，难免会有一些空洞的、任意夸大的、多余的表达，如上例中的"最具影响力""第一展"等。如果照单全译，会缺乏说服力，外商难以信服与接受，故不能起到应有的呼唤效果。其实，"中国最具影响力的"会展与"国家级"的会展内涵是相同的。因此，要解决这类问题，应该去掉或淡化这些表达，将口号改写成一般语言，并将多余的表达去除。

改译：CHTF is an international hi-tech trade fair with a history of eight years. It is one of the largest and most influential technology trade shows in China.

3. 内容表达上要言简意赅，传达足够信息

会展邀请函通常直接简练、开门见山，忌拖泥带水、过分修饰。一般会根据写信者所要表达的中心思想分段。正文每段的文字不宜过长，尤其是开头和结尾，更常以简短为妥。例如，"We are very much expecting to establish a long-term and good business relationship with your esteemed company in the near future."就不如"We expect to establish long-term business relations with your company in future."简洁、达意。

会展邀请函常用英文句型及翻译：

- You are invited to exhibit at ... Conference / Trade Fair / Expo, which will take place in ... on ... attracting more than ... from the ...

诚邀您加入××展会，在……与会观众……

- Please fill out the enclosed forms and return it to me by May 30 if you are interested in exhibiting or sponsoring a function during the conference.

如有兴趣参加或赞助本展，请填写附件中的表格并于5月30日前寄回。

- We look forward to your participation and support.

期待您的参与和支持。

- Exhibitors will be provided with a 6 ft. table.

将提供给参展商一个6英尺展台。

- Exhibitors wishing to include their product literature in the portfolio given to each registrant may do so.

参展商会加入这个项目，从而让每个注册展会的人了解他们的产品信息。

- Reservations should be made before September 16, 2012.

请在2012年9月16日前预订。

- This is the perfect chance to network with ... display ... and share ...

这将是您与……建立联系、展示……并分享……的绝佳机会。

- The ... Congress / Exhibition / Trade Fair / Expo offers a unique opportunity to promote your products and services to ...

本次会议/展览/交易会/博览会将提供一个独特的机会来向……推销您的产品和服务。

- The ... Congress / Exhibition / Trade Fair / Expo will attract ... that are leading within their field as scientists, manufacturers, business leaders or other users and the associated industry.

本次会议/展览/交易会/博览会吸引了××业界科学家、制造商、行业巨头、其他用户和相关行业。

鉴于会展邀请函强烈的信息和呼唤功能,根据纽马克的观点,可以采用交际翻译,其中特别需要指出的是套译的使用。套译指在翻译外国词汇时,既不音译,也不使用新词意译,而是采取折中方法,采用本国语言文字中已有的词汇进行套用。比如,现在广泛使用的中译名"博士""教授""冠军"等,其实都是古代的官名,虽然两者在具体意义上不同。具体而言,套译可以分为两大类:一是拟合性套译,如"几何学"(Geometry,徐光启译)、"运筹学"(Operational Research,取自"运筹帷幄",《史记》所载)、军队现代编制单位、爵位"公""侯""伯""子""男"(东西方在此方面制度比较相似,因而直接套用)等。二是传神型套译,如美国的"州"(state,与我国历史上的"州"的意义有很大不同),以及上述"博士""教授""冠军"等。这些词与其原来用法颇有差异,被赋予了新的含义。

1. 称呼语套译

会展邀请函中常用的称呼语包括 Dear Sir(s) / Madam / Gentlemen / Ladies 等,此处的 Dear 只是一种对收信人的尊称,是一种礼貌的习惯性表达方法,并不等同于汉语中的"亲爱的"。因此,根据汉语习惯,我们可以将其套译为"尊敬的(诸位)阁下/夫人/先生们/女士们",有时也可以套译为"敬启者/谨启者/执事先生/尊鉴/台鉴"。

2. 敬辞和谦辞套译

会展邀请函的一大特色就是措辞婉约、注重礼节、多用套语,其中频繁使用的单词有 appreciate, esteem, favor, grateful, kindly, oblige, please, pleasure, allow us ..., permit us to ..., may we ...。而汉语中常用的一些敬辞包括"您鉴""贵方""贵国""贵公司""阁下""敬复""敬悉""惠请""惠所""惠顾""赐复""奉告承蒙""恭候"等;常见的一些谦辞包括"敝人""敝公司""敝处""卑职愚见""拙见""拙作""拜读""过奖"等。在翻译时应采用功能意义相当的礼貌词语套译。

原文:我们诚挚邀请贵公司(贵单位/您)参加2022年服贸会展览展示、论坛会议,也可组织推介洽谈、成果发布和配套活动等,共襄展会盛举,共享发展商机!

译文:We sincerely invite you to participate in the exhibitions and displays as well as forums and conferences of the 2022 CIFTIS. Your organization for promotional business talks, achievements release, and supporting events in the 2022 CIFTIS will be also appreciated. Let us work together for this grand event and share business opportunities.

3. 结束语套译

结束语的表达方式有很多,如 Yours faithfully, Faithfully yours, Yours truly, Best regards, Sincerely, Best wishes, Yours sincerely, Kind regards 等。这类词不宜翻译成"您忠实的""您真诚的",不符合汉语习惯,可以直接套译为"谨上""敬上""谨启""顺致敬意"等。

另外,展会邀请函中常常需要介绍参展客户来自什么地区。根据中国人的习惯,通常介绍起来都含有长长的一串地名,常见的有"省、自治区、直辖市""中国大陆、中国台湾和中国内地、香港、澳门"等。其实,对外国投资者来说,他们并不关心中国的行政区域是如何划分的。如果都译出来,句子会又长又绕口,还可能造成外国人的理解困难。

原文:投洽会不仅全面展示和介绍中国内地各省、自治区、直辖市和香港特别行政区、澳门特别行政区的投资环境、投资政策、招商项目和企业产品,同时也吸引了数十个国家和地区的投资促进机构纷纷前来参展并举办投资说明会、推介会。

译文:CIFIT not only comprehensively showcases the investment environments, investment policies, investment projects and corporate products across China, and in all provinces, autonomous regions and municipalities directly under the Central Government in Mainland of China, as well as in Hong Kong and Macao Special Administrative Regions, but also attracts investment promotion agencies from dozens of regions and countries in the world to conduct investment briefings.

改译:CIFIT not only comprehensively showcases the investment environments, policies, projects and corporate products across China, but also attracts investment projects agencies abroad to conduct investment briefings.

二、支持信翻译

支持类信函(endorsement)的正文部分旨在阐释写信人对相关会展活动的全力支持,主体内容通常涉及三个方面:首先,陈述支持申办会展的态度;其次,阐述该地区作为会展东道主的优势;最后,表明成功举办会展的决心。这类信函虽有信息传递,但主要还是强调呼唤功能,即让受函人强烈地感受到写信人的态度,翻译时应采用交际翻译为主。

江泽民北京奥运会支持信

- 中文版

> 我以极大的热情,郑重向你们表示,全力支持北京申办2008年第29届奥运会。
>
> 如果能够在具有悠久文明并且迅速发展的、占世界人口22%的中国举办第29届奥运会,无论是对促进奥林匹克精神在中国和全世界的发扬光大与普及,还是促进东西方文化的交汇与融合都将产生极其重要的积极意义。中国人民愿意通过举办第29届奥运会,为人类和平、友谊和进步事业及发展奥林匹克运动,做出自己的贡献。
>
> 我热诚期望北京被国际奥委会选为举办第29届奥运会的城市。中国人民有热爱和平和热情好客的传统,你们和你们所领导的奥林匹克大家庭全体成员,届时将会受到我国举国上下的真诚欢迎。我深信北京市在中国政府和全国人民的支持下,将做出非凡的努力,一定能把第29届奥运会办成一届高水平的奥运会。

- 英文版

> With much enthusiasm, I solemnly convey to you my full support for Beijing's bid to host the Games of the XXIX Olympiad in 2008.
>
> It will be of extremely great significance to promote and carry forward the Olympic spirit in China and across the world and to facilitate the cultural exchanges and convergence between East and West if the Games of the XXIX Olympiad are held in China, a rapidly developing country with a long-standing civilisation and 22 percent of the world's population. The Chinese people are ready to contribute to the cause of peace friendship and progress of mankind and to the development of the Olympic Movement by hosting the XXIX Olympic Games.
>
> I sincerely hope that Beijing will be selected by the IOC as the Host City of the XXIX Olympic Games. The Chinese people have a peace-loving and hospitable tradition. You and all members of the Olympic Family under your leadership will be warmly welcomed by our whole nation for the occasion. I am convinced that with the support of the Chinese Government and all the Chinese people, Beijing will work very hard and will surely make the XXIX Olympic Games an extraordinary success.

(一)支持申办会展的态度

陈述支持申办会展的态度,惯常使用的中文句式是"我……(如何)表示全力支持……(东道国/城市)申办……(会展项目名称)"。

英文版将首段文字译成:

With much enthusiasm, I solemnly convey to you my full support for Beijing's bid to host the

Games of the XXIX Olympiad in 2008.

为更进一步提高支持信的正式程度，可采用目的语平行文本 It is that I write to endorse candidature for …。

（二）该地区作为会展东道主的优势

旨在说明区域优势的中文句式，最为常见的是"在……（东道国/城市）举办……（会展项目名称）将……（积极意义）"或其变体。

上面的英文版第二段第一处下划线部分可以视为条件复句，其中结果分句的主语实际上是隐含的，可添加指示代词"这"，指代"在具有悠久文明并且迅速发展的、占世界人口22%的中国举办第29届奥运会"，充任"无论是……还是……"的主语。该部分完全仿拟了源语句式结构：以 if 条件状语从句翻译"如果"分句，并增译代词 it 作为主句主语。问题是句式本身过于复杂，可读性较差，特别是 it 的指示对象极不明确。实际上，直接将 Hosting the Games in China, a rapidly developing country with a long-standing civilisation and 22 percent of the world's population 设置为主语，便能在保留原信息的同时使文本显得更简洁。

（三）成功举办会展的决心

为表明成功举办会展的决心，中文支持信末段经常使用"将""一定能"等能愿动词，前者的语气虽比后者弱，但它们的内涵是一致的。

参考目的语平行文本，将之译成 would 似乎比英文版中的 will 更能体现撰写者的意图。

- 改译

> It is with much enthusiasm that I solemnly write to endorse the Beijing candidature for the Games of the XXIX Olympiad 2008.
>
> Hosting the Games in China, a rapidly developing country with a long standing civilisation and 22 percent of the world's population, will significantly promote the Olympic spirit in China and across the world and facilitate the cultural exchange and convergence between East and West. The Chinese people are ready to celebrate the Games in 2008 and thus contribute to the peace, friendship and progress of mankind as well as the Olympic Movement.
>
> We sincerely hope that Beijing will be selected by the IOC as the Host City. The Chinese people have a peace-loving and hospitable tradition. You and all members of the Olympic Family under your leadership will be warmly welcomed by our whole nation for the occasion. We are fully convinced that with the support from the Chinese Government and all the Chinese people, Beijing would work very hard and would surely make the Games an extraordinary success.

三、担保信翻译

担保信(guarantee)的正文部分旨在确认写信人对相关会展活动的主管机构作出的必要承诺。常用的汉语句式包括"……将……""……保证……"等。

上海市代市长世博会担保信

- 中文版

上海市人民政府将全力支持中国2010年上海世博会申办委员会以及上海市申办工作领导小组为举办2010年世界博览会所制订的场馆土地使用、规划建设、财政预算、安全保障及其他方面的各项计划,满足为举办2010年世界博览会在资金、土地、人员、场馆等方面的需求,并保证遵守国际展览局的各项规定,履行有关义务,承担申办和举办2010年世界博览会活动的相关责任;保证采取一切为确保中国2010年上海世界博览会的顺利举办所需的其他必要措施和手段。

上海市代市长
×××
2001年12月10日于上海

- 英文版

Letter of Commitment from the Shanghai Municipal People's Government

Shanghai, December 10th, 2001

President Gilles Noghes,

Secretary General V. G. Loscertales,

Delegates to the Bureau International des Expositions,

The Shanghai Municipal People's Government hereby fully supports the plans put forward by the Expo 2010 Shanghai China State Bidding Commission and Expo 2010 Shanghai China Municipal Bidding Committee as regards land use, construction, budget, security guarantee and other projects for the Exposition. We hereby pledge to satisfy all and any requirements in terms of finance, space, personnel and pavilions, abide by all regulations set by BIE, fulfill relevant obligations on our part, and carry out responsibilities arising in the process of bidding for and hosting Expo 2010. We also promise to adopt other necessary means and measures to ensure the success of Expo 2010 Shanghai China.

×××

Acting Mayor of Shanghai

本例中文版以两种不同句式确认了上海市人民政府对国际展览局的四项保证。英文版除首句外,通过 guarantee, pledge, promise 等不同动词翻译相关承诺的内容。这样的处理本质上有悖于目的语平行文本的措辞习惯,可将源语各项保证统一译成以谓语动词 guarantee 为核心的句式。

- 改译

Shanghai
10 December 2001

Dear President Gilles Noghes,
Dear Secretary General V. G. Loscertales,
Dear Delegates to the Bureau International des Expositions,

Guarantee

The People's Municipal Government of Shanghai hereby guarantees full support for all plans made by the Shanghai 2010 World Exposition Bidding Commission and Shanghai Municipal Bidding Board with regard to land use, construction, budget, security and other aspects of the Exposition; guarantees to satisfy all requirements in terms of fund, land, labor and pavilions; guarantees the respect of all regulations set by BIE; guarantees to fulfill our obligations and undertake relevant responsibilities arising from bidding for and staging Expo 2010; and guarantees to adopt any other means and measures necessary to ensure the success of the World Exposition Shanghai China 2010.

Yours respectfully

×××

Acting Mayor of Shanghai

四、申请函翻译

申请函(application)的正文部分旨在说明申办特定会展项目,主体通常包括三方面内容:首先,提出举办会展的申请;其次,概述活动期限及主题;最后,表明履行义务的决心。

上海世博会申请函

- 中文版

尊敬的洛塞泰斯秘书长:

鉴于中国2010年上海世界博览会已在2002年12月举行的国际展览局全体大会上获得批准,中华人民共和国政府兹根据《国际展览公约》第6条的规定向国际展览局提出注册中国2010年上海世界博览会的申请,并递交相关的文件。

第六章 会展功能性文案翻译

中国2010年上海世界博览会将于2010年5月1日至10月31日在上海举行,其主题是"城市,让生活更美好"。

中华人民共和国政府将采取各种措施,根据《国际展览公约》履行主办国的各项义务,特别是遵循《公约》第10条的有关规定。

中华人民共和国国务院副总理
2010年上海世界博览会组织委员会主任委员
吴仪
2005年4月1日于北京

- 英文版

Mr. V. G. Loscertales

Secretary General of the Bureau International des Expositions

Beijing, April 1st, 2005

Dear Mr. Loscertales,

Following the approval of the date of the World Exposition Shanghai China 2010 by the General Assembly of the Bureau International des Expositions at its 132nd session held in December 2002, the Government of the People's Republic of China hereby applies for registration of the World Exposition Shanghai China 2010 and submits the required documents to the Bureau, in accordance with the provisions of Article 6 of the *Convention Relating to International Exhibitions*.

The World Exposition Shanghai China 2010 will be held from May 1st to October 31st 2010 on the theme "Better City, Better Life".

The Government of the People's Republic of China will make its utmost efforts and take all measures necessary to fulfill the obligations of the host country as prescribed in the provisions of the *Convention Relating to International Exhibitions*, particularly in Article 10 of the Convention.

Wu Yi

Vice-Premier of the State Council

People's Republic of China

Chairperson of

Shanghai 2010 World Exposition National Organizing Committee

这里需要强调的是,申请的提出、义务的履行都必须受到相关会展规章条文的约束。这方面汉语文本的常用术语主要包括"根据""按照"等,而英文中的 in accordance with, as provided/stipulated/stated, etc. in 等无疑是能够与之完全契合的短语结构。只是 in accordance with 可与 the provisions 搭配，而 as prescribed/provided/stipulated/stated, etc. in 再续接 the provisions 有点画蛇添足。

- 改译：

> Beijing
> 1 April 2005
>
> Mr. V. G. Loscertales
> Secretary General of the Bureau International des Expositions
> Dear Mr. Loscertales,
>
>   Following the approval of the date of <u>the World Exposition Shanghai China 2010</u> by the General Assembly of the Bureau International des Expositions at its 132nd session held in December 2002 the Government of the People's Republic of China hereby applies for registration of <u>the Exposition</u> and submits the required documents to the Bureau in accordance with the provisions of Article 6 of the *Convention Relating to International Exhibitions*.
>
>   <u>The Exposition</u> will be held from May 1st to October 31st 2010 on the theme of "Better City, Better Life".
>
>   The Government of the People's Republic of China <u>would</u> make its utmost efforts and take all measures necessary to fulfill the obligations of the host country as provided in the *Convention Relating to International Exhibitions*, particularly in Article 10 of the *Convention*.
>
>   Yours respectfully
> Wu Yi
> Vice Premier of the State Council
> Chairperson of
> Shanghai 2010 World Exposition National Organizing Committee

第三节　会议背景板标识语翻译

  背景板一般指会议的背景画面，也常用作会议宣传主画面，如产品发布会、周年庆、招商会、年会、颁奖典礼等都需要设计背景板。由于该语境具有一定的仪式感且受众较多，所以作为形象传播的重要元素，会议背景板语言表达呈现出严谨、庄重的特征，语言简短，形式紧凑，语义丰富，信息传递准确。有鉴于此，会议背景板文本属于信息类文本，兼具呼唤功能，翻译时要着重传达整个会议（活动）的意义和氛围。

作为背景板,图6.1中的英译文不仅错误频出,而且未能很好传递校庆理念,可谓不成功范例。因此,翻译时需要先确定以下三点:该背景板文本属于信息类文本,兼具呼唤功能;与之相应的翻译策略是交际翻译;主要采用的翻译方法是欠额翻译(under translation),译文通常具有通顺、简朴、清晰、直接等特征。针对上述英译文的相关错误,翻译时注意事项具体如下:

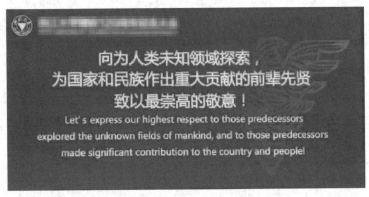

图6.1 会议背景板标识语翻译示例

1. 英汉标识语差异

一般来说,背景板中的英汉标识语表达方式不同,英语多为名词性结构,而汉语为动词性结构。Let's express … 结构为中式结构,不符合该语境表述。

2. 英汉搭配差异

英汉互译中经常出现的一个问题是"假朋友",即源语中的搭配组合不符合目标语的表达,如"吃苦"→eat bitterness(正确表达:endure/bear hardships)、"拳头产品"→fist product(正确表达:blockbuster/competitive product)。

因此,"致以……敬意"→ express respect to sb. 的表述不符合英语的搭配习惯,为中式搭配,正确的与 respect 搭配的动词有 pay、show、win、earn、gain 等。

3. 语用功能

根据词典释义 If you pay your respect to someone, you go to see them or speak to them. You usually do this to be polite, and not necessarily because you want to do it. , pay respect to 意为"探望、拜访(以示敬意)";respect 只是表示心中的敬意,不一定会有相应的行动,或纯粹就是一种礼节,而真实语境是大学校庆在向先贤致敬的同时,也想像先贤那样为国家做点贡献。因此,tribute 比 respect 更能传递这种含义,交际功能更强。(tribute: A tribute is something that you say, do, or make to show your admiration and respect for someone.)

另外,原译文中 predecessors 前加 those 也不合适,因为 those 是远指,从人际关系来看,有拉开距离、划清界限的功能。被 those 形容的人往往是说话者贬低的对象,这在汉语和英语中都一样。同时,从时间视角看,those 多用于事后描述或者事前计划,但事情正在发生时用 those 就很奇怪。出现在现场的标识语显然既非事后描述,也非事前计划。

4. 英汉句式差异

英汉句式差异主要体现在语言之间的连接方式,前者一般是显性的连接,即采用连词、关系代词、关系副词、非限定动词等形式进行连接;而后者常通过流水句这种没有非显性的连接标志来显示其关系并进行连接。因此,中文标语"前辈先贤"的修饰语"为人类未知领域探索"和"为国家和民族作出重大贡献"是通过流水句式进行呈现的,而英译文需要通过显性的连接方式(定语从句)进行表达。同时,原译文行文啰唆,to those predecessors 重复表达,违反英语忌重复的用语习惯,可以用省略的方法进行精简。

5. 原译文语法错误

对于文体极为正式的标识语,避免语法错误是翻译的最基本要求。翻译时不仅要确保语言的准确性,在版面设计时还要考虑排版、字数及显示效果,真正实现背景板的交际功能。

- 错误一:介词使用错误(the unknown fields of mankind)

该译文的字面意思不是"人类不知道的领域",而是关于人类的未知领域,因为介词 of 表示所属关系。如果要准确表达中文原文的意思,应该使用介词 for,即 the unknown fields for humankind(对人类来说未知的领域)。而且,该译文行文啰唆,不如直接删除介词短语,仅保留 explored the unknown。

- 错误二:单复数误用(made significant contribution)

contribution 是可数名词,要么用复数,要么用 a contribution。考虑到先贤们做出的贡献不止一个,所以这里应改为 made significant contributions 为妥。

- 错误三:时态误用(explored, made)

先贤的贡献已经做出,我们表示敬意,是由于这些贡献对我们有深远的影响。为了表达这层意思,应该使用完成时态,而不是原译文的过去时态。

6. 原文理解错误

这是整个标识语翻译最致命的错误。无论从什么样的翻译理论来看,"信"(忠实原文)都是最基本的要求。原文理解错误的直接后果就是交际失败。在"向为人类未知领域探索,为国家和民族作出重大贡献的前辈先贤致以最崇高的敬意"中有两个"为":一是"为人类未知领域探索",二是"为国家和民族"。在两个"为"后面是"作出重大贡献"。按照汉语的结构,"作出重大贡献"是前面两个状语的共同谓语,即"为人类未知领域探索作出重大贡献的"和"为国家和民族作出重大贡献的"两个定语,而原译文完全割裂了这层关系。

综上所述,该背景板标识语建议译为:

Our highest tribute to the predecessors who have made significant contributions to the cause of exploring the unknown and to the country and the people!

第四节　会议台签翻译

大型会议一般都会设置主席台,其中放置台签是会议主席台布置过程中非常重要的环节,这便于领导(嘉宾)一目了然,对号入座,也避免他们在主席台上互相谦让,既有利于维护会场秩序,又增强了会议的严肃性。

会议主席台一般应面对会场入口。每位参会领导(嘉宾)面前的桌子上均要摆放双向台签。台签的摆放应遵循"居中——左手"原则,即职务前排高于后排,中间高于两侧,左侧高于右侧。需要注意的是,左右之分,要以主席台1号领导(嘉宾)座位朝向为参照标准。

当参会领导人数为单数时,主要领导居中(主席台的中线位置),2号领导在1号领导左手位置,3号领导在1号领导右手位置,以下依次类推。

当参会领导人数为偶数时,1、2号领导同时居中(分别在主席台中线的右边和左边),2号领导依然在1号领导左手位置,3号领导依然在1号领导右手位置,以下依次类推。

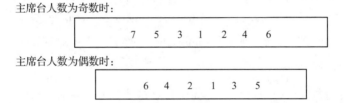

会议台签翻译主要涉及的文本包括姓名和头衔(职务),由于该语境具有一定的仪式感且受众较多,所以要求信息传递严谨、准确。有鉴于此,会议台签文本属于信息类文本,翻译时要着重注意信息传递功能,可以考虑纽马克的交际翻译策略。

一、姓名翻译

(一) 外国人名

虽然外国人名为名前姓后,但译成中文时一般不调换位置,如乔治·布什(George Bush)。在翻译外国人名时,大多采取音译法,但切忌用容易造成误解或歧义的音译,如Rich Santorum(李三多)等。

(二) 中国人名

目前,汉语姓名的翻译主要有以下三种方式:

▲ 汉语拼音直译

姓在前,名在后,双名的两个字要拼写在一起,中间不需要用连字符,首字母要大写,单名的两个字要分开,遇到复姓时,复姓的拼音要连在一起,如王建军(Wang Jianjun)、李强

(Li Qiang)、诸葛沂(Zhuge Yi)、欧阳中石(Ouyang Zhongshi)等。

▲ 遵照英美习惯

按照英美习惯,采用名在前、姓在后的次序拼写,但通常可在姓氏的前面加上逗号,与名字分开,也可以采用缩写,如王建军可以翻译成 Jianjun, Wang 或 J. J., Wang。

▲ 姓氏大写

人名中的姓全部大写,以起到突出醒目的作用,同时也表明大写部分是姓名中的姓,以免外国人将姓与名搞错,如王建军可以翻译成 WANG Jianjun,李江可以翻译成 LI Jiang。

二、头衔(职务)翻译

(一)正职头衔

▲ chief:总司令/总指挥(Commander-in-Chief)

▲ general:总书记(General Secretary)

▲ head:总教练(Head Coach)

▲ president:中国科学院院长(President of the Chinese Academy of Sciences)

▲ chairman:人大常委会委员长(NPC Chairman)

▲ director:亚洲司司长(Director of the Department of Asian Affairs)

▲ commissioner:行/公署专员(Commissioner)

(二)副职头衔

▲ associate:副教授(associate professor)、副研究员(associate research fellow)(associate 用作"副"时一般用于职称)

▲ assistant:副总经理(assistant general manager)

▲ deputy:副秘书长(deputy secretary-general)

▲ vice:副总裁(vice president)

▲ under:副国务卿(Under Secretary of State)

▲ sub:副编辑(subeditor)

根据翻译实践,表达"副"的含义最广泛的是 vice 和 deputy,二者并无本质区别,在实际使用时纯属搭配习惯。一般来说,vice 与 president, premier, chairman, minister, governor 搭配;deputy 与 director, chief, head, secretary, dean, mayor 搭配。从某种意义上来说,vice 比 deputy 的搭配级别高。

(三)其他

有些头衔含诸如"代理""常务""执行""名誉"等这类称谓。一般来说,"代理"可译为 acting,如代理市长(acting mayor);"常务"可译为 managing,如常务副校长(managing vice president,也可译为 first vice president);"执行"可译为 executive,如执行主席(executive chairman,也可译为 presiding chairman);"名誉"可译为 honorary,如名誉会长(honorary president，也可译为 emeritus president）。

还有些职称或职务带有"主任""主治""特级""特派""特约"等头衔，英译不尽相同。

▲ 主任编辑：associate senior editor
▲ 主任秘书：chief secretary
▲ 主任医师：senior doctor；chief physician
▲ 主任护士：senior nurse
▲ 主治医师：attending／chief doctor；physician；consultant
▲ 特级教师：special-grade senior teacher
▲ 特派记者：accredited correspondent；special correspondent
▲ 特派员／专员：commissioner
▲ 特约编辑：contributing editor
▲ 特约记者：special correspondent

思考题

1. 举例说明会议台签的摆放原则及翻译方法。
2. 翻译以下段落。

（1）

各位嘉宾、各位朋友！

"凡益之道，与时偕行。"互联网虽然是无形的，但运用互联网的人们都是有形的，互联网是人类的共同家园。让这个家园更美丽、更干净、更安全，是国际社会的共同责任。让我们携起手来，共同推动网络空间互联互通、共享共治，为开创人类发展更加美好的未来助力！最后，预祝大会取得圆满成功！

（2）

As we celebrate the success of these Games, let us altogether wish the best for the talented athletes who will soon participate in the Paralympic Games. They also inspire us. To the athletes tonight：You were true role models. You have shown us the unifying power of sport. The Olympic spirit lives in the warm embrace of competitors from nations in conflict. Keep that spirit alive when you return home. These were truly exceptional Games.

3. 翻译以下朱镕基总理北京奥运会申办支持信内容。

The Chinese Government gives all-out support to Beijing's bid to host the Games of the XXIX Olympiad in 2008.

I am confident that with the support of the Chinese Government and all the Chinese people, Beijing will be able to organize the 2008 Olympic Games successfully.

During the Olympic Games, the Chinese Government and all its relevant departments will respect the rules and by-laws of the Olympic Charter and the regulations of the International Federations related to the Olympic Games. I am personally ready to ensure the implementation of the rules and regulations.

China and the city of Beijing enthusiastically look forward to the hosting of the 2008 Olympic Games in Beijing.

第七章 会展合同与规章翻译

学习目标

- 了解合同与规章的内涵与外延
- 知晓会展合同的结构要素
- 了解会展合同与规章的语言特征
- 掌握会展合同与规章的翻译方法

核心词汇

* 合同(contract)
* 规章(regulation)
* 规定性文件(normative writing)
* 正式程度(formality)
* 专业术语(term)
* 古语词(archaic word)
* 外来词(loan word)
* 缩略词(abbreviation)

第一节　会展合同与规章概述

一、会展合同与规章的定义

合同(contract),也叫契约。"契",即意思相投或相合;"约"是用语言或文字订立共守的条件。合同和契约的含义一样,意思是愿意订立共同遵守的条件,合作共事。所谓会展合同,广义而言即平等主体之间围绕会展活动、依法订立的各类民事合同的总称;狭义的会展合同则主要包括会展组织机构与其他会展参与者之间依法签订的设立、变更、终止各方民事权利义务关系的书面协议(王平辉,2008:135)。一般而言,会展合同主要包括展会展位申请合同、展会展位租赁合同、展览设备购买合同、会展服务合同、会展买卖合同、会展物流服务合同六大类合同。

相对于基于双方协商的合同,规章(regulation)更多是单方作出的决定,是强调预先(即在行为发生之前)和法律效力,用于法律条文中的决定,一般具有约束性、权威性及稳定性。会展系列活动中为保证其顺利实施,会就相关事项作出具体的要求,特别在使用管理、安全保障、知识产权、特殊事项等领域。所谓会展规章,泛指在会展活动过程中,由会展管理机构和组织机构制定的,对有关团体与个人具有规范作用和约束力的文案,"包括涉及会展管理的行政法规、地方性法规、国务院部门规章、地方政府规章、会展行业规章、会展组织和会展企业内部规章、会展活动规则等"(向国敏,2008:64)。

尽管会展合同与规章的外延宽泛,但就会展英语和翻译的研究而言,最能反映此类文案语言风格特色的莫过于大型国际会展活动的筹备机构为确保事务纷繁、牵涉广泛的项目得以运作顺利而制定的活动规章及其与参展商之间就参展事宜签订的格式合同,这理所当然地成为本章的主要内容。

二、会展合同与规章的篇章布局

就篇章而言,会展合同与规章最明显的语用特点是其语言的法律效力,表现在结构布局上就是高度程式化的格式。大量的对比研究表明,"英、汉会展合同与规章语篇的结构大致相同,都由描写性成分过渡到规定性成分、由颁布命令和/或前言过渡到具体条文;其结构层次分明,都是采用从宏观到微观、从总论/总则到条文、从重要条文到次要条文的语篇结构"(张新红,2000:285)。立法机关通过并发布实施的各项法律法规必须遵照一定的立法方针,采用一定的立法技术,并借助格式较为固定的语篇模式将立法结果记录下来,其目的集中体现为:

其一,更加准确地传达立法者的意图和法律法规的具体内容,以便司法者和执法者在用法的过程中能够正确理解和使用法律;

其二,保持法律规范的庄严性及其内容的严谨合理和准确规范,使法律规范的内涵得到最充分的体现;

其三,为所涉及的法律条文、专业术语和概括性词语设定具体的阐释语境,减少曲解或误解法律条文和概括性词语的可能性,瓦解那些钻法律漏洞者的企图;

其四,符合专业用法者的阅读习惯和阅读期待,在理解和使用法律的过程中尽可能减少犯错误的机会。

(滕超、孔飞燕,2008:27)

当然,合同也可视为仅适用于特定协议当事人的行为规范,故其篇章结构亦是有章可循的,且主体部分与具有普遍适用性的法律法规无本质差别。

三、会展合同与规章的结构元素

(一)会展参展合同的结构元素

- 标题(Caption/Heading)
- 导言段落(Introductory Paragraph):当事人的名称或者姓名和住所
- 事实陈述部分(Recital):合同标的
- 正文(Main Body):包括当事人的权利义务、违约责任、解决争议的方法等
- 签名栏(Signature Block)
- 日期(Date)
- 附件(Appendix):构成合同正文条款的必要补充

(二)会展管理规章的结构元素

① 标题(Title):通常由适用范围、事由及规章类型构成,如《中国 2010 年上海世博会一般规章》(General Regulations of World Exposition Shanghai China 2010)。

② 制定条款(Enacting Clause):政府机关发布或会议通过的规章应当题注制定条款,包括发布机关名称或通过会议名称、发布或通过日期。但会展活动的管理规章通常不以题注形式标明制定机关和日期,如上海世博会一般规章就没有专门的制定条款,而是在封页标明发布日期为 2005 年 9 月,颁布机关为上海世博会事务协调局(Bureau of Shanghai World Expo Coordination)。

③ 目录(Content):内容较多、篇幅较长的规章应当设置目录,以便检索。不过,上海世博会一般规章仅有 39 款法条,故未编制目录。

④ 正文(Main Body):通常由总则、分则和附则三部分组成,可下设编、章、节、条、款、项、目。

有鉴于此,会展合同与规章的篇章结构是有章可循的,而且英、汉文本大致相同。

第二节　会展合同与规章翻译实践

国际会展的策划(展前)和运作(展中)阶段涉及大量的合同与规章内容,前者往往单独出现,而后者一般包含在参展商手册中。由于二者的文本类型基本相同,同属信息类文本,故二者翻译合并在本小节一并阐述,不再另行讨论。

从文本类型视角来看,会展合同与规章属于信息类文本,实施指令功能,相对应的翻译策略是交际翻译,即在内容上忠实传递源语信息,在形式上遵循目的语习惯,便于读者更直观地接收源语信息,可以采用对等翻译。

一、会展合同与规章词法翻译

会展合同与规章具有很强的法律兼容性,因而要求词汇专业、正式、严谨、准确且简洁明了。根据英国语言学家杰弗里·利奇(Geoffrey Leech)对英语词义的分类,专业术语、书面语、古语词、外来词都是具有正式含义风格的词汇(words with formal stylistic meaning)。另外,同义词连用和词项重复具有严谨的风格,而缩略词简洁明了,它们都能满足会展合同与规章对用词的要求。因此,会展合同与规章翻译时,需要采用换译法,尽量考虑选择一些正式的词汇,以凸显信息类文本的指令功能。

(一)专业术语

专业术语(term)是用来确切表达概念的词,要求具有单义性,排斥多义性和歧义性,且形式固定,不得随意更改,主要包括合同专业术语,如 rights and obligations(权利和义务)、breach of contract(违约)、arbitration binding force(仲裁)、force majeure(不可抗力)、binding force(约束力)等,以及较多的法律专业术语,如 action(诉讼)、party(当事人)、decision(裁决)、final(最终裁决)等。

例1　如展会由于不可抗力影响而不得不取消,参赛者被退还的最终金额数应为已付款总额减去主办方组织展会花费的直接成本后的差。

译文:In the case of cancellation because of a *force majeure* event, Participants shall be refunded the difference between the total amount already paid and the direct costs incurred by the Organizer in organizing the exhibition.

例2　每位承包商应于进场前以现金或抬头为"××会议中心"的非流通支票缴纳保证金×××元人民币。

译文:A contractor shall pay an entry deposit of RMB ＊＊＊ before entering the site, either in cash or by a *non-negotiable check* in favor of the ＊＊＊ Convention Center.

例3 根据《中华人民共和国合同法》及其他法律法规的规定，甲乙双方在自愿、平等、公平、诚实信用的基础上，就会展场地租赁的有关事宜达成如下协议。

译文：In accordance with "Contract Law of the People's Republic of China" and other relevant laws and regulations, the *Parties* have, based on the principles of equality, willingness, fairness, honest and credit, entered into the Contract concerning issues related to lease of exhibition place and agreed as follows.

上述译文中的 force majeure, non-negotiable check, Parties 都为合同或法律专业术语，无法用日常词汇替代。

（二）书面语

书面语（formal word）是指人们在书写和阅读文章时所使用的语言，具有法律效力的会展合同与规章用词都应正式、规范，不能太口语化。

例4 主办方一般会免费或依据流程统一发放入场许可证，参展人员进入会场时必须出示入场许可证方可入场。

译文：To gain admission to the event, Participants must show an admission pass, which the Organizer shall issue free of charge or for consideration *in accordance with* its own procedures.

例5 租用本中心会场办理活动而需自行雇用保安人员者，应于活动一周前向本中心报备，经同意后发给临时工作证。

译文：Those who need to hire their own security guards for activities at the venue of the Center should report to the Center for approval one week *prior to* the event. Temporary work badges will be issued upon the Center's prior approval.

上述译文中的 in accordance with, prior to 作为书面语，比口语形式 according to, before 在文体上显得更正式。需要特别指出的是，submit, confirm, endorse, abide by, maintain, promote 等词都是非常正式的书面语词汇。这些单词比较正式、庄重，在其他文体中较少使用，没有什么联想意义，词义明确，符合合同与规章这一文体对语言严谨的要求。此外，英文合同中常使用以下词汇（括号中的词是常用词汇，一般不出现在合同中）：assist（help）（帮助）、advise（tell）（通知）、render（give）（给予，提供）、rescind（cancel）（撤销）、commence（begin, start）（开始）、employ（use）（使用）、cease to do（stop doing）（停止做）、convene（hold）（召开）、construe（explain, interpret）（解释）、deem（think, believe, consider）（认为）、terminate（end）（终止）、partake in（join）（参与）、require（ask）（要求）、surrender（give）（递交）、conveyance（transfer of real estate）（不动产转让）、prior to（before）（在……之前）、provided that（if）（如果）、in accordance with（according to）（按照）、by virtue of（due to, because of）（因为）、as regards/concerning/relating to（about）（关于）、in effect（in fact）

（事实上）、miscellaneous（other matters）（其他事项）、pursuant to（according to）（依照/按照）。

（三）古语词

为体现文本正式、庄重的文体特征，英文合同与规章常使用一些古语词（archaic word）。这些词主要来源于古英语和中古英语，主要是由 here-, there-和 where-与一个或几个介词组成的复合副词，如 hereafter（此后，今后）、hereby（特此，兹）、herein（此中，于此，本合同中）、hereinafter（以下，此后，在下文）、hereof（于此，在本合同中）、hereto（于此）、hereunder（在下文，据此，根据本合同）、hereunto（于此）、herewith（与此一道）、thereafter（此后，后来）、thereby（因此，由此，在那方面）、therefrom（由此，从此）、therein（其中，在其中）、thereinafter（在下文）、thereof（关于，由此，其中）、thereto（此外，附随）、thereunder（在其下，据此，依据）、whereas（鉴于）、whereby（因此，由是，据此）、wherefore（为此，因此）、wherein（在那方面）、whereof（关于那事/人）等。在这些复合副词中，here 表示 this，there 表示 that，where 表示 what 或 which。使用这些单词能使语言精练、直观，使合同语言显得更为规范、严肃，体现合同语言的权威性和严密性。

例6 竣工时间是指合同规定从工程开工期算起到工程或其任何部分或区段施工结束并且通过竣工检验的时间。

译文："Time for Completion" means such time for completing the execution of the Works and passing the Tests on Completion of the Works or any Section or part *thereof* as is specified in the Contract from the Commencement Date（*thereof*：of the Works）.

例7 合同双方首先应通过友好协商，解决因合同而发生的或与合同有关的争议。

译文：The parties *hereto* shall, first of all, settle any dispute arising from or in connection with the contract through amicable negotiations.

（四）外来词

外来词（loan word）主要指来自法语、拉丁语等语言的词汇，它们比英语词汇更严谨、准确。例如，addiem（在指定日期）、status quo（现状）、null and void（无效）、vice versa（反之亦然）、adhoc（特别，临时）、as per（按照）、defacto（事实上的）、vis-à-vis（和……相比）等来源于拉丁语，force majuere（不可抗力）等来源于法语，del credere（信用担保）等来源于意大利语。

（五）缩略词

缩略词（abbreviation）主要由主干词的首字母构成。缩略词以其规范、简明、节时的特点而被广泛使用。会展领域常见和重要的机构、组织、公司、货币、度量衡、国家都常用缩略词表达，简洁明了。

例8　如果参展人员丢失了自己的参展证件,瑞德集团将另收80元人民币(含增值税)为其补办。

译文:If the participant loses his/her badge, Reed MIDEM will have to bill him/her 80 RMB Yuan(+VAT) for a duplicate.

例9　如果计划在其展台和/或指定区域和/或广告区间内播放音乐,参展商应以书面形式通知主办方,并填写所有必要的报告,特别是(但不限制)最好获得法国音乐版权组织(法国表演权利协会)和/或其他相关监管机构的许可,并支付相关的费用。

译文:The Participant shall inform the Organizer in writing if it plans to broadcast music at its stand and/or assigned location and/or in its advertising space, and shall file all required reports, in particular (but without limitation), with the *SACEM* (the French Performing Rights Society) and/or other relevant regulatory body and make the payments associated therewith.

(六) 词项重复

词项重复是指很少使用代词,而是重复关键词,这是为了准确。除了it is agreed as follows 和 it is understood that 两种结构外,代词 it 几乎不出现。此外,名词前常用 said, aforesaid, above-mentioned 等限定词,以增强准确性。

(七) 同义词连用

英语会展合同中经常使用成双成对的同义词,同义词之间用 and 或 or 连接。使用成对同义词是为了避免诉讼时双方律师利用词义间的细微差别大做文章。我们知道 term 和 condition 是同义词,都表示"条件,条款",但它们在合同中经常连用,因为在合同中这两个同义词连用比单个使用更显严谨。

例10　He/she *acknowledges and accepts* that personal data is accessible to participants or partners that may be located in states that may not provide a sufficient level of protection equivalent to the European Union Directives.

译文:当事人须认可,上传的个人资料能够被其他参展人员或公司浏览到,而这些个人或法律实体所在的国家也许不能提供与欧盟法令相同的保护力度。

例11　Certain of the Organizer's events may be sponsored by Participants pursuant to the *terms and conditions* set forth in the relevant participation contract which specifies the characteristics of the event.

译文:依据已明确界定展会类型的相关参展合同中列出的条款,主办方组织的展会应由参展商们进行赞助。

例 12　The contract is made *by and between* Oxford Publishing Limited, Great Clarendon Street Oxford and Foreign Language Teaching and Research Press, 29 Xisanhuan Beilu, Beijing P. R. China.

译文:本合同由坐落于牛津大克拉伦敦街的牛津出版有限公司与坐落于中华人民共和国北京西三环北路的外语教学与研究出版社签订。

同义词连用涉及介词、动词、名词、形容词等词类,如 by and between(由)、for and in consideration of(考虑到,鉴于)、for and on behalf of(为了,代表)、save and except(除了)、furnish and provide(提供)、make and enter into(达成)、fulfill or perform(履行)、procure and ensure(保证和确保)、force and effect(效力)、right and interest(权益)、power and authority(权利)、terms and conditions(条款)、goods and chattels(个人动产,有形动产)、losses and damages(丢失及损毁)、complaints and claims(投诉及索赔)、null and void(失效,无效)、sole and exclusive(唯一且排他的)、claims and debt(债务)、customs and usage(惯例)等。

另外,需要注意的是,为了行文的严谨,英语会展合同与规章文本除了使用 and 连接同义词之外,有时还会使用 or 连接的近义词,这些近义词往往并非意义完全相同的同义词,一般都需要翻译出来,以保证其精确性和内容的全面性,如 alteration, modification or substitution(变更、修改或替代)、compensation or damages(赔偿或赔偿金)、altered or amended(变更或修改)、agent or representative(代理或代表)、claim or allegation(声明或声称)等。

另外,根据美国《统一和标准法案起草规则》确定的立法语言文字使用制度,规定性法律文件应当"慎用代词,只有被指代的词不被误解并且是中性词时,或者是存在着一系列的名词如果不用代词则只能重复这些名词因而有明显的累赘毛病时,才可使用代词"。实际上,在英语会展规定性法律文件中,较为典型的是以 such, same, said 等词汇指代相关内容,因为这三个词能在很大程度上明确被指代的内容,减少模糊和歧义,但同时也会使语言变得臃肿,如以下节选自 BIE 发布的《注册博览会一般规章范本》的多项条款。

> ARTICLE 12—Admission of participants
> Exhibitors who do not come under any section shall deal directly with the Organiser, who shall inform the Government of the State of origin of the exhibitor concerned of their intention as soon as contact is established with such exhibitors.
> —Model General Regulations for International Registered Exhibitions

> ARTICLE 3
>
> The Organizer shall provide the Participant with the services set out in the Special Regulations designated in Article 34 of the Model General Regulations at the rate and on the following terms:
>
> —variant A: set out hereunder
>
> —variant B: mentioned in *said* special regulations
>
> —Registered Exhibition Model Participation Contract

这里需要特别指出的是,人称代词的使用也是会展合同与规章英文文本中必须特别注意的地方,要求使用者通过各种途径尽量在文本中实现性别平等,常用的策略包括使用被动语态、代词中性化(如 one,you)、重复名词、人称复数化或者 he 和 she 联用等。

在实际使用过程中,名词在会展合同与规章英文文本中出现的频率远高于其他词性,因为以名词作主语或宾语的中心词可附加较多的限定词。请看 BIE 提供给成员国参考的《注册博览会参展合同范本》第2条:

> TITLE II—THE PARTICIPANT'S EXHIBIT
>
> ARTICLE 2
>
> The Organizer places at the disposal of the Participant, which hereby accepts, the space designated on the plan annexed to the contract and made up as follows:
>
> covered space(s), of square _____, free of rent
>
> covered space(s), of square _____, at a rental of
>
> open space(s), of square _____, free of rent
>
> open space(s), of square _____, at a rental of
>
> This space shall be at the disposal of the Participant at the latest on.
>
> The structure and condition of the covered and open spaces placed at the Participant's disposal are described in the Special regulations designated in Article 34 of the Model General Regulations.
>
> The Participant shall be responsible for the furnishing, the maintenance and the cleaning of the space(s) at its disposal.
>
> —Registered Exhibition Model Participation Contract

所引合同条款不过120余词,却使用了多达31个名词,特别是该条款第一段中的 space,其冗长的修饰语 designated on the plan annexed to the contract 反而使行文更显严谨。同时,该条款还反映了会展合同与规章英文文本中名词使用的两个普遍特点:名词多用单数,复数极少使用;抽象名词较多。

由于会展合同与规章英文文本要求多采用客观描述性与解释性语言,特别是规定性文本侧重信息功能,所以会展合同与规章中很少使用带有强烈感情色彩的形容词和副词。

二、会展合同与规章句法翻译

会展合同与规章大多主题突出,表达以完整句子为主,其中陈述句居多,语义直接明确,不拖沓模糊,就所属对象进行精准的描述,如施事者、受事者、方式、时间、地点等,以便尽可能严谨地传达详尽的信息,同时语气上凸显严谨和庄重。由于该类文本具有普遍适用性,所以主要使用现在时态,阐述道理,确立规范或规定权利、义务等。

(一) 常用条件句

会展合同与规章除了规定双方履行的义务外,还设想了各种可能发生的情况和处理办法,尤其在有关付款、违约责任、不可抗力、财产处理和仲裁等方面更是详尽全面。英语中最常见的条件表达方式有 in the event that, in the case of, in case 等,而不是使用引导条件状语从句的连接词 if。这种结构虽然冗长,但表意明确,能杜绝歧义。

例13 如果法文条例和任何其他翻译版本的条例存在出入,应以法文版本为准。

译文:*In the event of* a discrepancy between the French and any other translated versions of the Regulations, the French version shall prevail.

例14 然而,如果展会取消,参展人员可以获赔展会取消之前其支付的所有费用。

译文:However, *in the case of* cancellation of the event, Participants may be refunded any amounts paid prior to the cancellation.

(二) shall 和 may

shall 是英语合同文本中重复率很高的法律用词,具有指示性和施为性的法律含义,表示"必须""应当"的含义;而 may 则表示许可性的法律规范,一般译为"可以""有权"等。

例15 举办地组委会应确保本届亚残运会的庄重及严肃性,并将其作为一项独立的残疾人体育赛事来举办,且不得与任何位于主办城市的国际或国内企业,或与位于该城市的其他任何活动(如交易会或展览)产生关联,但杭州亚运会除外。

译文:LOC *shall* organize the Asian Para Games in a dignified and solemn manner as an independent Para sport event, and not in connection with any other international or national enterprise or event in the City, such as a fair or exhibition, with the exception of Hangzhou 2022 Asian Games.

例16 如不遵守相关要求,主办单位可随时移除相关广告,恕不提前通知。

译文:In the event of non-compliance with these requirements, the Organizer *may* remove such advertising at any time without prior notice.

在英语会展合同与规章中，shall 在表示"应该"时，不可随便用 should 代替，shall 虽然也表示"应该"，但它没有 should 那样重的含义，因为 should 并不表示法律义务，只表示一般的义务或道义上的义务，有时甚至表示"原该"或"最好如此"。当 should 出现在合同与规章中时，它常被放在句子的开头，表示一个隐含的条件状语，类似于由 if, in case, in the event that 引导的状语从句，其含义相当于中文的"如果""万一"，而不是"应该"。

例17　本合同执行期间，如发生侵害第三方权利情形，要按照甲乙双方的过错确定责任，并由过错方依法进行赔付。

译文：*Should* any rights of the third Party be violated during the Contract period, both Parties *shall* determine the responsible Party who will be liable for reimbursement.

例18　参展期间如需变更参展人员，须交回原证件，按要求办理新证，每证收费200元。

译文：*Should* there be any alteration of the exhibitors during the exhibition, the original card needs to be returned to the Organizers to apply for a new one as required and 200 yuan is to be charged for each card.

（三）被动语态

会展合同与规章英文文本中的被动语态使用比较频繁，其目的是突出动作的对象，强调客观事实，从而使论述更为平实、客观。比较而言，会展合同与规章中文文本多非主谓句（无主句），使用被动语态较少。简而言之，英语使用被动语态的频率远高于汉语，翻译时须在英汉两种语言间进行灵活的主被动转换。

例19　如果合同如前述被终止，发包方应向承包方支付款项。

译文：If the Contract shall *be terminated* as aforesaid, the Contractor shall be paid by the Employer.

例20　参展人员不得以任何方式对契约文书做出任何修改或修订。

译文：No amendments or reservations may *be made* by the Participant to the Contract Documents in any manner whatsoever.

例21　参展人员必须在2018年10月15日上午9点后当场出示官方身份证后方可领取胸卡。

译文：Badges can only *be obtained* on site upon presentation of an official ID from 15 October 2018, 9:00 a.m. onwards.

（四）长句

毋庸置疑，会展合同与规章英文文本的句子就其长度和使用从句的连续性来看，比普通英语要频繁得多。这可以将各方的权利和义务明确、完整地表达出来，同时又可以确保逻辑严密，避免误解或歧义的出现。在陈述过程中，句子往往显示出扩展性，即输出信息时"先点睛后展开枝节"，是一种开门见山、先正后偏的逐渐外展形式。

由于英语逻辑性较强，而且是形合的（hypotactic）语言，所以在会展合同与规章英文文本中经常见到逐句对意义进行解释、限制或补充的定语（从句）、状语（从句）等附加成分，翻译时可以根据实际情况采取顺译、逆译或混译。

例22　参展商签署《参展合同》后，未征得承办单位书面同意退出参展或未能参展的，已缴纳的展位费用以及其他费用概不退还，且承办单位有权将相应的展位转给第三方。

译文：An exhibitor who has signed the Exhibition Contract but withdraws from or fails to participate in the Expo without the written consent of the Organizers shall forfeit the paid booth fee and other fees, and the Organizers have the right to transfer the corresponding booth to a third party.（顺译）

例23　当卖方完成了运输货物的责任，货物的丢失或损坏以及承受与货物相关的费用的责任便从卖方转移到买方。

译文：The risk of loss of or damage to the goods, as well as the obligation to bear the costs relating to the goods, passes from the seller to the buyer when the seller has fulfilled this obligation to deliver the goods.（逆译）

例24　由于如地震、台风、水灾、战争以及其他不能预见并且对其发生和后果不能防止或避免的不可抗力事件，影响任何一方履行合同时，遇有不可抗力的一方应立即用电报、传真通知对方，并应在15天内提供不可抗力详情及不能旅行或者部分不能履行、需要延期履行的理由的有效证明文件，此项证明文件应由不可抗力发生地区的公证机构出具。

译文：Should one of the parties to the contract be prevented from executing contract by force majeure, such as earthquake, typhoon, flood, fire, and war and other unforeseen events, and their happening and consequences are unpreventable and unavoidable, the prevented party shall notify the other party by cable or fax without any delay, and within fifteen days thereafter provide the detailed information of the events and a valid document for evidence issued by the relevant public notary organization for explaining the reason of its inability to execute or delay the execution of all or part of the contract.（混译）

（五）专用表达

在会展合同与规章中经常出现一些专用表达，这些单词或词组在日常交流中几乎不用,如 in witness whereof(特此作证,以资证明),know all men by these presents(特此宣布)。

例25 作为所协议事项的证据,双方授权代表于上面首次写明的日期正式签订本协议一式两份。

译文:*In witness whereof*, the parties have executed this Contract in duplicate by their duly authorized representatives on the date first above written.

另外,为更好地传递信息,会展合同与规章文本还大量采用平行结构进行阐述。如《注册博览会参展合同范本》的第12条第1款,该条款将表述手段的四项介宾状语结构以平行罗列的方式铺陈展开,层次分明、内容完整地诠释了政府总代表和组织者为最大限度确保世博会的成功举办,要求相关政府机构实施的行为。

ARTICLE 12

The Commissioner General of the Government and the Organiser will deal with the relevant governmental authorities so that they will act in a manner consistent with the best possible success of the Exhibition, particularly:

• by establishing the offices necessary for the performance of customs operations in the most convenient places;

• by facilitating the entry of all goods and items of any type used for the presentation of the Participant;

• by relaxing, if necessary, the import quotas on the products sold in the section of the Participant, including its restaurant;

• by communicating a list of agents approved by the Organiser to deal with customs matters on the Participant's behalf, for a specified charge

——Registered Exhibition Model Participation Contract

此类句式至少存在三方面的优势,即融合丰富的限定语,包含完整、清晰和详尽的信息;保持单句的性质;减少句子数目,简化、明确双方的法律责任与权利。

 思考题

1. 举例说明会展合同与规章文本中的法律特征在词法与句法层面上的体现。

2. 翻译以下句子。

(1) 未经组织者事先许可,任何参展者都不得更改会展场地的设施。

(2) 否则,发起争端的当事方的要求将被视为不正当。

(3) 经会展主办方批准,参展商可以分发各自产品的免费样品,或允许各自的食物在展区内供免费品尝。

（4）只有与第一条所描述主题相关的物品和展览材料才被允许进入世博会。上述产品的原产地必须符合《公约》第19条的规定。

（5）任何展区都可以组建餐厅和点心店，专门供所属人员使用。上述活动不要求向组织者支付任何费用。

(6) In this capacity, the Organizer is authorized to suspend or stop any activity, and to effect at any time the withdrawal of items of whatever origin which are incompatible with the proper standing of the exposition and which are likely to be a risk or liability.

(7) The Participant is entitled to sell exhibited goods and materials used to install presentations, as well as other items used within its section at the end of the Exposition.

(8) In the case where the Organizer has granted exclusive commercial rights to certain suppliers for the sale of goods or services, these rights must not be allowed to hinder the commercial activities of official participants whether these activities are restaurants or the sale of articles included in the national sections.

(9) Notwithstanding the time scale established for the approval of these Special Regulations, the Organizer shall make available early guidelines on costs or provisions necessary for assessing the financial implications of participation.

(10) If a Participant fails to fulfill his/her commitments towards the Organizer, the Organizer may proceed at the closing date of the exposition and at the Participant's cost and risk, with the dismantling removal, storage and sale of the Participants', goods located within the exposition grounds, with the exception of items considered as national heritage or of a nature of public property. The amount due to the Organizer of the exposition shall be deducted from the proceeds of such sale.

3. 修改以下译文，并作出相关说明。

（1）原文：本报告中如英文与法文出现语义差异，以英文为准。

译文：The English text of the Candidature File will prevail in the event of any difference of interpretation between the English and French versions.

（2）原文：如果上述空间在世博会开幕24个月前未全部配置，组织者可予以收回并自由处置未被预留空间的权利。

译文：If, however, this space has not been fully allocated 24 months before the opening of the Exposition, the Organizer shall recover the right to dispose freely of the unreserved space.

（3）原文：如果参展者不履行上述义务，则根据《一般规章》第18条的规定，世博会政府总代表有权代行组织者的职权。

译文：Should the Participant fail to fulfill the above obligation, the Commissioner General of the Exposition shall be authorized to exercise the Organizer's rights, under the terms of Article 18 of the General Regulations.

（4）原文：参展者与组织者签署《参展合同》后，组织者将授权给参展者在与世博会直接相关的非商业活动中使用世博会标志，此使用权不能转让。

译文：The Participants may use the Symbols of the Exposition solely for non-commercial purposes directly related to the Exposition after having concluded the Participation Contract with the Organizer and receiving the permission of the Commissioner General of the Exposition. This right of use is not transferable.

（5）原文：上述商品（建筑、家具、设备、个人财产和其他类似物品）被偷窃、损坏或破坏的保险认购责任应由上述商品的所有者全部承担。

译文：Insurance of such goods (buildings, furnishings, equipment, personal property and other such items) against the risks of theft deterioration or destruction of these goods, shall be the sole responsibility of the owner of these goods.

（6）原文：常规邀请或短期邀请的参展者的免费入场卡或特许经营证和员工服务卡等的发放，应按上述《特殊规章》第13号确定的条件颁发。

译文：Standing invitations or invitations for a limited period complimentary entrance cards for exhibitors or concessionaires and employees service cards shall be issued in accordance with the conditions laid down in the Special Regulation No. 13 mentioned above.

国际贸易合同签署注意事项

（以下提示信息仅供交易各方了解签署国际贸易合同相关信息参考使用）

1. 参展商和采购商达成交易后在确认合同内容方面需要注意哪些事项？

参展商和采购商通过协商达成交易后，应签订书面合同，明确双方在交易履行中的具体权利义务。为避免交易履行中的不确定，减少纠纷发生，双方应特别关注合同的内容。一是合同内容应充分反映双方在协商中达成的一致意见，未写入合同的各种承诺可能在后续的交易履行中不会得到认可或导致纠纷发生。二是合同内容应明确、具体、完整，避免出现相互矛盾、前后不一致的约定。三是合同使用不同语言时，应明确各种不同语言版本合同的效力顺序。双方在确定合同最终内容时应寻求专业律师的帮助。

2. 参展商和采购商签订的合同一般应有哪些主要内容？

参展商和采购商签订的合同应覆盖双方交易的各个环节和全过程，一般来讲，合同应包括以下主要条款：

(1) 合同主体条款：包括双方当事人名称、地址及相关联系信息等。

(2) 合同标的条款：包括双方交易标的名称、品牌、规格、数量、包装要求等。

(3) 价格条款：包括单价、总价款、计价货币等。

(4) 价款支付条款：包括支付方式、支付时间等。

（5）质量和检验条款：包括适用的质量标准、检验时间、检验方法、检验机构、质量保证期等。

（6）标的交付条款：包括标的交付的时间以及地点和方式等。

（7）运输和保险条款：包括标的运输和保险责任的承担等。

（8）违约责任条款：包括迟延付款、质量瑕疵等的救济和责任承担等。

（9）争议解决条款及法律适用条款：包括合同适用的法律及发生纠纷时的争议解决方式、地点等。

根据交易的具体需要，双方还可以约定安装条款、不可抗力条款、合同生效条款及交易双方的具体联系方式等内容。

3. 参展商和采购商签订合同时对于合同主体相关信息的确认有哪些需要注意的事项？

参展商和采购商在签订合同时应关注对方资质以及实际签约主体的基本信息，尤其是在交易方为集团公司或有多个关联企业的情况下。交易双方在签署合同之前应对签约主体的注册地、实际经营地、实际管理机构等相关信息有所了解和分析，确认签约主体名称与注册信息一致，注意中外当事人在合同签署或盖章上的差异。

4. 参展商和采购商是否需要在合同中明确交易双方的联系信息？

为便于合同履行和保障交易安全，交易双方应在合同中指定专门的联系人员、明确双方联系文件送达的具体地址、电话、电邮等其他联系信息，并对联系信息的变更通知提出明确要求。

5. 参展商和采购商签订合同时如何就合同标的的质量作出约定？

在国际贸易中，就同一标的，进口国和出口国的质量标准往往存在差异。双方在合同中明确约定合同标的适用的质量标准，尤其要关注进口国对合同标的的特殊要求，包括涉及动植物产品的检验检疫要求，避免因不符合进口国强制性质量要求而合同目的不能实现的情况。当选择中国的质量标准时，还要注意国家标准、部门标准和企业标准的区别。对于需要凭样品成交的合同，还应注意封存并妥善保管样品，以作为验收货物的最终依据。

6. 合同中约定检验或验收条款有什么意义？具体需要约定哪些内容？

检验或验收是确认合同标的质量是否符合合同约定的必经程序，检验时间不同、检验机构不同，合同标的是否符合质量要求的结论就可能不同。所以，参展商和采购商应在合同中约定明确的检验或验收条款，具体内容视标的物情况而有所区分，可包括检验时间、检验方法、检验机构、双方在检验过程中的权利义务、检验结果的通知等。

7. 在合同履行过程中如何组织合同标的的检验？

参展商和采购商应按合同检验条款的约定及时组织对合同标的的检验或验收，以确定合同标的是否质量相符。当发生质量问题，而合同未就检验作出约定时，双方应尽快协商确定检验机构，不能达成一致的，各方应及时委托相关专业领域内权威的第三方检验机构进行检验。

8. 参展商和采购商在合同中采用电汇方式支付货款时需要注意哪些事项?

电汇因具有手续简便、收汇快捷等特点,在国际贸易中被广泛采用。为有效控制交易双方在货款收付方面的风险,双方可根据合同履行的进程,结合合同标的的性质、价格条款、质量和检验条款等,确定合同签订、货物装运、货物接收、货物验收等不同时间节点的付款比例。

9. 选用信用证方式支付货款时不依约开立信用证会有什么样的法律后果?

参展商和采购商如选用信用证方式支付,采购商应按合同约定的时间和要求如期开立信用证,否则对方有权推迟交货,并将由采购商承担相应的违约责任或推迟交货可能带来的损失。如开立信用证有困难,需要更改开证时间等,采购商应及时和对方进行协商解决。

10. 参展商和采购商使用信用证支付时为什么要特别关注单证相符?

单证相符是卖方(参展商)获得信用证支付的前提条件,卖方应严格按信用证要求提供提单等单据,避免倒签提单或单据造假。如果因为装船时间的迟延或其他原因导致不能提供符合信用证要求的提单等单据,卖方应及时和对方联系,修改信用证要求。同时,单证相符也是银行议付的唯一条件,买方(采购商)如发现存在倒签提单、单据造假等情形,要及时通知银行或采取必要手段止付,以免单证不符给自己造成损失。

11. 使用国际贸易术语时应注意什么?

国际贸易术语在国际贸易合同中被广泛使用,不同的术语不仅涉及买卖双方在运输、保险、价格方面的权利义务,可能也会对合同标的的质量、验收等产生影响。参展商和采购商可在了解国际商会公布的《国际贸易术语解释通则》(Incoterms 2010)的基础上,结合合同标的的性质,选择适合的术语。如果不希望术语的使用影响到合同标的的质量或验收,应就质量或验收问题作出明确的特别约定。

12. 参展商与采购商如何在合同中约定违约责任,应特别注意哪些事项?

双方可以在合同中约定违约发生时违约方应支付违约金的具体数额,也可以约定违约赔偿的具体计算方法。没有对违约责任作出约定时守约方则须根据所适用法律的要求证明相关损失的存在。由于违约责任条款事关双方切身利益,参展商和采购商应按照公平合理原则协商确定违约责任条款,一方面避免约定不全面,只约定一方违约责任而忽略另一方的情况,另一方面也要注意违约责任的合理性,避免违约金或违约赔偿过高的情况。

13. 参展商和采购商在签订合同时能否自由约定合同适用的法律?

参展商和采购商在签订合同时,在不违反中国法律强制性要求的前提下,可以自由选择合同适用的法律,但涉及合同签订主体资格的问题仍应适用参展商或采购商注册登记地法律。双方可选择自己熟悉或符合国际惯例的法律,避免选择陌生的第三国法律,增加后续合同履行及争议解决的成本。

14.《联合国国际货物销售合同公约》(CISG)是否自动适用于参展商和采购商签订的合同?

中国是 CISG 成员国,如参展商的营业地亦处于 CISG 缔约国内,则 CISG 自动适用于参展商和采购商签订的国际货物买卖合同,除非双方当事人在合同中明确约定排除 CISG 的适用。在当事人选择适用中国法律的情况下,根据中国相关法律的规定,CISG 仍会优先适用,中国法律只有在 CISG 没有作出规定的情况下,如关于合同效力的认定等,才予以适用。

15. 参展商和采购商在签订合同中应如何选择有利的争议解决方式?

在合同中明确争议解决方式有利于交易风险的控制和实现双方对未来的预期,参展商和采购商可在综合考虑时间成本、纠纷解决费用、裁判结果的可执行性以及不同国家不同法域差异等因素的基础上,在合同中对争议解决方式作出明确约定。比较常见的约定是发生争议时应先通过友好协商解决,若无法通过友好协商解决,则在有强制执行力的诉讼或者仲裁中选择一种争议解决方式。

16. 参展商和采购商选择仲裁的方式解决纠纷具有哪些优势?

一般而言,当事人如选择了以仲裁方式解决相互之间的争议,则不可以再将争议提交诉讼解决。相比于诉讼,仲裁是更多使用的解决国际商事争议的方式。仲裁的优势主要在于:第一,充分尊重当事人意思自治。当事人享有选定仲裁员、仲裁地、仲裁语言以及适用法律的自由。第二,一裁终局。仲裁裁决一经作出即对双方当事人发生法律效力,一方不履行,另一方可向有管辖权的法院申请强制执行。第三,裁决的境外可执行性。仲裁裁决可以通过联合国《承认及执行外国仲裁裁决公约》在世界上 159 个国家和地区得到承认与执行。中国已于 1987 年加入该公约。第四,保密性。仲裁不公开进行,有利于保护当事人的商业秘密以及商业信誉。

17. 参展商和采购商应如何预防合同纠纷,减少纠纷带来的损失?

为减少合同纠纷的发生,推动纠纷的快速解决,参展商和采购商应注意合同履行过程中各种书面证据材料的留存,包括双方往来的函件、会议形成的纪要、传真或电子邮件等。

——https://www.ciie.org/zbh/gjmyht/

第八章 译后编辑

学习目标

- 了解机器翻译发展历史和技术更迭过程
- 知晓机器翻译的自动评价方法和人工评价方法
- 熟悉译后编辑的概念和类型以及会展文本译后编辑难点
- 掌握轻度译后编辑和深度译后编辑的原则

核心词汇

* 机器翻译（machine translation）
* 计算机辅助翻译（computer-aided translation）
* 自动语言处理咨询委员会（Automatic Language Processing Advisory Committee）
* 基于规则的机器翻译（rule-based machine translation）
* 基于转换的机器翻译（transfer-based machine translation）
* 中间语言机器翻译（interlingua machine translation）
* 基于实例的机器翻译（example-based machine translation）
* 基于统计的机器翻译（statistical machine translation）
* 神经网络机器翻译（neural machine translation）
* 自动评价（automatic evaluation）
* 人工评价（human evaluation）
* 质量评估（quality estimation）
* 单词错误率（word error rate）
* 位置无关的单词错误率（position-independent word error rate）
* 翻译错误率（translation error rate）
* 双语替换评测法（bilingual evaluation understudy）

* 明确排序的翻译评估指标(metric for evaluation of translation with explicit ordering)
* 可理解度(intelligibility)
* 忠实度(fidelity)
* 高级研究计划署(Advanced Research Project Agency)
* 充分性(adequacy)
* 流畅性(fluency)
* 可理解性(comprehension)
* 可懂度(comprehensibility)
* 译后编辑(post-editing)
* 轻度译后编辑(light post-editing)
* 深度译后编辑(full post-editing)
* 达到可理解水平的译后编辑(post-editing to understandable quality)
* 达到出版质量的译后编辑(post-editing to publishable level)
* 低可见度(low-visibility)
* 文化指涉项(cultural reference)

第一节　机器翻译的发展历史与技术更迭

所谓机器翻译(machine translation,简称MT),指的是使用计算机应用程序将一种自然语言(源语言)文本自动翻译成另一种自然语言(目标语言)文本的过程。人们常常将这一概念与"计算机辅助翻译""机辅翻译""机助翻译"(computer-aided translation,简称CAT)相混淆。主要差异在于实施主体的不同,前者是由计算机自动完成,无须人工参与,后三者以翻译人员为主体,计算机起辅助作用。

一、机器翻译的发展历史

机器翻译研究肇始于20世纪40年代,随后经历了五个阶段的漫长发展。

第一阶段:开创期(1946—1963)

早在1946年,美国人J. W. 莫奇利(J. W. Mauchly)和J. P. 埃克特(J. P. Eckert)就发明了世界上第一台电子计算机ENIAC(Electronic Numerical Integrator and Computer),为机器翻译的开展提供了必要的条件。1949年,美国科学家沃伦·韦弗(Warren Weaver)发表了一份以"Translation"为题的备忘录,提出了利用电子计算机实现自动翻译的想法,标志着机器翻译研究的开始。1954年,美国乔治敦大学与IBM公司合作用IBM-701计算机完成了世界上首次机器翻译实验,激起了世界范围内机器翻译的研究热潮。自此美、苏、英、日各国投入资金支持机器翻译研究项目,成功研发了首批实用的机器翻译系统,如欧洲原子能联营的俄英机器翻译等。我国机器翻译研究工作始于1956年,1959年成功研制出首个机器翻译系统,标志着中国成为第五个成功研发出机器翻译系统的国家。

第二个阶段:受挫期(1964—1975)

机器翻译的研究热潮并未持续太久。1964年,美国国家科学院设立了语言自动处理咨询委员会(Automatic Language Processing Advisory Committee,简称ALPAC),对机器翻译的性能进行了两年的调查分析,最后否认了机器翻译系统的发展潜力。自此,许多国家的机器翻译研发项目锐减,机器翻译研究进入了空前的萧条期。

第三阶段:恢复期(1976—1989)

尽管机器翻译研究受挫,但加拿大等欧洲国家依然坚持开展相关研究。与此同时,计算机硬件得到明显改善以及人工智能开始应用于自然语言处理领域,助推了机器翻译研究。1976年,加拿大蒙特利尔大学与加拿大政府翻译局联合研制成功机器翻译系统TAUM-METEO,该系统能够自动翻译天气预报文章,这标志着机器翻译研究开始复苏。

我国的机器翻译研究在20世纪中后期开始得到重视。1975年情报所、语言所等多家研究机构组成全国机器翻译协作研究组,测试了5000条冶金题录的英汉机器翻译方案。1987年中国人民解放军军事科学院开发的机器翻译系统"科译1号"问世,后来被商业开发成"译星"翻译软件。"译星"是我国第一个商业化的机器翻译系统,它的诞生有着特殊的历史意义。

第四阶段:快速发展期(1990—2013)

整个20世纪90年代,基于规则的机器翻译方法在理论上无法有所突破,在应用上受制于翻译质量而难以进步,反倒是基于翻译记忆技术的计算机辅助翻译迅速发展。20世纪90年代初,基于规则的方法不再占据主导地位,语料库技术和统计学习方法得到广泛应用。1990年在芬兰赫尔辛基召开的"第13届国际语言学大会"提出处理大规模真实文本的战略任务,即基于大规模语料库的统计自然语言处理,开启了机器翻译历史的新时期。

在中国,国家863计划专家组分别于1994年、1995年、1998年组织了三次全国机器翻译评测,在很大程度上促进了我国机器翻译研究的发展。2004年后,中科院计算所、中科院自动化所、厦门大学等单位开始从事统计机器翻译研究,并于2005年在厦门大学联合举办首次"全国统计机器翻译研讨会"。

第五阶段:蓬勃发展期(2014至今)

2014年,机器翻译迎来了巨大的变革。2014年,蒙特利尔大学的Kyunghyun Cho、约书亚·本古奥(Yoshua Bengio)等人发布了一篇关于在机器翻译中使用神经网络的论文,奠定了深度学习技术应用于机器翻译的基本架构。2015年,百度首次推出了神经网络机器翻译系统,使两种语言之间即使没有词典也能互相翻译理解第一次成为可能。2016年,谷歌神经网络机器翻译系统发布,其翻译质量已经接近人工翻译,标志着机器翻译进入神经网络机器翻译时期。

二、机器翻译的技术更迭

机器翻译的发展历史与其背后的技术更迭是密切联系在一起的。迄今为止,机器翻译经历了四次重大的技术革新,每次革新都促成了新一代机器翻译系统的诞生。

1. 基于规则的机器翻译(rule-based machine translation,简称 RBMT)

这一代机器翻译系统利用语言学规则和双语词典,对源语言文本的结构和语义进行分析,获得某种意义表示,然后将其转换为目标语言文本。根据分析、转换、生成模式的不同,可以将基于规则的机器翻译分为直接翻译(direct translation)、基于转换的机器翻译(transfer-based machine translation)和中间语言机器翻译(interlingua machine translation)。直接翻译法基本上不对源语言做分析,直接利用双语转换规则将源语言的单词翻译成目标语言;基于转换的机器翻译的完整过程可分为六个步骤:源语词法分析、源语句法分析、源语—目标语词汇转换、源语—目标语结构转换、目标语句法生成、目标语词法生成。中间语言机器翻译将中间语言作为独立源语言分析和独立目标语言生成的桥梁,真正实现独立分析和独立生成。

20 世纪 70 年代到 90 年代前,机器翻译采用的是基于语言规则的方法。这种方法的优势在于保留了原文结构,对符合词法、句法等语法规则的句子的处理能力较强,以至于很多语言学家认为,随着对自然语言语法规则的概括越全面、越深入和计算机的性能逐步增强,这种方法有望解决自然语言理解的问题。但实际上这类翻译系统的翻译质量并未如意料般地得到不断提升,而且由于规则编写成本高、维护成本高等劣势,基于语法规则的机器翻译方法最终走上了末路。

2. 基于实例的机器翻译(example-based machine translation,简称 EBMT)

20 世纪 80 年代,基于实例的方法的出现为陷入死寂的机器翻译研究带来了一丝希望。1984 年,日本京都大学的计算机科学家长尾真(Makoto Nagao)提出了"使用准备好的短语代替重复翻译"的想法(Nagao,1984),其核心理念是,利用计算机在对齐的双语实例库中查找与待翻译句子相似的实例,之后对实例的译文进行修改(替换、增加、删除、移位等),从而得到最终译文。这种方法的优势在于,它摆脱了对语言规则的极度依赖,但要求翻译实例库的规模要足够大,不然很难匹配到相似度高的句子,因此其实际可应用性并未如设想般理想。

3. 基于统计的机器翻译(statistical machine translation,简称 SMT)

这种方法的理念是,把翻译当作概率问题,利用平行语料库中学习到的概率模型,将源语言文本中的语言单位转换生成概率最高的配对译文,可分为基于单词的统计机器翻译、基于短语的统计机器翻译和基于句法的统计机器翻译。基于统计的机器翻译给出的译文都是基于数据统计和概率计算的,既不需要双语转换规则和双语对照词典,又不需要大规模的翻译实例库,较好地弥补了基于规则的机器翻译和基于实例的机器翻译的缺陷。

4. 神经网络机器翻译(neural machine translation,简称 NMT)

这种方法是通过利用计算机神经网络技术模仿人类大脑神经元进行语言翻译,主要采取"编码器—解码器"的运行模式,即由编码器把源语言句子编码成一个实数向量,解码器负责把该向量再重新解码成目标语言。神经网络机器翻译具有两大优点:直接从标注过的数据中学习翻译规律,规避了人工归纳翻译规律时的片面性;不同语言可以共用一个算法模型,极大减少了多语种翻译研究的工作量。然而,虽然该类翻译系统可以自动学习平行语料,理解句子细微的语言特征,但仍需要海量的语料,完全由人工智能自动控制,人工无法干预,一旦出现错误也难以纠正,只能通过深度学习正确的语料加以改善。

近 80 年来,机器翻译经历了四次重大的技术更迭,人工对机器翻译过程的干预程度不断降低,其翻译质量也有了显著的提升,甚至在某些专业领域已经替代了人工翻译,但若想全面达到乃至超越人工翻译的水平,依然任重道远。

第二节 机器翻译评价方法

机器翻译评价是根据某种评测规范或标准,对机器翻译生成的译文进行评分,以评估机器翻译系统性能的一种评测活动。《计算机科学技术名词》(第三版)将"机器翻译评价"定义为:人工或自动评价机器翻译系统译文质量的过程、技术和方法。一般而言,机器翻译评价方法大致分为自动评价和人工评价。

一、自动评价

自动评价(automatic evaluation)方法运用特定算法和程序自动评估机器译文质量,可进一步分为基于参考译文和不基于参考译文两种方式。其中,基于参考译文的自动评价指的是将机器译文与参考译文的近似程度作为评价结果,即译文与参考译文越接近,评价结果越好;反之,评价结果越差。无参考译文自动评价在机器翻译领域又被称为质量评估(quality estimation),旨在不参照参考译文的情况下对机器翻译系统产出的译文在单词、短语、句子、文档等层次上的翻译错误进行标记和统计,然后构建质量评估模型来评测其译文的整体质量。限于理论深度与难度,本节仅对基于参考译文的自动评价方法进行简要介绍。

(一)基于词串比对的评价方法

这种方法的基本思路是将译文看作字符序列,通过计算译文字符序列与参考译文字符序列的相似性来评价机器译文的质量。

1. 基于距离的方法

所谓"距离",指的是将一个字符序列转换成另一个序列所需的最少编辑操作次数。这种评价方法是通过计算机器译文改成参考译文所需的最小编辑量来评价机器译文质量。编辑量越小,距离越小,意味着机器译文越容易改写成参考译文,即机器译文的质量越好;相反,机器译文的质量越差。常用的计算方法主要有单词错误率(Word Error Rate)、位置无关的单词错误率(Position-Independent Word Error Rate)和翻译错误率(Translation Error Rate)。下面重点介绍翻译错误率计算方法。

翻译错误率计算公式:翻译错误率 = 编辑距离/参考译文字符长度(包括标点符号)

其中,翻译错误率所计算的编辑操作包括移位、增加、删除、替换四大类,这四类操作的次数被称为编辑距离,翻译错误率值的范围是 0~1,值越小,机译质量越好。

例1 Journalism became a subject in the twentieth century.(机器译文)

译文:Journalism became an academic subject early in the 20th century.

在实例中,将机器译文修改为参考译文,需要经过两次替换操作(将 a 替换成 an,将 twentieth 替换成 20th)和两次增加操作(增加 academic 和 early 两个单词),参考译文长度为 11 个字符,因此翻译错误率 = 4/11。

单词错误率、位置无关的单词错误率与翻译错误率的计算思路基本相同,唯一的区别在于,单词错误率所计算的编辑操作只包括增加、删除和替换,不包括移位,当机器译文出现词序调整情况时会把移位问题视作多次替换操作,因而会低估译文质量;而与位置无关的单词错误率只关注增加和删除两种操作,会计算机器译文与参考译文中出现相同单词的次数,把其他内容的改变视作插入词或删除词的操作,忽略词序错误,往往会高估译文质量。

2. 基于 n-gram 的方法

n-gram 是指文本中连续出现的 n 个字符或单词。基于 n-gram 的自动评价方法的代表是双语替换评测法(Bilingual Evaluation Understudy,简称 BLEU),其原理是比较机器译文和参考译文里的 n-gram 的重合程度,通常将 n 的范围设为 1~4,然后对所有重合的 n-gram 进行加权平均得到评测结果。双语替换评测值的范围为 0~1,数值越大,表示机器译文越接近参考译文。双语替换评测方法易于计算且速度快,评测精度较高,被广泛使用,但由于这种方法主要基于 n-gram 的重合程度,它不考虑语义、句子结构的准确性。

(二)基于词对齐的评价方法

基于词对齐的方法就是根据机器译文中的单词与参考译文中的单词之间的对齐关系对机译质量进行评价。此类方法中较为典型的方法是明确排序的翻译评估标准(Metric for Evaluation of Translation with Explicit Ordering,简称 METEOR)。明确排序的翻译评估标准的基本原理是先在机器译文的单词与参考译文的单词之间建立对齐关系,再根据其对应关系计算准确率(机器译文中命中单词数与机器译文单词总数的比值)和召回率(机器译文中命中单词数与参考译文总数的比值)。相比于双语替换评测法,明确排序的翻译评估标准引入了词干匹配和同义词匹配,扩大了词汇匹配的范围,而且由于召回率反映了参考译文覆盖机器译文的程度,明确排序的翻译评估标准评测结果与人工评价更为接近,但它需要借助同义词表、功能词表等外部数据,对汉语等与英语差异较大的语言的评价面临很多挑战。

在机器译文质量评价工作中,有参考答案的自动评价具有效率高、成本低的优点,但其可靠性、置信性及参考价值仍有待商榷。因此,当需要对机器译文的质量做出准确可信的评价时,往往采用人工评价的方式。

二、人工评价

顾名思义,人工评价(human evaluation)是指由人类专家依据一定的评价指标对机器译文进行评价。合理的评价指标或标准是人工评价得以顺利进行的保障。早在1966年,美国自动语言处理咨询委员会(Automatic Language Processing Advisory Committee,简称ALPAC)就提出将可理解度(intelligibility)和忠实度(fidelity)作为机器译文质量的人工评价标准。2006年,美国高级研究计划署(Advanced Research Project Agency,简称ARPA)将充分性(adequacy)、流畅性(fluency)和可理解性(comprehension)制定为机器译文评测标准,该标准被后续机器翻译竞赛采纳。充分性反映了对原文的忠实性,需要对比源语言文本的内容;流畅性指机器译文的句法和语法的正确性和流利程度,不需要参考原文内容;可理解性反映信息度,即机器翻译系统能否给用户提供充分有效和必要的信息。

依据中国国家语言文字工作委员会制定的《GF 2006——机器翻译系统评测规范》,对机器译文进行人工评测时,可以分别就忠实度(表8.1)和可懂度(表8.2)制定评测标准,也可以综合地采用可理解度进行评测(表8.3)。具体打分依据如下:

忠实度评测译文是否忠实地表达了原文的内容。按0~5分打分,打分可含一位小数。最后的得分是所有打分的算术平均值。

表8.1 人工评测的忠实度打分标准

分数	得分标准
0	完全没有译出来。
1	译文中只有个别单词与原文相符。
2	译文中有少数内容与原文相符。
3	译文基本传达了原文的信息。
4	译文表达了原文的绝大部分信息。
5	译文准确完整地表达了原文的信息。

可懂度(comprehensibility)评测译文是否流畅和地道,按0~5分打分,打分可含一位小数。最后的得分是所有打分的算术平均值。

表 8.2　人工评测的可懂度打分标准

分数	得分标准
0	完全不可理解。
1	译文晦涩难懂。
2	译文很不流畅。
3	译文基本流畅。
4	译文流畅但不够地道。
5	译文流畅而且地道。

综合地采用可理解度进行评测时按 0~5 分打分,可含一位小数,最后采用百分制换算评测结果。

表 8.3　人工评测的综合可理解度打分标准

分数	得分标准	译文可理解度
0	完全没有译出来。	0%
1	看了译文不知所云或者意思完全不对,只有小部分词语翻译正确。	20%
2	译文有一部分与原文的部分意思相符,或者全句没有翻译对,但是关键的词都孤立地翻译出来了,对人工编辑有点用处。	40%
3	译文大致表达了原文的意思,只与原文有局部的出入,一般情况下需要参照原文才能改正译文的错误。有时即使无须参照原文也能猜到译文的意思,但译文的不妥明显是翻译程序的缺陷造成的。	60%
4	译文传达了原文的信息,不用参照原文,就能明白译文的意思,但是部分译文在词形变化、词序、多义词选择、得体性等方面存在问题,需要修改。不过这种修改无须参照原文也能有把握地进行,修改起来比较容易。	80%
5	译文准确流畅地传达了原文的信息,语法结构正确,除个别错别字、小品词、单复数、地道性等小问题外,不存在很大的问题,只需对这些问题进行很小的修改,或者译文完全正确,无须修改。	100%

中国电子工业标准化技术协会制定的《信息技术、人工智能、机器翻译智能能力等级评估》(T/CESA 1039—2019)对上述评价模型进行了拓展和细化,提出了机器翻译译文质量和机器翻译系统功能的综合评价体系(表 8.4)。

表8.4 机器翻译译文质量和机器翻译系统功能综合评价体系表

一级指标	二级指标	指标项说明	评分方法	权重	说明
机器翻译译文质量	译文忠实度	翻译结果是否忠实表达了源语言的内容	—完全没有翻译出来,0分。 —译文中只有个别词被孤立地翻译出来,1分。 —译文中有少数短语或比词大的语法成分被翻译出来,2分。 —源语言中60%的概念及其之间的关系被正确翻译,或原文中的主谓宾及其关系被正确翻译,3分。 —源语言中80%的概念及其之间的关系被正确翻译,4分。 —源语言中100%的概念及其之间的关系被正确翻译,5分。	0.3	
	译文流畅度	翻译结果是否流畅和地道	—完全不可理解,0分。 —译文晦涩难懂(只有个别短语或比词大的语法成分可以理解),1分。 —译文40%的部分基本流畅(少数的短语或比词大的语法成分可以理解),2分。 —译文60%的部分基本流畅,3分。 —译文80%的部分基本流畅,或译文中的主谓宾部分基本流畅,只是个别词语或搭配不地道,4分。 —译文流畅而且地道,5分。	0.3	
	综合差错率	翻译结果与源语言内容的综合差错率	—译文综合差错率≥90%,0分。 —70%≤译文综合差错率<90%,1分。 —50%≤译文综合差错率<70%,2分。 —30%≤译文综合差错率<50%,3分。 —10%≤译文综合差错率<30%,4分。 —译文差错率≤10%,5分。	0.15	
	语用符合性	翻译结果是否符合目标语言的语用规则	—译文结果不符合,0分。 —译文结果符合,5分。	0.05	
	文化符合性	翻译结果是否符合目标语言的文化背景和观念	—译文结果不符合,0分。 —译文结果符合,5分。	0.05	
	情感符合性	翻译结果是否符合源语言表达的情感	—译文结果不符合,0分。 —译文结果符合,5分。	0.05	

续表

一级指标	二级指标	指标项说明	评分方法	权重	说明
机器翻译系统功能	多语言模态输入输出能力	是否支持文本以外的多种语言模态输入输出功能	—支持除文本以外的多种语言模态输入输出,包括但不限于语音、图像、视频、文档(网页、PDF)等,即翻译的源语言和目标语言可以通过语音、图像、视频、文档等形式输入和输出,其性能应满足评估对象所标称的性能值,每支持一种类型得1分,最高不超过5分。 —仅支持文本输入、输出,即翻译的源语言和目标语言仅能以文本的形式输入和输出,0分。	0.02	
	多语种翻译能力	是否支持多语种翻译	—支持两个以上语种之间的相互翻译,其翻译性能应满足评估对象所标称的性能值,5分。 —仅支持两个语种之间相互翻译,0分。	0.02	
	离线翻译	是否支持网络连接状态下的离线翻译	—支持无网络连接状态下的离线翻译,其翻译性能应满足评估对象所标称的性能值,5分。 —不支持无网络连接状态下的离线翻译,0分。	0.02	
	翻译模式	是否支持同传翻译模式	—支持评估对象所标称的同传翻译模式,其翻译性能应满足评估对象所标称的性能值,5分。 —不支持同传翻译模式,0分。	0.02	
	响应时间	是否在规定的时间内响应用户的翻译请求	—系统翻译引擎响应时间应符合附录B的要求,5分。 —系统翻译引擎响应时间不符合附录B的要求,0分。	0.02	

注:测评指标以反映机器翻译译文结果质量为主,侧重评价机器翻译系统的翻译能力,该部分指标权重占整体评价结果的90%;系统相关的功能测评指标占整体评价结果的10%。

此外,《机器翻译服务质量评价规范——中英双向》(T/CAQ XXXXX—2023)也制定了类似的机器译文人工评价标准(表8.5)和机器翻译错误分类(表8.6)。

表8.5 人工评价得分区间和评分标准

得分区间	标准
0~20	译文语义不明或完全错误,只有小部分字、短语正确且可读性极差,难以理解。
21~40	译文与原文极小部分语义相同但关键信息缺失或错误且可读性极差,大量不地道、不流利表达和语法错误。
41~60	译文能体现部分关键词义,但大量非关键语义错误且流利度、地道性欠佳。
61~80	译文基本能传达原文关键词义,但存在部分非关键信息错误,同时存在语法错误和非地道性表达。
81~100	译文可呈现原文词义,只存在少量非关键信息错误且表达较地道流畅。

表 8.6 机器译文错误分类

错误大类	错误子类
忠实度	术语/命名实体错误
	错译
	漏译(原文中内容在译文中未出现)
	过译
	未译(原文内容直接搬在译文中,未翻译)
流利度	语域/风格错误
	拼写错误
	标点错误
	语法错误
	晦涩拗口

人工评价可以准确反映机器译文的质量,是最权威、可信度最高的评价方法,但人工评价没有统一的标准。在实际应用中,研究人员可以根据实际情况选择不同的人工评价指标模型。

第三节 译后编辑的类型与原则

2014 年召开的第 20 届世界翻译大会以"人工翻译与机器翻译——翻译工作者与术语学家的未来"为议题,指出"机器翻译+译后编辑"已成为常见的翻译工作,预见到计算机辅助翻译走向云端,最终和机器翻译技术融合成为"机器翻译+翻译记忆"(MTM)或者"机器翻译+译后编辑"(PEMT)。2016 年美国卡门森斯咨询公司(Common Sense Advisory)发布的全球语言服务市场调研报告指出,"机器翻译+译后编辑"业务占全球语言服务行业市场的 3.94%,25.39% 的语言服务供应商提供这项服务,并认为该项服务发展前景良好。中国翻译协会最新发布的《2023 中国翻译及语言服务行业发展报告》显示,机器翻译技术的发展对当今的中国语言服务行业产生了重大影响。截至 2022 年年底,国内具有机器翻译与人工智能业务的企业达 588 家,相较于 2021 年实现了快速增长,年增长率为 113%,90.1% 的翻译及语言服务企业认为"机器翻译+译后编辑"模式提高了效率,其中有 24.2% 的受访企业认为"极大地提高了效率";有 65.9% 的受访企业认为"提高了一些效率"。该报告指出,"机器翻译+译后编辑"生产模式大幅提高了工作效率,使得传统翻译及语言服务行业焕发新生,增加了业务量与提升市场竞争力的空间。可见,"机器翻译+译后编辑"已经成为国内语言服务行业的新业态。

一、译后编辑的概念

译后编辑(post-editing)与机器翻译密切相关。依据国家标准《翻译服务:机器翻译结果的译后编辑——要求》(GB/T 40036—2021)的定义,机器翻译是"使用计算机应用程序将文本从一种自然语言自动翻译成另一种自然语言",而译后编辑是"编辑和更正机器翻译结果"。机器翻译研究学者丹尼尔·马库(Daniel Marcu)给出的定义更为详细:译后编辑是指语言专家对机器翻译输出进行编辑以生成人工质量翻译的过程。译后编辑是将机器翻译和高水准专业人工译后编辑人员相结合,以生成达到发布标准的高质量翻译的过程。(SDL,2013)崔启亮(2014)教授对于"译后编辑"的界定较为全面:他将上述编辑行为归为"狭义的译后编辑",把对翻译记忆、机器翻译、翻译管理系统等集成翻译环境下得到的译文进行译后编辑的行为称为"广义的译后编辑"。简言之,译后编辑是基于人机协作模式衍生出的翻译现象。作为语言服务行业积极采用的新的翻译实践方式,译后编辑正在逐渐改变人们对翻译实践活动的认识。

二、译后编辑的类型

依据不同的质量要求,译后编辑一般分为轻度译后编辑(light post-editing)和深度译后编辑(full post-editing)。轻度译后编辑又称"要旨翻译",根据国家标准(GB/T 40036—2021)的界定,轻度译后编辑适用于最终文本不用于发布而主要用于掌握文本核心信息的情况,其编辑结果应可理解并准确,但不要求风格适当。SDL 译后编辑官方培训手册中将其定义为"达到可理解水平的译后编辑"(post-editing to understandable quality),其目的是为用户提供解决问题的办法或(常见问题解答、博客、知识库等)低可见度(low-visibility)内容的译文。

深度译后编辑又称"达到出版质量的译后编辑"(post-editing to publishable level),其目的是产生与人工翻译结果相同的译文,要求编辑后的译文准确、可理解、风格适当,句法、语法和标点符号使用正确。

三、译后编辑的原则

国家标准"翻译服务:机器翻译结果的译后编辑——要求"(GB/T 40036—2021)从译后编辑人员角度给出了轻度译后编辑的原则:

① 尽可能多地使用原始机器翻译结果。
② 确保未添加或遗漏信息。
③ 修改任何不恰当的内容。
④ 在意思不正确或不清楚的情况下重组句子结构。

相比之下,SDL 译后编辑官方培训手册对于轻度译后编辑原则的总结更为具体:

① 重视意义的传达,不关注语法或风格方面的问题。

② 保持基本的行文风格,无须关注流畅度。
③ 保持基本的语域和语气,无须依据文本类型或目标读者进行改编。
④ 保证句子结构的可读性,无须保证拼写和语法正确无错。

此外,SDL 译后编辑官方培训手册指出,将机译文本编辑到可理解的水平,不能期望产出一个语法完全正确或语体风格完全规范的文本;只要不影响意义的传达,语法和拼写错误无须更正。

① 轻度译后编辑后文本中的操作指令必须是可执行的,不必保证其措辞完全妥帖地道。轻度译后编辑后的译文不应当是完美无缺的,而应当是可执行的。例如,将一篇知识库文章或常见问题帮助文档译后编辑成可理解的质量水平后,读者通过阅读该文档应当理解如何解决某个具体问题。
② 保证术语适用于当前语境,不使用用户特定术语。
③ 修订阻碍最终用户理解概念的严重术语错误。
④ 轻度编辑产出的文本应当是可理解的,不必做到语义连贯;轻度译后编辑人员无须检查语篇连贯性。
⑤ 保证信息准确,无须为了适应国内规范而进行本地化处理。
⑥ 不纠正标点符号错误用法。

对于深度译后编辑,国家标准"翻译服务:机器翻译结果的译后编辑——要求"(GB/T 40036—2021)给出的编辑原则是:

① 确保未添加或遗漏信息。
② 修改任何不恰当的内容。
③ 在意思不正确或不清楚的情况下重组句子结构。
④ 生成语法、句法和语义均正确的目标语言内容。
⑤ 遵循客户和/或领域专业术语规范。
⑥ 遵循拼写、标点符号和断字规则。
⑦ 确保使用适合文本类型的风格,并遵守客户提供的风格指南。
⑧ 遵循格式规则。

SDL 译后编辑官方培训手册给出的深度译后编辑的基本原则是:

① 译文应当准确传达原文本内容。
② 保证拼写和标点符号用法正确。
③ 保证译文句法和语法正确,并且符合目标语言的惯例。
④ 使用正确的术语,保证其一致性(包括针对高频出现的术语使用优选译文)。
⑤ 使用正确的文化指涉项(cultural reference)(如日期和时间格式、度量衡单位、数字格式、货币单位等)。
⑥ 保证译文的语体风格和语域与译文的文本类型相符合。
⑦ 再现原文本的格式。

⑧ 遵循项目风格指南。

⑨ 保证译文可读性强,适合于最终用户。

四、会展文本的译后编辑难点

"机器翻译+译后编辑"之所以能够取代纯人工翻译,成为当今语言服务行业的主流工作模式,是因为它最大限度地利用了机器翻译速度快、效率高的巨大优势。选择轻度译后编辑还是深度译后编辑,完全取决于产出文本的质量需求。然而,在译后编辑实践中,难点在于如何掌握好译后编辑的尺度。现在的一种普遍现象是,很多译后编辑人员混淆轻度译后编辑和深度译后编辑,无论客户对译文的质量有何种要求,他们都倾向于选择深度译后编辑,把机器译文改得"面目全非""体无完肤",希望用质量最好的译文留住客户,但这实际上取消了"机器翻译+译后编辑"模式在提高翻译效率方面的核心竞争力。此外,很多自身翻译水平较高的学习者容易将"纯人工翻译"的标准用于衡量深度译后编辑的译文,把不符合个人语言风格和措辞偏好的内容认定为必须修改的错误,甚至会把机器译文"推倒重来",这些都是不可取的做法。

对于会展文本的"机器翻译+译后编辑"而言,译后编辑人员除了要具备基本的翻译能力、语言能力、技术能力、文化能力之外,这必须熟悉各类会展文本的文体特点、功能和格式规范,具备相关术语知识和术语管理能力,尤其要了解轻度译后编辑和深度译后编辑的基本原则并加以实践。对会展文本进行译后编辑时,译后编辑人员依然要面临两方面的难题:一方面,进行轻度译后编辑时如何判断译文是否达到了可理解的水平以及进行深度译后编辑时如何判断译文是否达到了出版质量都必须依赖译后编辑人员的主观性评价;另一方面,无论是选择轻度译后编辑,还是选择深度译后编辑,译后编辑人员所要面临的首要挑战都是评价机器译文的质量,辨别出机器译文中出现的错误,确定哪些部分是值得保留的,然后依据轻度译后编辑或深度译后编辑的质量要求,以最恰当的方式将这些不正确的翻译改为正确的翻译。

 思考题

1. 简述机器翻译的应用场景。

2. 简述轻度译后编辑的应用场景。

3. 计算下列实例中的翻译错误率。

机器译文:The Huangpu River is the "Mother River" of Shanghai and one of the birthplaces of the national industry of China.

参考译文:The Huangpu River is not only the "Mother River" of Shanghai, but also a birthplace of the national industry of China.

4. 对下列 DeepL 的翻译结果分别进行轻度译后编辑和深度译后编辑。

第八章 译后编辑

原文	DeepL 翻译结果
技术装备展区秉承"引领创新发展，融合全产业链"的发展目标，以高端及智能装备为基础，重点围绕"双碳"、数字化、集成电路、人工智能等题材，融入"高端＋智能＋绿色"发展理念，设立工业、科技、环保三大板块。以先进技术为中心，引领行业创新趋势，集中展示前沿技术和高端装备，为全球制造业提供高端展示和交流平台。展期重点打造人工智能体验区和低碳高峰论坛。	Adhering to the development goal of "leading innovative development and integrating the whole industry chain", the Technology and Equipment Zone is based on high-end and intelligent equipment, focusing on topics such as "dual-carbon", digitization, integrated circuits and artificial intelligence, and incorporating the development concept of "high-end + intelligent + green". High-End + Intelligent + Green" development concept, the establishment of industrial, science and technology, environmental protection three plates. Centering on advanced technology and leading industry innovation trends, the exhibition will focus on displaying cutting-edge technology and high-end equipment, providing a high-end exhibition and communication platform for the global manufacturing industry. During the exhibition period, it will focus on creating an artificial intelligence experience zone and a low-carbon summit forum.
创新孵化专区以"跨越边界，孵化创新力量，引领未来科技"为主题，邀请全球创新企业、跨国企业内部孵化平台、创新孵化园区参展，帮助创新企业释放创新激情，与行业领袖交流碰撞，共同探索创新之道。	With the theme of "Crossing Boundaries, Incubating Innovative Power, Leading Future Technology", the Innovation Incubation Zone invites global innovative enterprises, internal incubation platforms of multinational enterprises and innovation incubation parks to participate in the exhibition, which will help the innovative enterprises to release their passion for innovation, communicate and collide with the industry leaders, and explore the way of innovation together.
服务贸易展区以数字化为轴，关注商业活动全生命周期，形成"绿色低碳、稳链强链、数智未来"三位一体的展区主题。展区致力于服务全行业数字化转型，深入打造为五大货物贸易展区输送智力支持与潜在客户的转换平台，持续为实体经济聚智赋能。	The Trade in Services Zone takes digitization as its axis, focuses on the whole life cycle of business activities, and forms the theme of "Green and Low Carbon, Stabilizing and Strengthening the Chain, and Digital Future". The zone is committed to serving the digital transformation of the whole industry, creating a conversion platform for the five major trade in goods zones to deliver intellectual support and potential customers, and continuing to gather wisdom and empowerment for the real economy.
医疗器械及医药保健展区以"健康中国，美好生活"为主题，把助力健康中国建设作为重中之重，聚焦全球医疗行业最新发展趋势和共性话题，紧贴广大人民群众对健康美好生活的向往，集中展示国际领先的医疗创新产品、尖端技术和服务。	With the theme of "Healthy China, Better Life", the Medical Devices and Pharmaceuticals & Healthcare Pavilion places top priority on helping the construction of a healthy China, focuses on the latest development trends and common topics in the global healthcare industry, and closely follows the aspirations of the general public for a healthy and better life, and centrally showcases the world's leading medical innovations, cutting-edge technologies and services.

The Ultimate Guide to Machine Translation Post-Editing (MTPE)

Ofer Tirosh

The founder and CEO of Tomedes, a language technology and translation company that supports business growth through a range of innovative localization strategies. He has been helping companies reach their global goals since 2007.

What Is Machine Translation Post-Editing?

Machine translation post-editing (or post editing or postediting, if you prefer) is when a human takes a machine translation (MT) and brings it up to scratch. MT post editing blends the skill and accuracy that the post editor brings to the task with the speed and convenience of using machine translation.

Done well, MTPE can result in high-quality translations that save businesses time and money compared with translations that are carried out in the usual way.

In simple terms, machine translation refers to the use of computer software to translate text (either written or spoken) from one language to another. In practice, creating a machine that translates with the nuance and finesse of a human translator has proven tricky.

Machine translation quality took a leap forward with the introduction of deep learning and neural networks from around 2014 onwards and it continues to improve today. It delivers impressive time savings, even with the need for MT post editing services factored in.

At Tomedes, our skilled post editors work hard to enhance the quality of machine translations. To do so, they focus on tone, flow, clarity and accuracy, as well as on grammar. They add their nuanced translation expertise to the work that the machine has undertaken.

Tomedes' MT post editors also take account of cultural sensitivities. Based around the globe, our post editors don't just deliver linguistic expertise but in-depth local knowledge. This is key to ensuring that translations don't offend local sensitivities.

Appropriate technical knowledge is also a must. Tomedes pairs its MT post editing specialists with work that matches their experience, so that they can apply the right terminology (I'll explore this in more detail below). It's all about blending state-of-the-art tech with highly skilled human input—this is the key to successful MTPE.

Why Can Translators Benefit from Embracing MTPE?

Machine translation can deliver substantial cost savings to businesses, so many are embracing it as a core part of their translation workflow. This means that translators have a choice between sticking with their traditional methods of translation or adding a new service to their repertoire: post editing of machine translation.

When it comes to embracing MTPE, the key benefit for translators is that it opens the door to more work. That includes more work from direct clients and through translation agencies that are looking to recruit post editors.

Working with a document that has been produced by a machine, to produce a hybrid translation, is a different kind of work than translating a source document from scratch. It's ideally suited to those who enjoy editing work as well as translation, as it blends the skills of both roles.

Translators who offer MT post editing services display to their clients that they are embracing technology and its benefits and that they are keeping one eye on the future of the language services industry.

How to Get Post Editing of Machine Translation Right—for Businesses

Does your business need to connect with people (whether customers, investors, manufacturers, suppliers or anyone else) on a regular basis in other languages? If so, then it's likely you've been tempted to use machine translation. It's also likely that you have been disappointed with the results if you did not use a post editor.

If you have taken the decision to use post editing machine translation services, then there are steps that you can take to drive up the quality of the resulting translation. These include everything from carefully choosing which machine translation engine and post editor you use, to preparing your document for translation in the right way. I will run through some machine translation post editing best practise tips now, to ensure that you have every chance of success when it comes to your business translations.

Choose Your Machine Translation Engine

Let's start with how to choose your machine translation engine. This decision can make a major difference to the quality of the translations that you receive. Using a machine translation engine that delivers high-quality results can lead to a significant reduction in the amount of time that your post-editor will need to work with your translation. As such, it can be worth looking at premium machine translation engines as well as free software, as the investment can pay off through a reduction in MT post editing hours.

The machine translation engine that is right for your business will also depend on which language you need to translate. Some MT engines deliver better results with European languages, for example, while others specialise in Asian languages. It's a question of finding the right machine translation engine to meet your needs, just as you will need the right post editor.

As a general rule of thumb, neural machine translation engines will outperform statistical and rules-based translation engines, though results will vary depending on the content of your translation as well as the languages. DeepL, NMT Systran and Modernmt could all be of interest to you if you are working with languages such as English, French, German, Italian, Portuguese or Spanish. Tencent or Baidu might be a better choice, however, if you're working with Chinese.

Regardless of which language you need, be sure to research your machine translation options well. The tech side of the languages industry is improving fast, so there may be new entrants into the marketplace that can help you, or more established machine translation tools that have improved their abilities with different languages since I wrote this.

Appoint Your Post Editor

Just as you put care into choosing the best machine translation engine for your business, the quest to find the perfect MT post editor is also deserving of your time and attention. Several factors come into play here. First, clearly, you will need a translator who has experience of providing machine translation post editing. But that's not all …

Your post editor will also need to be a fluent speaker of both your source and target languages—preferably a native speaker of the target tongue. They will also need to have experience of working in your particular sector. Whether you manufacture medical devices, provide financial services or anything else, your translator will need to be familiar with the terminology that people in your industry and in your business frequently use.

You have a couple of options open to you here. You can work through a translation agency or seek to engage a post editor directly. In either case, ensure that the individual who will be providing post editing machine translation services is suitably experienced. And if you plan to use a translation management system, now is the time to discuss that with your potential post editor, to ensure they are experienced/comfortable with it.

Agree Your Machine Translation Post Editing Guidelines

If you have chosen a neural machine translation tool, you should have the option to feed data into it before the translation work begins. This means you can furnish it with glossaries and translation memories that relate to the terminology used in your industry.

Doing so should enhance the results of the translation process.

Likewise, it is helpful to furnish your post editor with all of the relevant linguistic information prior to them beginning their MT post editing work. Your post editor will also need to know about any elements of the document that you do not want to be translated: company strap lines, product names or anything else that you want to keep in the original language.

A discussion with your post editor on how any queries should be handled, in addition to the above-mentioned machine translation post editing guidelines, is also useful at this stage, as it can save time once the post edit begins.

Prepare Your Document for Translation

Another way to achieve successful results when using MTPE is to engage in a post of pre-editing. This is where you get your document ready for translation. Key to this is checking it for any errors. After all, the machine will not be able to pick up on them. It only has the chance to compound them and create confusion. The same goes for any content that is ambiguous.

It's also well worth running some sample copy through your machine translation engine. Doing so will give you an idea of the kind of results you can achieve and whether the document you are working with is suited to this type of translation or not. I will expand on the kinds of documents that are not suitable for MTPE in a moment.

Post Postediting Editing

Finally, remember that the process does not end after the post editor finishes their first pass of the document. There will be an element of back and forth required after the MT post editing process takes place, a kind of "post postediting editing" if you will.

This final element of the post editing translation process can reasonably be expected to take less time once the machine translation engine and editor are both more familiar with your terminology. However, it is always worth monitoring how long each element of the MTPE process takes, so that you can assess its efficiency. For more on quality assessment of machine translation, you can click the link below.

Machine Translation Post Editing Guidelines for Translators

Successful post editing of machine translation involves the translator working closely with the client. This relates to many of the points I've included above—terminology, queries and so on—and also to the kind of MTPE service being provided.

There is more than one way that post editors can approach this kind of hybrid translation work. Some of the most common MT post editing strategies that translators

can use include:
- Light post editing—this involves making as few edits as possible while still ensuring the clarity and legibility of the text. It's a cost-effective approach to MT post editing that delivers speedy results.
- Full post editing—as the name suggests, this approach involves a thorough post edit, with the post editor working on everything from style and tone to cultural sensitivities. This will result in a higher quality document than light post editing, so is ideal for customer-facing documents.
- Project-specific post editing—some translation projects will include a range of documents, some of which will require a heavier edit than others. In these instances, it can be helpful to devise a strategy that focuses post editing work appropriately on the documents that need the most attention.

Note that the kind of strategy the MT post editor uses will impact how long the task takes to complete. This has clear implications for the client's budget and so must be discussed with the client prior to the post editing taking place.

When Not to Use MTPE

Just before I wrap this up, I wanted to add a quick word about when not to use post editing of machine translation. While MTPE is suitable for the majority of translations, if the best practice tips above regarding preparing documents and choosing the right MT engine are followed, it may not be best for more creative types of translation—or rather, for transcreation.

Transcreation is a creative type of translation that marketing translators may use when preparing documents for foreign audiences. Doing so can involve creative design work and a great deal of local adaptation, as well as translation. In these instances, it may be better to avoid using machine translation with a post edit and instead opt for using a marketing translation professional to undertake the entire job. As ever, it will depend on the document in question and the company it's for—I'm just adding this in by way of a final thought.

MTPE can save businesses a great deal of time and money but it's important to get it right. Hopefully the advice above should help with that. And if you're inspired to learn more about machine translation and its role in helping businesses connect with the world, why not check out my thoughts on the top machine translation trends for 2022?

参考文献及重要会展网站

参考文献

Hatim, B. & Mason, I. *Discourse and the Translator* [M]. London / New York: Longman, 1990.

Joos, M. The five clocks [J]. *International Journal of American Linguistics*, 1962(5): 28–41.

Munday, J. *Introducing Translation Studies: Theories and Applications* [M]. London: Routledge, 2001.

Nagao, M. A framework of a mechanical translation between Japanese and English by Analogy Principle. In A. Elithorn and R. Banerji (eds), *Artificial and Human Intelligence*. Amsterdam: North-Holland, 1984: 173–180.

Newmark, P. *Approaches to Translation* [M]. London: Prentice Hall, 1988a.

Newmark, P. *A Textbook of Translation* [M]. London: Prentice Hall, 1988b.

Reiss, K. Text types, translation types and translation assessment [A]. In Chesterman, A. (ed.), *Readings in Translation Theory* [C]. Helsinki: Oy Finn Lextura Ab, 1977/1989: 105–115.

Shevlin, C. *Writing for Business* [M]. London: Penguin Books Ltd., 2005.

北京2008年奥林匹克运动会申办委员会.北京2008年奥林匹克运动会申办报告(中英文版).北京:奥林匹克出版社,2001.

崔启亮.论机器翻译的译后编辑[J].中国翻译,2014(6):68–73.

冯全功,刘明.译后编辑能力三维模型构建[J].外语界,2018(3):55–61.

高飞雁.从功能翻译理论看汉语会展文本英译[J].广西教育学院学报,2014(6):67–70.

全国语言与术语标准化技术委员会.翻译服务 机器翻译结果的译后编辑 要求GB/T 40036—2021[S].北京:中国标准出版社,2021.

何刚强.会展、仪式横幅名称英译刍议[J].上海翻译,2008(3):25–28.

黄忠廉.变译理论[M].北京:中国对外翻译出版公司,2001.

孔飞燕.英义会展规章与合同的规定性语言特征[J].新余高专学报,2010(6):51–54.

李静,朱献珑.基于文本类型学的英语专业人才会展文案翻译能力培养[J].常州工学院学报(社科版),2016(6):75–79.

李燕华. 会展英语翻译技巧与教学实践研究[M]. 西安:世界图书出版公司,2018.
马国志. 国际会展文本的功能及翻译[J]. 海外英语,2019(19):147-148,175.
SDL. 塑造内容翻译的未来:机器翻译和译后编辑简介[EB/OL]. (2013-03-29). http:www.sdl.com/cn/download/shaping-the-future-of-content-translation-an-introduction-to-machine-translation-and-postediting/25205.
滕超. 会展翻译研究与实践[M]. 杭州:浙江大学出版社,2012.
滕超,孔飞燕. 英汉法律互译:理论与实践[M]. 杭州:浙江大学出版社,2008.
万丽,倪筱燕. 语域论视域下的国际商务合同翻译[J]. 企业经济,2012(11):71-74.
王华树. 翻译技术研究[M]. 北京:外语教学与研究出版社,2023.
王平辉. 会展文案写作:规范与范例[M]. 南宁:广西人民出版社,2008.
向国敏. 会展文案写作与评改[M]. 上海:华东师大出版社,2008.
肖桐,朱靖波. 机器翻译:基础与模型[M]. 北京:电子工业出版社,2021.
杨艳霞,魏向清. 基于认知范畴观的机器翻译译后编辑能力解构与培养研究[J]. 外语教学,2023(1):90-96.
俞华,朱立文. 会展学原理[M]. 北京:机械工业出版社,2005.
张美芳. 文本类型、翻译目的及翻译策略[J]. 上海翻译,2013(4):5-10.
张霄军,贺莺. 翻译的技术转向——第20届世界翻译大会侧记[J]. 中国翻译,2014(6):74-77.
张新红. 汉语立法语篇的言语行为分析[J]. 现代外语,2000(3):283-295.
赵璧. 翻译技术基础教程[M]. 上海:上海外语教育出版社,2023.
周勇祥. 英汉致辞的语言对比分析与翻译实践[J]. 上海理工大学学报(社会科学版),2013,35(3):208-212.

重要会展网站

https://aipc.org/

https://cn.wicinternet.org/

https://exhibitions.org.hk/

https://library.olympics.com/

https://olympics.com/en

https://olympics.com/en/olympic-games/beijing-2008

https://olympics.com/ioc/theme-paris-2024

https://olympics.com/ioc/theme-tokyo-2020

http://www.battery-expo.com/

https://www.bie-paris.org/site/en/

https://www.boaoforum.org/

http://www.caec.org.cn/

https://www.cantonfair.org.cn/

https://www.ccpit.org/

https://www.chtf.com/

http://www.ciec-expo.com.cn/

https://www.ciie.org/zbh/index.html

https://www.ciif-expo.com/

https://www.cnexpo.com/

https://www.iaee.com/

https://www.iapco.org/

http://www.iccaworld.org/

https://www.tubechina.net/Tube China

https://www.ufi.org/

https://www.yiwufair.com/

http://www.zjceia.com/index.html

参考答案

第一章

1. "会展"概念的内涵是指在一定地域空间,许多人聚集在一起形成的定期或不定期、制度或非制度地传递和交流信息的群众性社会活动;外延包括各种类型的博览会、展览展销活动、大型会议、体育竞技运动、文化活动、节庆活动等。

2. 优势:G20峰会的成功举办、良好的自然环境和人文环境、优越的地理位置及便利的交通、政府政策的大力支持;劣势:专业人才缺乏,培养机构不足,会展行业组织管理体制不完善,品牌化展会不多,国际影响力不够,区域之间合作相对较少。

第二章

1. 语义翻译是指译者在语义规则和句法结构允许的前提下,把表达内容限制在原文文化范围内,不改变原文中富有民族文化色彩的概念,力图保留原作者的语言特色和独特的表达方式,试着再现原文的美学价值。这种翻译在结构和词序安排上更接近原文,尽可能准确地再现原文的上下文意义。它以原文为依归,倾向于以源语为中心,集逐字翻译、直译和忠实翻译的优势为一体,力求保留源语文本的语言特点和表达方式,因而译文与原文的形式和风格更为接近。因此,这种翻译通常适用于文学、科技文献和其他视原文语言与内容同等重要的语篇体裁。

从理论上讲,语义翻译为了表现原作的思维过程,力求保持原作的语言特色和独特的表达方式,增强了语言的表达功能。语义翻译比较客观,讲究准确性,屈从源语文化和原作者,翻译原文的语义,只在原文的内涵意义构成理解的最大障碍时才加以解释。但是,语义翻译也不能忽视向读者传达信息,因此原文如果不是现代作品,也要用现代语言来翻译,以使译文更接近读者。

总之,语义翻译注重对原作的忠实,处理方法带有直译的性质,而交际翻译则强调译文应符合译入语的语言习惯,处理方法带有意译的性质。二者又不是截然分开的,语义翻译和交际翻译的区别是相对的,在一部作品的翻译过程中,往往语义翻译和交际翻译相辅相成、互为补充。两种翻译方法都建立在认识性翻译的基础上,都必须反映原文的思想内容,都必须服从译入语的语法结构和某些固定的文体特征。

2. (1)信息型,交际翻译;(2)表达型,语义翻译;(3)呼唤型,交际翻译;(4)信息型,交际翻译;(5)信息型,交际翻译。

3. 分析:这是一家企业宣传资料中的一段文字,语言夸张渲染、气势豪迈,是中文宣传文本中烙有民族文化思维特征的文字运用。从汉语文字运用角度看,原文似乎很"美",但从对外宣传效度看,若按照汉语的语言文字和行文结构翻译,势必造成文字臃肿、句子堆砌,一大堆过度渲染的夸张的文字掩盖了宣传的信息意图,国外读者会质疑使用这样极度夸张渲染文字的企业宣传的可信度;再者,对外宣传文字要求应尽量运用实事求是的客观性语言,文字应简洁明快,即简洁美。从信息传递角度看,上述文字能让国外读者感兴趣的或能说明该企业特色的内容主要有6项:(1)成立时间;(2)能抓住商机求发展;(3)精益求精;(4)汇集世界顶尖生产技术装备;(5)引领服装潮流;(6)产品质量高。综上所述,译文2比译文1

更简洁直观,更符合目标语读者的阅读习惯,呼唤功能也就实现得更强烈。

译文1：Founded in the late 1980's and striving for ceaseless development, the Hubao Group has achieved great successes in the fashion-manufacturing sector. It is outstanding for being well-equipped with the world's most advanced technologies and is renowned for its maintenance of a high-standard quality system. It is now taking the lead in fashion designs and enjoys a good market share with quality products. The Hubao people have been keeping updating their products with their diligence and intelligence.

译文2：Founded in the late 1980's, the Hubao Group has now well developed into a leading enterprise in garment-fashion manufacturing by its great efforts for continuous progress. Enhanced by the most advanced technologies and its ceaseless technical innovation, it is now taking the lead in the world fashion designs for its good quality productions.

第三章

1. (略)

2.

(1) Beijing "Two Zones" International Cooperation and Investment Beijing Summit Enterprises Supply and Demand Matchmaking Event

(2) China International Import Expo Signing Ceremony

(3) Australian National Field Days

(4) The "Samaranch Cup" International Snow-Themed Contest Online Launching Ceremony

(5) Jiangsu-RCEP Online Matching Meeting

(6) Dalian Science and Technology Finance Docking Conference

(7) 韩国渔具钓具展览会

(8) 德国科隆国际促销产品贸易博览会

(9) 马来西亚吉隆坡特许经营展览会

(10) 荷兰广播电视影视及摄影设备展览会

3.

(1) 中国国际中小企业博览会(简称"中博会")于2004年10月18日—22日在广州花城会议展览中心举行,设1860个展位,有来自中国大陆与港澳地区30个贸易代表团共1950家中小企业参展,吸引11.8万人次(其中包括4.6万名国内买家和5600名国际买家)到场参观、洽谈、采购,达成意向总金额320亿元。

(2) 因在长途运输途中展品会被承运各方频繁装卸,并且会被多次置于露天场所或展览中心的露天仓库,所以包装箱应坚固耐用,以避免损坏或雨淋,尤其必须适用于展览会结束后重新包装和回运。

(3) 如果单件展品重量超过1000千克,请在箱子外面注明重心点、前面和后面、吊点。对于所有易碎和不能倒立的展品,也必须在箱外清楚注明。其他唛头必须适用于国际惯例和包装符号。

(4) 为安全起见,所有展场内接驳总电源之电力装置必须由大会指定承建商执行。如要求的电力超出租用表中列出的范围,参展商须于截止日期前直接联系大会指定承建商以作安排。

(5) 个别展台获照明及电力供应之前,若参展商需要电力作测试之用,须与大会指定承建商联络,以便提早安排,该服务将收取额外费用,并视乎技术上是否可行方可落实。

(6) 100% surcharge of inbound movement and outbound movement charges for handling of dangerous,

refrigerated or high-value cargo will be levied.

(7) Upon requirement, exhibits' bandage, fixing, and pad cushion in container (including dry container, flat rack and open top), the charges will be as per outlay.

(8) All exhibits, materials and fittings used or displayed in the stand must be properly fireproofed and be in accordance with all applicable fire prevention and building regulations.

(9) Exhibitors must make their own arrangements for removal of their packing materials, cartons, boxes, crates, construction debris, etc. and be responsible for any expenses incurred.

(10) Please note that all the electric power listed in the order form can NOT be combined as one to use. For example, 300 Amp power main * 2 nos ≠ 600 Amp.

4. (1)

INTRODUCTION OF THE VENUE

National Exhibition and Convention Center (Shanghai) is the world's largest convention and exhibition complex with a total construction area of more than 1.5 million m^2. Facilities at NECC (Shanghai) include exhibition halls, the conference center, the commercial plaza, office buildings and a high-end hotel, integrating functions of exhibition, conference, activity, business, office and hotel.

1.5 km away from Hongqiao Transportation Hub, NECC (Shanghai) is linked to Hongqiao Airport and Hongqiao Railway Station by the city's metro line. Because of the convenient national expressway network, the major cities in the Yangtze River Delta region are easily accessed within 2 hours.

• Exhibition Hall: The area available to exhibitions at NECC (Shanghai) is nearly 600,000 m^2, including 500,000 m^2 of indoor exhibition hall and 100,000 m^2 outdoor area in North Square, which are all accessible to trucks.

• Convention Center: NECC (Shanghai) has witnessed the opening ceremony of the CIIE as well as the Hongqiao International Economic Forum. A total of 78 conference rooms of different sizes together with a conference area of 56,000 m^2 constitute a facility "community" for international modern conferences.

---

(2)

---

9. Exhibitor's Badges

9.1 The Exhibitor shall only be granted three exhibition badges for free after full participation payment has been made. Request of the Exhibitor for any extra badges shall be settled according to the *Exhibitors Manual of the Import and Export Fair*.

10. Stand Setting-Up

10.1 Only if the Exhibitor, prior to entering the Exhibition Area for setting up stands during the preparation period, present to the managing staff at site of the Organizer the customs clearance of all exhibits or other original documents such as ATA Certificate and submit relevant copies, can enter Exhibition Area.

In case relevant documents are failed to be submitted, the Organizer reserves the right to reject the Exhibitor from entering the Exhibition Area, and the loss caused therefrom shall be borne by the Exhibitor.

10.2　All premium stands shall be set up by the contractor nominated by the Organizer. Raw space shall be set up by the Exhibitor's entrusted contractor recommended by the Organizer or the Exhibitor's own contractor accredited by the Organizer.

10.3　In case of entrusting any company to set up his stand, the Exhibitor shall then be responsible for the design, setting-up and relevant safety and fireproofing of such activities. The Exhibitor shall furthermore guarantee that all constructional work to be strictly complying with the operational and technical requirements stipulated in the *Exhibitors Manual of the Import and Export Fair* and relevant governmental laws and regulations.

5.

Item 1　Standard Stands

The Canton Fair provides standard stand packages.

Basic Furnishings

Including (as is shown in the picture):

Panels for walls on three sides

1 Fascia Board/Header

1 Carpet

4 Spotlights

1 Fluorescent Light

1 Table

4 Chairs

1 Box of Mineral Water (Note: 24 bottles per box. Quality Supervision Telephone of SQC mineral water: 0086 - 20 - 86676702)

1 Telephone

Stand Dimensions

Size: 2,970 mm * 2,970 mm

Height of Panels: 2,500 mm

Height at the nadir of fascia board: 2,200 mm

Construction Specifications

(1) The spotlights and the fluorescent light will be installed as indicated in the above picture.

(2) For corner stands, panels will only be set up on two sides while the other two sides are open to aisles.

第四章

1. (略)

2. 信息型文本一般采用交际翻译策略(欠额翻译),表达型文本采用的多为语义翻译策略(超额翻译),而呼唤型文本采用的翻译策略是交际翻译,常用的翻译方法是等效再创作。

3. (1) Beijing, with its ancient past, dynamic present and exciting future, has the honour to deliver its

second bid to host the Olympic and Paralympic Games.

（2）Besides, relevant ministries and commissions under the State Council together with the Shanghai Municipal Government have signed guarantees in support of the Expo.

（3）To establish a coordination mechanism among the BIE, the Organizer and participating countries.

（4）The Chinese Government encourages competition and liberalization. This has already resulted in better customer service, lower prices and more advanced networks and facilities.

（5）A reasonable and fair proportion of seats will be allocated for public audience in as many events as possible.

4. 翻译以下段落。

（1）主餐厅位于电影城（220 m×24 m）正厅，紧连着露天平台。正厅高度达18m，目前已经完成翻修，充分彰显了其工业时代的特色。主餐厅内可容纳就餐人数5000人，离奥运村东侧的运动员交通中心仅有150米的距离。

（2）戴高乐机场开通了直飞全球319个城市的航线，旅客吞吐量位居全球前十。机场距离主媒体中心12千米，距奥林匹克村和残奥村不到20千米。到2024年，登机口数量将从226个增加到259个，机场容量提升19%。除了现有的郊区快铁B线，日后还可乘坐地铁17号线以及戴高乐机场快线抵达机场。值得一提的是，戴高乐机场快线是机场直达专线，从市中心到机场在20分钟之内。

（3）场馆规划理念：无限精彩

2020年东京奥运会和残奥会场馆规划主要由两个主题和运营区组成："遗产区"包括1964年东京奥运会的标志性场馆，并进一步继承1964年东京奥运会的悠久遗产；"东京湾区"是创新城市发展的典范，象征着这座城市激动人心的未来。

（4）严管街头贩卖行为

《道路交通法》对街头贩卖商贩进行严格管理，奥运会期间也将采取相应措施，确保其依法接受管控。

严管门票转售

东京奥组委将按照国际奥委会的规定，实施官方门票转售方案，并将严禁官方渠道外的门票转售行为。

根据各地政府的条例，严禁在公共场所向民众转售门票。

（5）除东京以外，参与本次奥运会的其他地方政府也将通过类似条例严格规范广告投放区域。

东京奥组委将在奥运会开幕前夕和比赛期间密切关注户外、公共交通、机场和其他地区的广告投放情况。如有违规情况，东京奥组委将即刻发布禁令，以维护赞助商和特许商的合法权益。

第五章

1.（略）

2.（略）

3.（1）

Section Ⅰ Project Introduction

1. Summary for the Investigation Information

（1）Explanation of the Evaluation Module

There are 3 modules concerning satisfaction and effects assessment: satisfaction rate and effects assessment, special investigation (the satisfaction of forum and activities, satisfaction investigation on Release of New Products & Technologies) and popularity index statistics.

(2) Implementation Introduction

We planned to finish 2,600 samples; however, we did 2,836 copies, of which, 2,719 copies are valid, with the availability to 95.87%.

2. Major Analysis Methods

There are 5 methods concerning satisfaction and effects assessment: comparative analysis, frequency analysis, single factor analysis of variance, improvement priority index analysis and structural equation modeling.

3. Questionnaire Reliability Explanation

According to the evaluation statistics, we can get respectively that the questionnaire reliability of exhibitors is 0.967, of visitors is 0.912, of investors is 0.730, of forum and activities is 0.884, of Release of New Products & Technologies is 0.887, all of which indicate that the evaluation result is quite reliable.

(2)

Exhibition Effect Evaluation of IT, Energy Saving Exhibition and New Energy Exhibition

Because this survey is from the perspective of exhibition business, among which indices are independently designed, there is no direct comparison meaning with overall satisfaction rate.

(1) Exhibitors' Satisfaction Rate

As for the exhibitor's satisfaction rate, the IT exhibition exhibitors is 95.82%, Energy Saving Exhibition and New Energy Exhibition exhibitors is 96.05%. As for the various indicators of satisfaction rate, the exhibition service of IT is the highest, accounting for 98.91%; Energy Saving Exhibition and New Energy Exhibition's influence towards the industry is the highest, accounting for 99.25%. For details, see Figure 21 below.

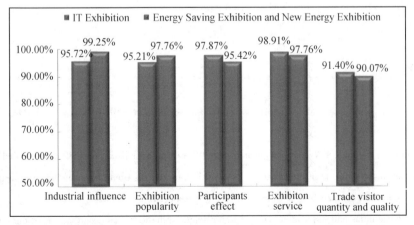

Figure 21 Evaluation of Exhibitor Index of IT, Energy Saving Exhibition and New Energy Exhibition

（3）

> 相较于往届冬季奥林匹克运动会,北京奥运会通过电视直播及数字媒体报道,为世界各地粉丝播报的时间更长。
>
> 奥运会官方媒体及持权转播商的线上参与人数达到数十亿次,此届冬奥会也成了数字化程度最高的一届。
>
> 总的来看,2022北京冬奥会吸引全球观众约20亿人次;电视直播及数媒播放总时长高达120亿小时,平均每名观众观看5.9小时。
>
> 其中,数媒观看及消费增速迅猛,线上观看人数较2018平昌冬奥会增加了123.5%;但电视直播占全球播放总量的92%,仍居于主导地位。

第六章

1.（略）

2.（1）

Distinguished Guests,

Dear Friends,

"All good principles should adapt to changing times to remain relevant." While the Internet is invisible, Internet users are visible. The Internet is the common home of mankind. Making it better, cleaner and safer is the common responsibility of the international community. Let us work hand in hand to promote an interconnected cyberspace shared and governed by all, and make contribution to a better future for the progress of all mankind. In conclusion, I wish the conference a complete success.

（2）

在庆祝奥运会圆满成功之际,让我们一起祝福才华横溢的残奥会运动健儿们,希望他们在即将到来的残奥会上取得优异的成绩。今晚在场的每位运动员们,你们是真正的楷模。你们充分展示了体育的凝聚力。来自冲突国家竞技对手之间的热情拥抱闪耀着奥林匹克精神的光辉。希望你们回国后让这种精神生生不息,世代永存。这是一届真正的无与伦比的奥运会!

3.（略）

第七章

1.（略）

2.

（1）No participant may make alterations within the exposition grounds without the Organizer's prior approval.

（2）Otherwise, the request of the party which raised the dispute shall be considered unjustified.

（3）Subject to the approval of the Organizer, the exhibitors may distribute free samples of their products, or allow their foodstuffs to be tasted free of charge within their respective sections.

（4）Only those items and Exposition material which relate to the theme as described in Article 1 herein shall be admitted to the Exposition. The origin of these products shall comply with the provisions of Article 19 of the Convention.

（5）A section may organize a restaurant and refreshment services for the exclusive use of its own personnel.

Such activities shall not require the payment of any dues to the Organizer.

（6）在这一权力范围内,主办方有权推迟或阻止任何活动,有权撤掉与展会的正常展示相矛盾或可能成为危险隐患的物品,不管该物品来源于何处。

（7）参展者有权在世博会结束时出售自己的展品和用于安装展示的材料,在本区域中使用的其他物品也可出售。

（8）如果组织者授予特定供应商销售商品或服务的排他性商业权利,上述权利不得妨碍官方参展者的商业活动,不管上述商业活动是指餐馆营业还是指国家展区内物品的销售。

（9）尽管有对上述《特殊规章》的批准时间表,组织者仍应提早为估算参展费用提供必要的成本指南或规定。

（10）如果参展者不能履行对组织者的承诺,主办方可以在会展闭幕之日对展会场馆之内属于该参展者的物品进行拆除、转移、储存或出售,被认为具有国家传统或公共财产性质的物品除外。一切成本和风险皆由参展者自行承担。主办方应得的部分从上述销售所得中扣除。

3.

（1）In case of discrepancy between the English and French versions of the Candidature File, the English version shall prevail.

（2）If, however, such space has not been fully disposed 24 months before the opening of the Exposition, the Organiser may recover the right to dispose freely of the unreserved space.

（3）If the Participant fails to fulfil the above obligation the Commissioner General of the Exposition shall be authorized to exercise the Organiser's rights, under the terms of Article 18 of the General Regulations.

（4）Participants shall be authorized to use the Symbols of the Exposition solely for non-commercial purposes directly related to the Exposition after having concluded the Participation Contract with the Organizer. This right of use is not transferable.

（5）Subscription to any insurance against theft deterioration or destruction of such goods, including buildings, furnishings, equipment, personal property and other similar items, shall be the sole responsibility of their owner.

（6）Complimentary entrance cards for exhibitors with standing invitations or invitations for a limited period or for concessionaires and employees' service cards shall be issued in accordance with the conditions laid down in the Special Regulation No. 13 mentioned above.

第八章

1. 翻译自动化用户协会（TAUS）分析了专业翻译项目使用机器翻译的四种应用场景:(1) 时间较紧的内容。(2) 译文质量要求不高的内容(如在线商店展示的产品信息)。(3) 需要人工译后编辑的翻译初稿。(4) 作为检测译文问题的途径,需要审校人员进一步修改的翻译场景。

2. 轻度译后编辑为用户提供解决问题的办法或（常见问题解答、博客、知识库等）低可见度（low-visibility）内容的译文,只用于组织内部传阅,不用于对外发布,而且在保证传达主旨大意的前提下尽量多使用原始机器翻译结果,此时就需要对机器翻译产出的译文进行最少或较少的译后编辑。

3. TER = 7/25 （① 增加 not；② 增加 only；③ and 替换为",";④ one 替换为 but；⑤ of 替换为 also；⑥ the 替换为 a；⑦ birthplaces 替换为 birthplace）

4.

原文	轻度译后编辑结果	深度译后编辑结果
技术装备展区秉承"引领创新发展,融合全产业链"的发展目标,以高端及智能装备为基础,重点围绕"双碳"、数字化、集成电路、人工智能等题材,融入"高端+智能+绿色"发展理念,设立工业、科技、环保三大板块。以先进技术为中心,引领行业创新趋势,集中展示前沿技术和高端装备,为全球制造业提供高端展示和交流平台。展期重点打造人工智能体验区和低碳高峰论坛。	Adhering to the development goal of "leading innovative development and integrating the whole industry chain", the Technology and Equipment Zone is based on high-end and intelligent equipment, focusing on topics such as <u>peak carbon dioxide emissions and carbon neutrality</u> "dual-carbon", digitization, integrated circuits and artificial intelligence, and incorporating the development concept of "high-end + intelligent + green". High-end + Intelligent + Green" development concept, The three sectors establishment of industries industrial, science and technology, environmental protection are established three plates. Centering on advanced technology and leading industry innovation trends, the exhibition will focus on displaying cutting-edge technology and high-end equipment, providing a high-end exhibition and communication platform for the global manufacturing industry. During the exhibition period, it will focus on creating an artificial intelligence experience zone and a low-carbon summit forum.	Committed to the goal of "leading innovative development and integrating the whole industry chain", this area focuses on high-end and intelligent equipment, and addresses key topics such as peak carbon dioxide emissions and carbon neutrality, digitization, integrated circuits and artificial intelligence. The "high-end + intelligent + green" development concept is incorporated and presented in three sectors: industries, science and technology, and environmental protection. Centering on advanced technology, this exhibition leads the innovation trends of related industries and showcases cutting-edge technology and high-end equipment, providing a high-end exhibition and communication platform for the global manufacturing industry. Highlights of this exhibition will be an AI experience area and a low-carbon summit.
创新孵化专区以"跨越边界,孵化创新力量,引领未来科技"为主题,邀请全球创新企业、跨国企业内部孵化平台、创新孵化园区参展,帮助创新企业释放创新激情,与行业领袖交流碰撞,共同探索创新之道。	With the theme of "Crossing Boundaries, Incubating Innovative Power, Leading Future Technology", the Innovation Incubation Zone invites global innovative enterprises, internal incubation platforms of multinational enterprises and innovation incubation parks to participate in the exhibition, which will help the innovative enterprises to release their passion for innovation, communicate <u>and collide</u> with the industry leaders, and explore the way of innovation together.	Innovation Incubation Special Section focuses on the theme of "Crossing Boundaries, Incubating Innovative Forces and Leading Future Technologies". Innovative enterprises, incubation platforms of global top enterprises and innovation incubation parks are welcomed to participate in this special section. We aim to offer opportunities to unleash the passion for innovation, interact with industry leaders, and explore the way of innovation together.

续表

原文	轻度译后编辑结果	深度译后编辑结果
服务贸易展区以数字化为轴,关注商业活动全生命周期,形成"绿色低碳、稳链强链、数智未来"三位一体的展区主题。展区致力于服务全行业数字化转型,深入打造为五大货物贸易展区输送智力支持与潜在客户的转换平台,持续为实体经济聚智赋能。	The Trade in Services Zone takes digitization as its axis, focuses on the whole life cycle of business activities, and forms the theme of "Green and Low Carbon **Development**, Stabilizing and Strengthening the Chain, and Digital **and Smart** Future". The zone is committed to serving the digital transformation of the whole industry, creating a conversion platform for the five major **exhibition trade in goods** zones to deliver intellectual support and potential customers, and continuing to gather wisdom and empowerment for the real economy.	Emphasizing digitalization and focusing on the whole life cycle of business activities, the theme of Trade in Services Exhibition Area represents an integration of "Green and Low-Carbon Development, Stable and Strong Chains, and Digital and Smart Future". The exhibition area aims to facilitate the digital transformation of the entire industry by creating a platform for the other five exhibition areas to deliver intellectual support and potential customers, thus pooling wisdom and enhancing capability for the real economy.
医疗器械及医药保健展区以"健康中国,美好生活"为主题,把助力健康中国建设作为重中之重,聚焦全球医疗行业最新发展趋势和共性话题,紧贴广大人民群众对健康美好生活的向往,集中展示国际领先的医疗创新产品、尖端技术和服务。	With the theme of "Healthy China, Better Life", the Medical Devices and Pharmaceuticals & Healthcare **Exhibition Zone** ~~Pavilion~~ places top priority on helping the construction of a healthy China, focuses on the latest development trends and common topics in the global healthcare industry, and closely follows the aspirations of the general public for a healthy and better life, and centrally showcases the world's leading medical innovations, cutting-edge technologies and services.	The Medical Equipment & Healthcare Products Exhibition Area centers on the theme of "Healthy China, Better Life". It is dedicated to promoting a healthy China and highlighting the latest development trends and common topics in the global healthcare industry. The exhibition closely follows the aspirations of the public for a healthy and better life by featuring international leading medical innovation products and cutting-edge technologies and services.

附录一

国际标准化组织标准规范 25639-1:2008：
展览、展会、交易会和大会——第 1 部分：词汇

Exhibitions, shows, fairs and conventions—Part 1: Vocabulary	展览、展会、交易会和大会——第 1 部分：词汇
1. Scope This part of ISO 25639 specifies terms and definitions that are commonly used in the exhibition industry. They are grouped into the following four categories: • individual and entity, which lists and classifies the various types of people involved in the exhibition industry • type of event, which defines the different types of exhibitions and their related meetings • physical item, which describes the various component sizes of the exhibition, the types of facility and print material • miscellaneous	1．范围 ISO 25639 这一部分规定会展业中常用的术语和定义，可分为以下四类： • 个人和实体，列出与分类参与会展业的各种类型人群 • 活动类型，定义不同类型展会及相关会议 • 实物，描述展会的各种组件大小、设施类型和印刷材料 • 其他
2. Individual and entity **2.1** **exhibitor** entity that displays products or services accepted by the **organizer** (2.23), with personnel present at the **exhibition** (3.1), including **main exhibitors** (2.2) and **co-exhibitors** (2.3). NOTE 1：An entity can be a company, a body or an organization. NOTE 2：An exhibitor is sometimes also known as a "direct exhibitor".	2．个体和实体 **2.1** **参展商** 展示**主办方**(2.23)认可的产品或服务的实体，且有人员参加**展会**(3.1)，包括**主参展商**(2.2)和**联合参展商**(2.3)。 注1：实体可以是公司、机构或组织。 注2：参展商有时也被称为"直接参展商"。
2.2 **main exhibitor** **exhibitor** (2.1) contracting directly with the **organizer** (2.23)	**2.2** **主参展商** 直接与**主办方**(2.23)签约的**参展商**(2.1)。

续表

Exhibitions, shows, fairs and conventions—Part 1: Vocabulary	展览、展会、交易会和大会——第1部分：词汇
2.3 **co-exhibitor** **exhibitor** (2.1) on the **main exhibitor's** (2.2) **booth** (4.1), with its own products or services and personnel, having the approval of the organizer NOTE：A co-exhibitor is sometimes known as a "share exhibitor".	**2.3** **联合参展商** 经主办方同意，在**主参展商**(2.2)的展位(4.1)上展示自己的产品或服务，有人员的**参展商**(2.1)。 注：联合参展商有时被称为"共享参展商"。
2.4 **represented company** entity whose products or services are displayed on an **exhibitor's** (2.1) **booth** (4.1), without personnel present NOTE 1：An entity can be a company, a body or an organization. NOTE 2：A represented company is not considered to be an "exhibitor" even though it can appear in an exhibition directory. NOTE 3：A represented company is sometimes known as an "indirect exhibitor and it is not considered an "exhibitor".	**2.4** **被代表公司** 以**参展商**(2.1)展位(4.1)展示产品或服务，无人员在场的实体。 注1：被代表公司可以是公司、机构或组织。 注2：被代表公司可以出现在会展目录中，但它不被视为"参展商"。 注3：被代表公司有时被称为"间接参展商"，而不被视为"参展商"。
2.5 **international exhibitor** **foreign exhibitor** **exhibitor** (2.1) whose contractual address with the **organizer** (2.23) is outside the host country NOTE：Where the contractual address of an exhibitor does not represent its nationality, a written declaration by the exhibitor of its nationality can be accepted.	**2.5** **国际参展商** **外国参展商** 与**主办方**(2.23)的合同地址不在主办国境内的**参展商**(2.1)。 注：如参展商的合同地址不代表其国籍，则可以接受参展商关于其国籍的书面声明。
2.6 **national exhibitor** **domestic exhibitor** **exhibitor** (2.1) whose contractual address with the **organizer** (2.23) is inside the host country NOTE 1：A national exhibitor is sometimes also known as a "local exhibitor". NOTE 2：Where the contractual address of an exhibitor does not represent its nationality, a written declaration by the exhibitor of its nationality can be accepted.	**2.6** **本国参展商** **国内参展商** 与**主办方**(2.23)的合同地址在主办国境内的**参展商**(2.1)。 注1：本国参展商有时也被称为"本地参展商"。 注2：如参展商的合同地址不代表其国籍，则可以接受参展商关于其国籍的书面声明。
2.7 **exhibitor staff** **exhibitor personnel** person working on the **exhibition** (3.1) **booth** (4.1) during the official opening hours, employed by the **exhibitor** (2.1) NOTE：Exhibitor staff excludes third-party service providers.	**2.7** **参展员工** **参展人员** 在官方**展览**(3.1)开放期间，受雇于**参展商**(2.1)在展位(4.1)工作的人员。 注：参展员工不包括第三方服务供应商。

Exhibitions, shows, fairs and conventions—Part 1: Vocabulary	展览、展会、交易会和大会——第1部分：词汇
2.8 **visitor** person who attends an **exhibition** (3.1), with the purpose of gathering information, making purchases or contacting **exhibitor**(s) (2.1) NOTE 1: Visitor excludes exhibitor staff, media personnel, service provider and organizer staff. NOTE 2: A speaker/delegate is a visitor only if attending the exhibition.	**2.8** **观众** 以收集信息、购买商品或与**参展商**(2.1)接触为目的参加**展会**(3.1)人员。 注1：观众不包括参展员工、媒体人员、服务供应商和主办方员工。 注2：发言人/代表仅在参展情况下可被称为观众。
2.9 **trade visitor** **visitor** (2.8) who attends an **exhibition** (3.1) for professional or business reasons NOTE 1: Trade visitor excludes media representatives. NOTE 2: A trade visitor is sometimes also known as a "buyer".	**2.9** **专业观众** 因职业或商务原因参加**展会**(3.1)的**观众**(2.8)。 注1：专业观众不包括媒体代表。 注2：专业观众有时也被称为"买家"。
2.10 **general public visitor** **visitor** (2.8) who attends an **exhibition** (3.1) for personal reasons NOTE 1: A public visitor is sometimes also known as a "private visitor" or a "consumer show visitor". NOTE 2: Public visitor excludes media representatives.	**2.10** **普通观众** 由于个人原因参加**展会**(3.1)的**观众**(2.8)。 注1：普通观众有时被称为"私人观众"或"消费展观众"。 注2：普通观众不包括媒体代表。
2.11 **international visitor** **foreign visitor** **visitor** (2.8) whose address provided to the **organizer** (2.23) is outside the host country	**2.11** **国际观众** **外国观众** 提供给**主办方**(2.23)的地址是在主办国境外的**观众**(2.8)。
2.12 **national visitor** **domestic visitor** **visitor** (2.8) whose address provided to the **organizer** (2.23) is inside the host country NOTE: A national visitor is sometimes also known as a "local visitor".	**2.12** **本国观众** **国内观众** 提供给**主办方**(2.23)的地址在主办国境内的**观众**(2.8)。 注：本国观众有时也被称为"本地观众"。
2.13 **visit** entry into an **exhibition** (3.1) made by a **visitor** (2.8), with a maximum count of one entry per day	**2.13** **参观** **观众**(2.8)进入**展会**(3.1)的行为,每天最多入场一次。

Exhibitions, shows, fairs and conventions—Part 1: Vocabulary	展览、展会、交易会和大会——第1部分：词汇
2.14 **hosted visitor** **visitor** (2.8) who is invited and sponsored to attend the **exhibition** (3.1)	2.14 受邀观众 受邀并受赞助参加**展会**(2.8)的**观众**(3.1)。
2.15 **delegate** person who attends a **conference** (3.7), **convention** (3.8), congress, meeting, **workshop** (3.11), seminar (3.9) or **symposium** (3.10)	2.15 代表 出席**专业会议**(3.7)、**大会**(3.8)、代表会议、一般会议、**专题报告会**(3.11)、**研讨会**(3.9)或**专题研讨会**(3.10)的人员。
2.16 **international delegate** **foreign delegate** **delegate** (2.15) whose address provided to the **organizer** (2.23) is outside the host country	2.16 国际代表 外国代表 提供给**主办方**(2.23)的地址在主办国境外的**代表**(2.15)。
2.17 **national delegate** **domestic delegate** **delegate** (2.15) whose address provided to the **organizer** (2.23) is inside the host country NOTE：A national delegate is sometimes also known as a "local delegate".	2.17 本国代表 国内代表 提供给**主办方**(2.23)的地址在主办国境内的**代表**(2.15)。 注：本国代表有时也被称为"本地代表"。
2.18 **accompanying person** spouse or guest present with a **visitor** (2.8) or **delegate** (2.15) during an event	2.18 陪同人员 参观期间与**观众**(2.8)或**代表**(2.15)一起出席的其配偶或客人。
2.19 **media representative** journalist or reporter attending the **exhibition** (3.1)	2.19 媒体代表 参加**展会**(3.1)的记者或新闻工作者。
2.20 **service provider** third-party entity that provides products or services related to the **exhibition** (3.1) NOTE：An entity can be a company, a body or an organization.	2.20 服务供应商 提供与**展会**(3.1)相关的产品或服务的第三方实体。 注：实体可以是公司、机构或组织。
2.21 **official contractor** **service provider** (2.20) appointed by the **organizer** (2.23) to supply goods or services to the **exhibition** (3.1)	2.21 指定承建商 由**主办方**(2.23)指定的为**展会**(3.1)提供货品或服务的**服务供应商**(2.20)。

Exhibitions, shows, fairs and conventions—Part 1: Vocabulary	展览、展会、交易会和大会——第1部分：词汇
2.22 **sponsor** entity that supports or endorses the **exhibition**（3.1）or related activities NOTE 1：An entity can be a company, a body or an organization. NOTE 2：A sponsor is sometimes known as a "supporting or endorsing organization".	**2.22** 赞助商 为**展会**(3.1)相关活动提供支持或认可的实体。 注1：实体可以是公司、机构或组织。 注2：赞助商有时可被称为"支持或认可组织"。
2.23 **organizer** entity that produces and manages the event NOTE 1：An entity can be a company, a body or an organization. NOTE 2：The organizer is not necessarily the owner of the event.	**2.23** 主办方 组织、管理展会活动的实体。 注1：实体可以是公司、机构或组织。 注2：主办方不一定是项目的所有权人。
2.24 **co-organizer** entity that forms a partnership with the **organizer**（2.23）to produce and/or manage the event NOTE：An entity can be a company, a body or an organization.	**2.24** 协办方 与**主办方**(2.23)共同组织、管理展会活动的实体。 注：实体可以是公司、机构或组织。
2.25 **show management** entity that manages an event NOTE：An entity can be a company, a body or an organization.	**2.25** 管理方 管理展会活动的实体。 注：实体可以是公司、机构或组织。
2.26 **attendee** person attending an **exhibition**（3.1）including **visitor**（2.8）, **exhibitor staff**（2.7）, speaker, **delegate**（2.15）, **media representative**（2.19）and any other verified **admission category**（2.28） NOTE 1：Attendee does not include staff from the organizer and service provider. NOTE 2：When quoting figures for attendees, it is advisable to provide a full breakdown of admission categories.	**2.26** 与会者 参加**展会**(3.1)人员，包括观众(2.8)、参展员工(2.7)、发言人、代表(2.15)、媒体代表(2.19)及其他经认证准许入内人员。 注1：与会者不包括主办方与服务供应商的工作人员。 注2：统计与会者人数时，建议提供完整的入场类别明细。
2.27 **total attendance** total number of individual **attendees**（2.26） NOTE：When quoting figures for attendees, it is advisable to provide a full breakdown of admission categories.	**2.27** 与会总人数 个体**与会者**(2.26)总人数。 注：统计与会者人数时，建议提供完整的入场类别明细。

Exhibitions, shows, fairs and conventions—Part 1: Vocabulary	展览、展会、交易会和大会——第1部分：词汇
2.28 **admission category** criteria defining the type of **attendee** (2.26) permitted to enter the **exhibition** (3.1) by the **organizer** (2.23)	2.28 入场类别 主办方(2.23)允许进入展会(3.1)的与会者(2.26)类别界定标准。
3. Types of events **3.1** **exhibition** **show** **fair** event in which products, services or information are displayed and disseminated NOTE：Exhibition excludes flea market and street market.	3．活动类型 3.1 展览会 展会 交易会 展示或传播产品、服务、信息的一种活动。 注：展会不包括跳蚤市场和街边市场。
3.2 **trade exhibition** **exhibition** (3.1) that promotes trade and commerce and is attended primarily by **trade visitors** (2.9) NOTE：A trade exhibition can be opened to the public at specific times.	3.2 贸易展 推动贸易和商业发展的展览(3.1)，参观者主要为专业观众(2.9)。 注：贸易展可在特定时间向公众开放。
3.3 **international exhibition** **exhibition** (3.1) that attracts a significant presence of **exhibitors** (2.1) and/or **visitors** (2.8) from outside the host country NOTE：Generally speaking, at least 10% of international exhibitors or 5% of international visitors constitutes "significant presence".	3.3 国际展 吸引大量来自主办国境外的参展商(2.1)和/或观众(2.8)的展会(3.1)。 注：一般来说，有至少10%的国际参展商或5%的国际观众才构成国际会展。
3.4 **public exhibition** **exhibition** (3.1) open primarily to the **general public visitor** (2.10) NOTE：A public exhibition is sometimes also known as a consumer show.	3.4 公共展会 该展会(3.1)主要面向普通观众(2.10)。 注：公共展会有时也被称为"消费展"。
3.5 **general exhibition** **exhibition** (3.1) that comprises multiple business or consumer product and service sectors NOTE：These sectors are not necessarily related to each other.	3.5 综合展会 涵盖多种业务或消费品和服务领域的展会(3.1)。 注：各个领域无须相关。

续表

Exhibitions, shows, fairs and conventions—Part 1: Vocabulary	展览、展会、交易会和大会——第1部分：词汇
3.6 **specialized exhibition** exhibition (3.1) that focuses either on a specific business sector, or on several business sectors that are closely linked to each other NOTE：Specialized exhibition is often open to the trade visitor, but can also be open to the general public visitor.	**3.6** **专业展会** 聚焦一个特定的商业领域或若干关联性较强的商业领域的展会(3.1)。 注：专业展会通常面向专业观众，但也向普通观众开放。
3.7 **conference** organized formal meeting, or series of meetings, comprising of groups of representatives belonging to a common interest group, in which issues, ideas and policies are discussed	**3.7** **专业会议** 一系列有组织的、正式的议事活动，具有共同利益的各方代表在会议上就各项议题进行讨论、交流思想、商议政策。
3.8 **convention** organized meeting of industry, profession or organization to share knowledge and experience NOTE：A convention is sometimes also known as a "congress".	**3.8** **大会** 各行业、专业或机构所组织的会议，用于分享知识与经验。 注：大会有时也被称为"代表会议"
3.9 **seminar** organized meeting to discuss specialized and focused topics	**3.9** **研讨会** 讨论专业或特定话题的有组织的会议。
3.10 **symposium** organized meeting with presentations of papers on a specific subject and debated by multiple experts NOTE：A symposium is typically scientific or medical.	**3.10** **专题研讨会** 就某一特定主题进行论文报告，并由多位专家进行辩论的有组织的会议。 注：专题研讨会通常为科学或医学类。
3.11 **workshop** organized meeting conducted by experts to achieve a predefined goal that can be accessible to interested parties	**3.11** **专题报告会** 由专家组织召开的会议，利益相关方都能实现预先设定的目标。
4. Physical item **4.1** **booth** **stand** structure occupied for the display of products or services	**4. 实物** **4.1** **展位** 供展示产品或服务的结构体。

续表

Exhibitions, shows, fairs and conventions—Part 1: Vocabulary	展览、展会、交易会和大会——第1部分：词汇
4.2 **booth space** **stand space** area indoors and/or outdoors, occupied and contracted by an **exhibitor** (2.1), whether paid or unpaid, for the display of products or services NOTE：Booth space is sometimes also known as "exhibit space".	**4.2** 展位空间 **参展商**(2.1)订约并使用的室内和/或室外空间，用于有偿或无偿展示其产品或服务。 注：展位空间有时也被称为"展示空间"。
4.3 **raw space** **booth space** (4.2) without structure that is to be constructed by the **exhibitors** (2.1) NOTE：Raw space is sometimes also known as "bare space".	**4.3** 光地 不附带任何配置的展位空间(4.2)，**参展商**(2.1)须自行搭建。 注：光地有时也被称为"空地"。
4.4 **contra booth** **contra stand** **booth** (4.1) with an identified commercial value, provided by the **organizer** (2.23) to an **exhibitor** (2.1) in exchange for a commercial benefit NOTE：Contra booth is sometimes also known as "barter booth".	**4.4** 对销展位 一种由**主办方**(2.23)提供给**参展商**(2.1)，具有确定的商业价值，以换取商业利益的**展位**(4.1)。 注：对销展位有时也被称为"易货展位"。
4.5 **pavilion** collection of **exhibitors** (2.1) under a common identity EXAMPLE：national pavilion; association pavilion	**4.5** 展馆 共同身份下的**参展商**(2.1)集合。 例如：国家展馆、协会展馆
4.6 **gross indoor exhibition venue space** total permanent indoor space available for **exhibitions** (3.1)	**4.6** 总室内展览场馆空间 长期可用于**展会**(3.1)的室内空间。
4.7 **gross outdoor exhibition venue space** total outdoor space available for **exhibitions** (3.1)	**4.7** 总室外展览场馆空间 可用于**展会**(3.1)的室外空间。
4.8 **gross exhibition space** total space used for the **exhibition** (3.1), including circulation areas NOTE：Facilities that need to be built within the exhibition area can be considered as gross exhibition space.	**4.8** 总展览空间 供**展会**(3.1)使用的总空间，包括流通区域。 注：展览区域内搭建的设施也应被包括在总展览空间内。

Exhibitions, shows, fairs and conventions—Part 1: Vocabulary	展览、展会、交易会和大会——第1部分：词汇
4.9 net exhibition space sum of **booth space** (4.2) and any space utilized by the **organizer** (2.23) for features that have a direct relation to the theme of the **exhibition** (3.1)	4.9 净展览空间 展位空间与**主办方**(2.23)为**展会**(3.1)主题相关特色而使用的所有**空间**(4.2)总和。
4.10 rented exhibition space **booth space** (4.2) that is rented and paid for by the **exhibitors** (2.1)	4.10 租赁展览空间 通过**参展商**(2.1)有偿租赁获得的**展位空间**(4.2)。
4.11 floor plan map or layout plan of the **exhibition** (3.1)	4.11 展会平面图 **展会**(3.1)地图或平面布置图。
4.12 exhibitors' manual electronic or physical document containing event information, rules and regulations, service order forms, and other information pertinent to the **exhibitors** (2.1) participation in an **exhibition** (3.1)	4.12 参展商手册 电子或实物文档，包括活动信息、规章制度、服务订购表，以及其他**展会**(3.1)中与**参展商**(2.1)参展相关的信息。
4.13 exhibition directory exhibition catalogue electronic or physical document containing a listing of **exhibitors** (2.1), their contact details, stand numbers and any other information related to the **exhibition** (3.1) NOTE：Exhibition directory is sometimes also known as "show directory".	4.13 展会名录 包括**参展商**(2.1)名单、联系方式、展位号，以及其他**展会**(3.1)相关信息的电子或纸质文档。 注：展会名录有时也称"展示名录"。
4.14 convention centre permanent facility used primarily for meetings, **conferences** (3.7) and exhibitions (3.1)	4.14 会展中心 长期并主要用于会议、**专业会议**(3.7)与**展会**(3.1)的场馆。
4.15 congress centre permanent facility used primarily for congresses, meetings and **conferences** (3.7) NOTE：A congress centre can also have facilities for exhibition.	4.15 会议中心 长期并主要用于大会、会议及**专业会议**(3.7)的场馆。 注：会议中心亦可有展会设施。
4.16 exhibition centre fairground permanent facility used primarily for **exhibitions** (3.1) NOTE：An exhibition centre can have meeting facilities.	4.16 展览中心 展销会场地 主要用于**展会**(3.1)的永久性场所。 注：展览中心亦可有会议设施。

Exhibitions, shows, fairs and conventions—Part 1: Vocabulary	展览、展会、交易会和大会——第1部分：词汇
5. Miscellaneous 5.1 **build up** period defined by the **organizer** (2.23) for set-up or preparation onsite prior to **exhibition** (3.1) NOTE 1：The build up period is not open to visitors. NOTE 2：Build up is sometimes also known as "move-in".	5. 其他 5.1 搭建期 主办方(2.23)在展会(3.1)前确定的用于搭建和准备现场的时间段。 注1：搭建期展馆不对观众开放。 注2：搭建有时亦称"布展"。
5.2 **tear down** **break down** period defined by the **organizer** (2.23) for dismantling after the **exhibition** (3.1) NOTE 1：The tear down period is not open to visitors. NOTE 2：Tear down is sometimes also known as "move-out".	5.2 拆卸期 主办方(2.23)在展会(3.1)后拆卸现场的时间段。 注1：拆卸期不对观众开放。 注2：拆卸有时亦称"撤展"。
5.3 **duration of exhibition** period during which an **exhibition** (3.1) is open to **visitors** (2.8) NOTE：It is not advisable to include build up and tear down periods in the duration of exhibition.	5.3 展期 展会(3.1)对观众(2.8)开放的时间段。 注：展期不包括搭建期和拆卸期。

附录二

会展翻译实训项目 A

场景设定：

2023 第五届中国国际茶叶博览会，杭州惠农茶叶有限公司（展位号：杭州国际博览中心 3 楼 C 馆 225#）与匈牙利阿若尼布拉（ARANYBULLA）农业综合开发公司商业谈判（主题：千岛湖高山有机茶购销）

就上述场景完成以下三项文本翻译内容：

- 中外方人员名片（中英文）
- 公司宣传手册（中英文）
- 买卖合同（中英文）

（1）中外方人员名片

（2）公司宣传手册

In pursuit of high-quality tea products, the company emphasizes strict quality control and meticulous craftsmanship, providing consumers with a fresh and authentic range of teas. As a company valuing technological innovation, Huinong continually introduces advanced tea planting and processing technologies, striving to enhance the efficiency and quality of the tea industry chain. The company's tea gardens employ modern planting techniques, emphasizing ecological environmental protection, adhering strictly to green and eco-friendly principles from tea cultivation to processing.

王牌产品 STAR PRODUCT

千岛湖高山有机茶以其优良的生长环境和有机种植方式而著称。这种茶叶常常遵循有机农业的生产标准，不使用化学肥料和农药，采用天然有机的方式种植和管理茶园。千岛湖高山有机茶的种类包括了绿茶、红茶、乌龙茶等不同类别。这些茶叶品种多样，口感丰富，常常受到茶叶爱好者的欢迎。千岛湖高山有机茶通常具好较高的品质和口感，富含丰富的天然营养成分，并且没有人工添加物的残留。

Qian Dao Lake Mountain Organic Tea is renowned for its excellent growing environment and organic cultivation methods. This type of tea often adheres to the production standards of organic agriculture, refraining from the use of chemical fertilizers and pesticides, employing natural organic methods for tea garden cultivation and management. Varieties of Qian Dao Lake Mountain Organic Tea include different types such as **green tea, black tea, oolong tea**, among others. These teas are diverse, offering rich flavors, and are often welcomed by tea enthusiasts. Qian Dao Lake Mountain Organic Tea usually boasts higher quality and flavor, rich in natural nutritional elements, and free from residual artificial additives.

千岛玉叶 QIAN DAO YU YE

产于淳安县青溪一带，原称"千岛湖龙井"。1982年创制，1983年7月，浙江农业大学教授庄晚芳等茶叶专家到淳安考察，品鉴了当时的千岛龙井茶后，根据千岛湖的景色和茶叶粗壮 又白毫的特点，亲笔题名"千岛玉叶"。

"Qian Dao Yu Ye" is a tea produced in the Qingxi area of Chun'an County, originally known as Qian Dao Lake Longjing. It was created in 1982 and in July 1983, Professor Zhuang Wanfang, among other tea experts from Zhejiang Agricultural University, visited Chun'an for inspection. After tasting the Qian Dao Longjing tea at that time and considering the scenery of Qian Dao Lake and the robustness of the tea leaves along with the characteristic of white fuzz, Professor Zhuang personally named it "Qian Dao Yu Ye".

（3）买卖合同

茶叶出口合同
Contract（Sales Confirmation）

买卖双方同意按照下列条款签订本合同：

The Seller and the Buyer agree to conclude this Contract subject to the terms and

签订日期（Date）： 2023 - 5 - 23

签订地点（Signed at）： 杭州国际博览中心

买方： 阿若尼布拉农业综合开发公司

The Buyer： ARANYBULLA

地址： 匈牙利布达佩斯市4区22号

Address： No. 22, Zone 4, Budapest, Hungary

电话（Tel）： (36) 1301221660

传真（Fax）： (36) 1301221666

电子邮箱（E-mail）： ARANYBULLA@google.com

卖方：＿＿＿＿＿＿杭州惠农茶叶有限公司＿＿＿＿＿＿

The Seller：＿＿＿＿Hangzhou Huinong Tea Co., Ltd.＿＿＿＿

地址：＿＿＿浙江省杭州市上城区吴兴路188号荣安中心＿＿＿

Address：＿＿Rong'an Center, No. 188 Wuxing Road, Shangcheng District, Hangzhou City, Zhejiang Province, China＿＿

电话（Tel）：＿＿＿＿＿（86）57160804520＿＿＿＿＿

传真（Fax）：＿＿＿＿＿（86）57160804550＿＿＿＿＿

电子邮箱（E-mail）：＿＿＿＿HuinongTea@163.com＿＿＿

Conditions stated below：

1. 货物名称和质量（Name and Quality of Commodity）：

货号 Art No.	名称及规格 Descriptions	单位 Unit	数量 Quantity	单价 Unit Price	金额 Amount
A级产品一号 NO. A01	龙井 500克/小包 10小包/盒 Longjing Tea 500g/packet and 10 packets/boxes	盒 box	30箱（10盒/箱） 30 cases（10 boxes/cases）	（1750美元/盒） （17500美元/箱） （1,750 dols/case） （17,500 dols/box）	合计：525000美元 Totally：525,000 dols
A级产品二号 NO. A02	银针 200克/小包 10小包/盒 Scented Tea 200g/packet and 10 packets/boxes	盒 box	25箱（20盒/箱） 25 cases（20 boxes/cases）	（588美元/盒） （11760美元/箱） （588 dols/case） （11,760 dols/box）	合计：294000美元 Totally：294,000 dols

总值（大写）：捌拾壹万玖仟美元

Total value：(in words)：Eight hundred and nineteen thousand US dollars

2. 数量（Quantity）：

允许＿4%＿的溢短装（＿4＿% more or less allowed）

3. 单价（Unit Price）：

龙井（Longjing）：350 $/kg

银针（Yinzhen）：294 $/kg

4. 总值（Total Amount）：

2,500 kg,

819,000 $

5. 交货条件（Terms of Delivery）：＿FOB＿

6. 原产地国与制造商（Country of Origin and Manufacturers）：

中国杭州惠农茶叶有限公司
Hangzhou Huinong Tea Co., Ltd., China

7. 包装及标准(Packing):

货物应具有防潮、防锈蚀、防震并适合于远洋运输的包装,由于货物包装不良而造成的货物残损、灭失应由卖方负责。卖方应在每个包装箱上用不褪色的颜色标明尺码、包装箱号码、毛重、净重及"此端向上""防潮""小心轻放"等标记。

The packing of the goods shall be preventive from dampness, rust, moisture, erosion and shock, and shall be suitable for ocean transportation / multiple transportation. The Seller shall be liable for any damage and loss of the goods attributable to the inadequate or improper packing. The measurement, gross weight, net weight and the cautions such as "Do not stack upside down", "Keep away from moisture", "Handle with care" shall be stenciled on the surface of each package with fadeless pigment.

8. 保险(Insurance):

由 __买方__ 按发票金额110%投保 __协会货物(A)__ 险和 __一般附加__ 险。

Insurance shall be covered by the Buyer for 110% of the invoice value against ICC (A) Risks and General Additional Risks.

9. 付款条件(Terms of Payment):

(1) 信用证方式:买方应在装运期前/合同生效后 __10__ 日,开出以卖方为受益人的不可撤销的议付信用证,信用证在装船完毕后 __15__ 日内到期。

Letter of Credit: The Buyer shall __10__ days prior to the time of shipment / after this Contract comes into effect, open an irrevocable Letter of Credit in favor of the Seller. The Letter of Credit shall expire __15__ days after the completion of loading of the shipment as stipulated.

(2) 付款交单:货物发运后,卖方出具以买方为付款人的付款跟单汇票,按即期付款交单(D/P)方式,通过卖方银行及 __中国__ 银行向买方转交单证,换取货物。

Documents against payment: After shipment, the Seller shall draw a sight bill of exchange on the Buyer and deliver the documents through Sellers bank and __Bank of China__ to the Buyer against payment, i.e D/P. The Buyer shall effect the payment immediately upon the first presentation of the bill(s) of exchange.

(3) 承兑交单:货物发运后,卖方出具以买方为付款人的付款跟单汇票,付款期限为 __2023-6-20__ 后 __6__ 日,按即期承兑交单(D/A 全日)方式,通过卖方银行及 __中国__ 银行,经买方承兑后,向买方转交单证,买方在汇票期限到期时支付货款。

Documents against Acceptance: After shipment, the Seller shall draw a sight bill of exchange, payable __6__ days in June 20, 2023 after the Buyer delivers the document through the Seller's bank and ___Bank of China___ to the Buyer against acceptance (D/A days). The Buyer shall make the payment on date of the bill of exchange.

（4）货到付款：买方在收到货物后___5___天内将全部货款支付卖方（不适用于 FOB、CRF、CIF 术语）。

Cash on delivery (COD)：The Buyer shall pay to the Seller total amount within ___5___ days after the receipt of the goods (This clause is not applied to the Terms of FOB, CFR, CIF).

10. 单据（Documents Required）：

卖方应将下列单据提交银行议付/托收：

The Seller shall present the following documents required to the bank for negotiation/collection：

（1）标明通知收货人/收货代理人的全套清洁的、已装船、空白抬头、空白背书并注明运费已付/到付的海运/联运/陆运提单。

Full set of clean on board Ocean / Combined Transportation / Land Bills of Lading and blank endorsed marked freight prepaid / to collect；

（2）标有合同编号、信用证号（信用证支付条件下）及装运唛头的商业发票一式___3___份；

Signed commercial invoice in ___3___ copies indicating Contract No., L/C No. (Terms of L/C) and shipping marks；

（3）由___杭州惠农茶叶有限公司___出具的装箱或重量单一式___3___份；

Packing list / weight memo in ___3___ copies issued by ___Hangzhou Huinong Tea Co., Ltd.___；

（4）由___杭州惠农茶叶有限公司___出具的质量证明书一式___3___份；

Certificate of Quality in ___3___ copies issued by ___Hangzhou Huinong Tea Co., Ltd.___；

（5）由___杭州惠农茶叶有限公司___出具的数量证明书一式___3___份；

Certificate of Quantity in ___3___ copies issued by ___Hangzhou Huinong Tea Co., Ltd.___；

（6）保险单正本一式___2___份（CIF 交货条件）；

Insurance policy/certificate in ___2___ copies (Terms of CIF)；

（7）___杭州惠农茶叶有限公司___签发的产地证一式___2___份；

Certificate of Origin in ___2___ copies issued by ___Hangzhou Huinong Tea Co., Ltd.___；

（8）装运通知（Shipping Advice）：卖方应在交运后___24___小时内以特快专递方式邮寄给买方上述第1项单据副本一式一套。

The Seller shall, within ___24___ hours after shipment effected, send by courier each copy of the above-mentioned documents No. 1.

11. 装运条款(Terms of Shipment)：

（1）FOB 交货方式

卖方应在合同规定的装运日期前 30 天，以　传真　方式通知买方合同号、品名、数量、金额、包装件、毛重、尺码及装运港可装日期，以便买方安排租船/订舱。装运船只按期到达装运港后，如卖方不能按时装船，发生的空船费或滞期费由卖方负担。在货物越过船舷并脱离吊钩以前一切费用和风险由卖方负担。

The Seller shall, 30 days before the shipment date specified in the Contract, advise the Buyer by ___FAX___ of the Contract No., commodity, quantity, amount, packages, gross weight, measurement, and the date of shipment in order that the Buyer can charter a vessel/book shipping space. In the event of the Seller's failure to effect loading when the vessel arrives duly at the loading port, all expenses including dead freight and/or demurrage charges thus incurred shall be for the Seller's account.

（2）CIF 或 CFR 交货方式

卖方须按时在装运期限内将货物由装运港装船至目的港。在 CFR 术语下，卖方应在装船前 2 天以　传真　方式通知买方合同号、品名、发票价值及开船日期，以便买方安排保险。

The Seller shall ship the goods duly within the shipping duration from the port of loading to the port of destination. Under CFR terms, the Seller shall advise the Buyer by ___FAX___ of the Contract No., commodity, invoice value and the date of dispatch two days before the shipment for the Buyer to arrange insurance in time.

12. 装运通知(Shipping Advice)：

一俟装载完毕，卖方应在　24　小时内以　传真　方式通知买方合同编号、品名、已发运数量、发票总金额、毛重、船名/车/机号及启程日期等。

The Seller shall, immediately upon the completion of the loading of the goods, advise the Buyer of the Contract No., names of commodity, loading quantity, invoice values, gross weight, name of vessel and shipment date by ___FAX___ within ___24___ hours.

13. 质量保证(Quality Guarantee)：

货物品质规格必须符合本合同及质量保证书之规定，品质保证期为货到目的港　1　个月内。在保证期限内，因卖方在茶叶制造过程中的缺陷造成的货物损害应由卖方负责赔偿。

The Seller shall guarantee that the commodity must be in conformity with the quality, specifications and quantity specified in this Contract and Letter of Quality Guarantee. The guarantee period shall be ___1___ month(s) after the arrival of the goods at the port of destination, and during the period the Seller shall be responsible for the damage due to the defects in designing and manufacturing of the manufacturer.

14. 检验（Inspection）：

卖方须在装运前 __30__ 日委托 __中科检测__ 检验机构对本合同之货物进行检验并出具检验证书，货到目的港后，由买方委托 __TÜV 南德意志集团__ 检验机构进行检验。

The Seller shall have the goods inspected by __30__ days before the shipment and have the Inspection Certificate issued by __CAS TESTING__. The Buyer may have the goods reinspected by __Technischer Überwachungs-Verein__ after the goods' arrival at the destination.

15. 索赔（Claim）：

买方凭其委托的检验机构出具的检验证明书向卖方提出索赔（包括换货），由此引起的全部费用应由卖方负担。若卖方收到上述索赔后 __30__ 天未予答复，则认为卖方已接受买方索赔。

The Buyer shall make a claim against the Seller (including replacement of the goods) by the further inspection certificate and all the expenses incurred therefrom shall be borne by the Seller. The claims mentioned above shall be regarded as being accepted if the Seller fail to reply within __30__ days after the Seller received the Buyer's claim.

16. 迟交货与罚款（Late Delivery and Penalty）：

除合同第21条不可抗力原因外，如卖方不能按合同规定的时间交货，买方应同意在卖方支付罚款的条件下延期交货。罚款可由议付银行在议付货款时扣除，罚款率按每 __7__ 天收 __0.5__ %，不足 __7__ 天时以 __7__ 天计算。但罚款不得超过迟交货物总价的 __5__ %。如卖方延期交货超过合同规定 __70__ 天，买方有权撤销合同，此时，卖方仍应不迟延地按上述规定向买方支付罚款。

Should the Seller fail to make delivery on time as stipulated in the Contract, with the exception of Force Majeure causes specified in Clause 21 of this Contract, the Buyer shall agree to postpone the delivery on the condition that the Seller agree to pay a penalty which shall be deducted by the paying bank from the payment under negotiation. The rate of penalty is charged at __0.5__ % for __7__ every days, odd days less than __7__ days should be counted as __7__ days. But the penalty, however, shall not exceed __5__ % of the total value of the goods involved in the delayed delivery. In case the Seller fail to make delivery __70__ days later than the time of shipment stipulated in the Contract, the Buyer shall have the right to cancel the Contract and the Seller, in spite of the cancellation, shall nevertheless pay the aforesaid penalty to the Buyer without delay.

买方有权对因此遭受的其他损失向卖方提出索赔。

The Buyer shall have the right to lodge a claim against the Seller for the losses sustained if any.

17. 不可抗力(Force Majeure)：

凡在制造或装船运输过程中,不可抗力致使卖方不能或推迟交货时,卖方不负责任。在发生上述情况时,卖方应立即通知买方,并在__14__天内,给买方特快专递一份由当地民间商会签发的事故证明书。在此情况下,卖方仍有责任采取一切必要措施加快交货。如事故延续__70__天以上,买方有权撤销合同。

The Seller shall not be responsible for the delay of shipment or non-delivery of the goods due to Force Majeure, which might occur during the process of manufacturing or in the course of loading or transit. The Seller shall advise the Buyer immediately of the occurrence mentioned above and within __14__ days thereafter the Seller shall send a notice by courier to the Buyer for their acceptance of a certificate of the accident issued by the local chamber of commerce under whose jurisdiction the accident occurs as evidence thereof. Under such circumstances the Seller, however, is still under the obligation to take all necessary measures to hasten the delivery of the goods. In case the accident lasts for more than __70__ days, the Buyer shall have the right to cancel the Contract.

18. 争议的解决(Arbitration)：

凡本合同引起的或与本合同有关的任何争议应协商解决。若协商不成,应提交中国国际经济贸易仲裁委员会浙江分会,按照申请仲裁时该会现行有效的仲裁规则进行仲裁。仲裁裁决是终局的,对双方均有约束力。

Any dispute arising from or in connection with the Contract shall be settled through friendly negotiation. In case no settlement is reached, the dispute shall be submitted to China International Economic and Trade Arbitration Commission (CIETAC), Zhejiang Commission for arbitration in accordance with its rules in effect at the time of applying for arbitration. The arbitral award is final and binding upon both parties.

19. 通知(Notices)：

所有通知用__中/英__文写成,并按照如下地址用传真/电子邮件/快件送达给各方。如果地址有变更,一方应在变更后__3__日内书面通知另一方。

All notice shall be written in __Chinese or English__ and served to both parties by fax/email-courier according to the following addresses. If any changes of the addresses occur, one party shall inform the other party of the change of address within __3__ days after the change.

20. 本合同使用的 FOB、CFR、CIF 术语系根据国际商会《2000 年国际贸易术语解释通则》。

The terms FOB, CFR, CIF in the Contract are based on INCOTERMS 2000 of the International Chamber of Commerce.

21. 附加条款(Additional Clause):

本合同上述条款与本附加条款抵触时,以本附加条款为准。

Conflicts between Contract clause hereabove and this additional clause, if any, it is subject to this additional clause.

22. 本合同用中英文两种文字写成,两种文字具有同等效力。本合同共 2 份,自双方代表签字(盖章)之日起生效。

This Contract is executed in two counterparts each in Chinese and English, each of which shall be deemed equally authentic. This Contract is in 2 copies, effective since being signed/sealed by both parties.

买方代表(签字):

Representative of the Buyer

(Authorized signature):

卖方代表(签字):

Representative of the Seller

(Authorized signature):

附录三

会展翻译实训项目 B

场景设定：

2023 慕尼黑国际车展

（1）整车企业，如比亚迪、上汽名爵、小鹏汽车、零跑汽车、东风柳汽等；

（2）动力电池企业，如宁德时代、孚能科技、亿纬锂能等；

（3）智能驾驶方案供应商，如地平线、亿咖通、轻舟智航、亮道智能、商汤、纵目科技等。

请以上述某一品牌企业（任选）完成以下三项翻译任务：

（1）申请函（中英文——文本）；

（2）展位搭建方案（设计图及方案说明——英文 PPT）；

（3）产品发布会（情景模拟——交传中英文文本）。

案例：

（1）申请函

尊敬的慕尼黑国际汽车展组委会：

非常荣幸有机会向您申请参加 2023 年德国慕尼黑车展。我代表阿维塔科技，衷心向您致以最诚挚的问候与祝福。

作为欧洲规模最大的国际性汽车盛会之一，德国慕尼黑车展一直以来都是全球顶级车展。我们深知，这是一个展示最新科技、创新产品和未来趋势的绝佳平台。因此，我们希望能够参展并向全世界用户展现阿维塔的独特魅力。

阿维塔科技成立于 2018 年，公司总部位于中国重庆，并在上海及德国慕尼黑设有分部，致力于探索面向未来的人性化出行科技，为用户创造情感智能出行体验。作为智能电动汽车（SEV）新赛道的探索者，阿维塔科技致力于打造国际化高端 SEV 品牌。

我公司计划在贵展上展示全球首发的新一代产品——阿维塔 12，由位于慕尼黑的阿维塔全球设计中心设计，秉承"未来美学"的整体设计理念，十分契合本届 IAA MOTOBILITY "体验互联移动"（Experience Connected Mobility），聚焦可持续性及最新移动科技的主题。作为中大型车纯电动轿车，阿维塔 12 采用 Shootingbrake 的车身造型，并配备有电子外后视镜、HUAWEI ADS 2.0 高级智能驾驶辅助系统、三颗激光雷达及主动式升降尾翼等最新移动科技。在动力系统上，阿维塔 12 采用华为提供的电机，配合宁德时代电池组，支持高压超快充技术，续航里程或将达到 700 千米，完美契合本届博览会的主题。

慕尼黑国际车展素来被视为全球汽车产业趋势的指针。阿维塔在这里的精彩亮相，不仅能向世界展示中国汽车制造业的创新实力与综合竞争力，还标志着中国汽车工业已准备好携手全球，共同迎接一个全新的时代，迈向更加美好的出行未来。我们公司的参与无疑进一步提升了慕尼黑车展的国际影响力和吸引力。

  我公司诚挚地希望组委会能考虑阿维塔科技的参展申请，期待能够与您共同努力，共创慕尼黑车展更加辉煌的未来！

  再次感谢您给予我们宝贵的时间与机会。

  顺颂

时祺！

阿维塔科技
2023 年 12 月 17 日

Avatr Technology
Chongqing Liangjiang New District Internet
Industrial Park Phase III
Tel：4001754113－9588

Committee of the IAA MOTOBILITY 2023

Messe Munich Exhibition Center

Chongqing，December 17，2023

Your Excellency Committee of the IAA MOTOBILITY 2023：

  It's a great honor to submit our application to participate in the esteemed IAA MOTOBILITY 2023. As the representative of Avatr Technology，I would like to extend our warmest greetings and heartfelt wishes to you.

  Renowned as one of Europe's largest international automotive events，the IAA MOTOBILITY has consistently held the title of the world's premier auto show. Recognizing its exceptional capacity for highlighting cutting-edge technology，pioneering products，and forthcoming trends，our company aspire to partake in this exhibition and showcase Avatr's distinctive allure to a global audience.

  Founded in 2018，Avatr Technology is based in Chongqing，China，and operates branches in Shanghai and Munich，Germany. Our company is dedicated to researching and developing advanced，user-centric mobility technology that caters to the needs and emotions of consumers. As a pioneer in the field of Smart Electric Vehicles（SEV），Avatr Technology strives to establish itself as a leading global brand in the high-end SEV market.

The Avatr 12, a next-generation product set to make its debut at this year's IAA MOTOBILITY, has been meticulously designed by Avatr's Global Design Center in Munich. It embodies the overarching design concept of "Future Aesthetics", which seamlessly aligns with the theme of this year's IAA MOTOBILITY, "Experience Connected Mobility". This theme places a strong emphasis on sustainability and the latest advancements in mobile technology. As a fully electric sedan catering to mid-size and large vehicles, the Avatr 12 boasts a sleek Shootingbrake body style and is equipped with cutting-edge mobility technologies. These include electronic exterior mirrors, the HUAWEI ADS 2.0 Advanced Intelligent Driver Assistance System, three LIDARs, and an active lifting tailgate. In terms of powertrain, the Avatr 12 utilizes an electric motor provided by Huawei, coupled with a CATL battery pack that supports high-voltage ultra-fast charging technology. With a potential range of up to 700 kilometers, the Avatr 12 perfectly aligns with the sustainability-focused theme of this year's expo.

The IAA MOTOBILITY has always been recognized as a key indicator of global automotive industry trends. Avatr's impressive presence at the event not only showcases China's automotive manufacturing industry's innovative prowess and comprehensive competitiveness to the world but also signifies China's readiness to collaborate with the global community in embracing a new era and advancing towards a better future of transportation. Our company's participation will undoubtedly further elevate the international influence and allure of the IAA MOTOBILITY 2023.

We sincerely hope the committee to kindly consider Avatr's application to participate in the show. And we will eagerly grasp the opportunity to collaborate with IAA MOTOBILITY in creating an even more remarkable future!

Heartfelt gratitude for your valuable time and the opportunity provided for us.

Yours sincerely,

Avatr Technology

（2）展位搭建方案

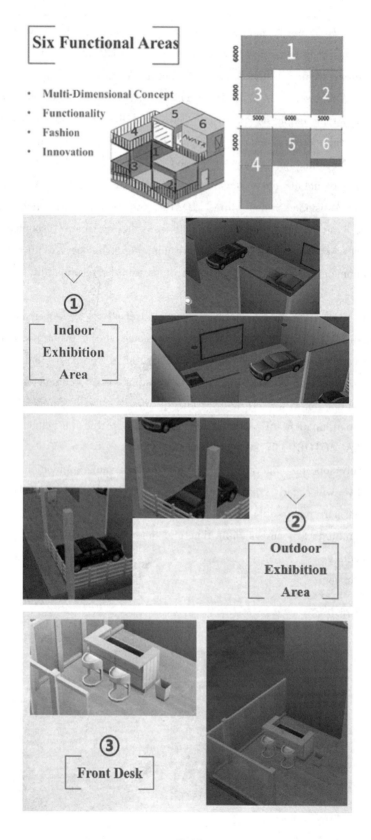

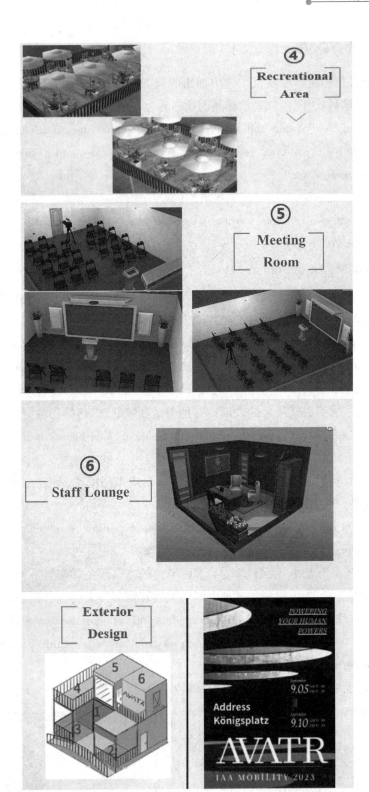

(3) 产品发布会(交传中英文文本)

大家晚上好!感谢各位在百忙之中抽出时间参加阿维塔12的新品发布会。在这里,我代表阿维塔科技,向各位表示热烈的欢迎和衷心的感谢!

Good evening, everyone, and thank you for taking the time to attend the Avatr 12 launch event. On behalf of Avatr Technologies, I would like to extend a warm welcome and heartfelt thanks to all of you!

今天,我们齐聚一堂,共同见证阿维塔品牌全新力作——阿维塔12的全球首发。

Today, we are gathered here to witness the world premiere of Avatr 12, the brand-new masterpiece of the Avatr brand.

一、未来美学(Art of Tomorrow)

阿维塔12的外观设计由位于德国慕尼黑的阿维塔全球设计中心操刀,秉承未来美学的整体设计理念,坚持前瞻、极致、纯粹的设计哲学。

The appearance design of Avatr 12 is operated by the Avatr Global Design Center in Munich, Germany, adhering to the overall design concept of future elegance and showing the forward-looking, extreme, pure design philosophy.

如您所见,它拥有极其美丽的外形。这种美是独特的、成熟的和自信的。

As you can see, it has an extremely beautiful shape. This beauty is unique, mature, and confident.

在车身侧面,我们特别甄选最佳比例,采用隐藏式车门把手,呈现出悬浮感十足的流线型车身线条。

On the side of the car, we specially select the best proportion, use hidden door handles, presenting a floating streamlined body lines.

阿维塔12还具有豪华、精英、运动等多种丰富的内饰颜色和配置选择,并从设计哲学的个性层角度出发,为用户提供各种大胆前卫的装饰套件来展现自我个性。

Avatr 12 also has a variety of rich interior colors and configurations such as luxury, elite and sports, and it provides users with a variety of bold and avant-garde decorative kits to show their own personality.

同时,我们也采用可持续发展的创新材料践行环保理念。

At the same time, we also use innovative materials of sustainable development to practice the concept of environmental protection.

二、智能与全能(Intelligent and Versatile)

阿维塔在诞生之初就明确要打造超越出行的智慧生活。

At the beginning, we have determined to create a smart life beyond travel.

1. 上车即上手(User-Friendly from the Start)

基于华为高阶智能驾驶系统 ADS 2.0 技术,阿维塔12 具备"辅助泊车"功能。

Based on the HUAWEI ADS 2.0 technology, Avatr 12 has the function of "auxiliary parking".

该功能对于一些新手司机可以说是十分友好,能够做到车位识别"狠准稳",车位泊入"多快顺",支持160 + 车位类型。

This function can be said to be very friendly to some novice drivers. It can provide accurate parking space identification, including more than 160 types of parking space, for your smooth and safe parking.

2. 应用皆好用(User-Centric Applications)

搭载鸿蒙系统,支持华为投屏等一系列操作。有海量应用软件,多元需求全满足。

With Harmany OS, we support Huawei Share and offer rich applications, as to meet the needs in infotainment, games, and others catering to all your entertainment needs.

用户只需登录一个华为账号,就可以实现华为手机、平板、电脑等设备之间的无缝连接,一键即可解锁第三方生态应用,不需要烦琐的操作。

After logging into a Huawei account, you can realize seamless connection between Huawei mobile phones, tablets, computers and other devices, and third-party ecological applications can be unlocked with one click without tedious operations.

三、性能(Performance)

1. 高环极速(High Loop Speed)

阿维塔12 具有0.21 Cd 的超低风阻系数,以及智能主动进气格栅的自动开关功能。搭配华为 Drive ONE 高压电驱动系统,最高功率可达425 kW,零百加速仅需3.9 秒。

Avatr 12 has 0.21 Cd ultra-low wind resistance coefficient of vehicle & automatic opening and closing of intelligent active air intake grille. With HUAWEI Drive ONE HV electric drive system, the max power could be 425 kW, and the acceleration time from 0 km/h to 100 km/h is only 3.9 s.

2. 续航补能(Battery and Charging)

在最高充电速度下,充电20 分钟即可增加 350 千米行驶里程。

At the maximum charging speed, charging 20 mins can realize additional 350 km driving range.

3. 电池安全(Battery Safety)

电池机械测试一次性通过率为100%,累计通过150 多项专项安全和性能试验。

Our battery features 100% one-off passing rate in mechanical test, accumulatively passing more than 150 special safety and performance tests.

看了这么多细节,大家觉得如何?凭借上述优点,我相信阿维塔12一定会遥遥领先。

After seeing all the details, what do you think? With the above advantages, I believe that the Avatr 12 is far ahead.

阿维塔作为中国高端品牌的践行者,自然也肩负着中国品牌向上发展的责任与决心。今年9月,我们就带着阿维塔12在慕尼黑完成了首秀,让全世界为之倾心。

As a practitioner of high-end brands of Chinese brands, Avatr naturally shoulders the responsibility and determination of Chinese brands to go upward. In September, we made the Avatr 12 in Munich, inspiring the world.

一路走来,离不开各位用户、朋友们的大力支持,感谢你们的支持与厚爱。再次感谢大家。

Without the strong support of all users and friends, we would not have made such achievements. Thank you for your support and love. Thank you all again.